Céline, Gadda, Beckett

CROSSCURRENTS

Florida A&M University, Tallahassee
Florida Atlantic University, Boca Raton
Florida Gulf Coast University, Ft. Myers
Florida International University, Miami
Florida State University, Tallahassee
University of Central Florida, Orlando
University of Florida, Gainesville
University of North Florida, Jacksonville
University of South Florida, Tampa
University of West Florida, Pensacola

CÉLINE, GADDA, BECKETT
Experimental Writings

Crosscurrents
Comparative Studies in European Literature and Philosophy
Edited by S. E. Gontarski

OF THE 1930s

NORMA BOUCHARD

University Press of Florida

Gainesville · Tallahassee · Tampa · Boca Raton

Pensacola · Orlando · Miami · Jacksonville · Ft. Myers

Copyright 2000 by the Board of Regents of the State of Florida
Printed in the United States of America on acid-free paper
All rights reserved

05 04 03 02 01 00   6 5 4 3 2 1

Library of Congress Cataloging-in-Publication Data
Bouchard, Norma, 1960–.
Céline, Gadda, Beckett: experimental writings of the 1930s / Norma Bouchard.
p. cm.
Includes bibliographical references and index.
ISBN 0-8130-1818-8 (alk. paper)
1. Literature, Experimental–Europe–History and criticism. 2. Literature,
Modern–20th century–History and criticism. 3. Céline, Louis-Ferdinand, 1894–
1961–Criticism and interpretation. 4. Gadda, Carlo Emilio, 1893–1973–Criticism
and interpretation. 5. Beckett, Samuel, 1906–Criticism and interpretation.
I. Title.
PN771.B68   2000
809'.911–dc21   00-056784

The University Press of Florida is the scholarly publishing agency for
the State University System of Florida, comprising Florida A&M University,
Florida Atlantic University, Florida International University, Florida Gulf Coast
University, Florida State University, University of Central Florida, University of
Florida, University of North Florida, University of South Florida, and
University of West Florida.

University Press of Florida
15 Northwest 15th Street
Gainesville, FL 32611–2079
http://www.upf.com

To Carl, Fabian, and Raphael

To Raymond Bouchard (in memory)

Contents

FOREWORD

Norma Bouchard's archaeology of the postmodern through *Experimental Writing of the 1930s* is a cogent, incisive study of how postwar narrative dispersal, as characterized by the *nouveau roman* and other postmodern ventures, is already in place with a series of "anomalous" writers, French, Hiberno-English, Italian, and German, of the 1930s. These are writers working beyond the dominant symbolist aesthetics, offering "alternative practices of representation," and who collectively constitute, in Foucaultian terms, "'a discursive event'; a historically locatable moment of change . . . into a new phase." Rather than accepting Jean-Paul Sartre's postwar challenge in *What Is Literature?* to transform the age ideologically and so redeem it, these "anomalous" writers probe "a problematic relationship to language." It is a position Samuel Beckett champions at the very beginning of his literary career, in a biting, albeit youthful, 1934 essay for *Bookman* magazine called "Recent Irish Poetry." Writing under the pseudonym Andrew Belis (it was a Dublin periodical, after all), Beckett scolds the "antiquarians" and "Celtic Twilighters" of his homeland for their lack of awareness "of the new thing that happened, or the old thing that happened again" — that is, "the breakdown of the object" or "the breakdown of the subject. It comes to the same thing—rupture of the lines of communication." Beckett in 1934 is already leading the assault against, in Bouchard's phrase, "modernism's ordering subject."

Although these "anomalous" writers of the 1930s are as far-ranging as Nathalie Sarraute in *Tropismes*, Lawrence Durrell in *Black Book*, Flannery O'Brien in *At Swim-Two-Birds*, Vladimir Nabokov in *Despair*, and Robert Musil in the monumental *The Man without Qualities*, Bouchard focuses on three writers: Louis-Ferdinand Céline, Carlo Emilio Gadda, and Samuel Beckett, "To demonstrate the parallel changes occurring in the French, Italian and English traditions." On the contrary, what may be the most outwardly experimental linguistic novel of the age, James Joyce's *Finnegans Wake*, remains aligned with modernist figuration: "While the novel is an epic of metamorphosis and change, it also embodies the ultimate dream of mastering figurality by setting into place an abstract, complex machine of archetypal identity and circular history cast in 'Wakese,' the language of the novel and an idiom which attempts to contain plural and open-ended signs." It is on this point that the acolyte Samuel Beckett finally distances himself from Joyce: "the difference," says Beckett, "is that Joyce was a superb manipulator of material, perhaps the greatest. He was making words do the absolute maximum of work. There isn't a syllable that's superfluous. The kind of work I do is one in which I am not master of my material. The more Joyce knew the more he could. His tendency is towards omniscience and omnipotence. I'm working with impotence, ignorance." Beckett finally would take as his subject the unpresentable—subject and object.

Such insights as Bouchard offers, then, constitute an exemplary addition to the *Crosscurrents* series, which is designed to foreground comparative studies in European art and thought, particularly the intersections of literature and philosophy, aesthetics and culture. *Céline, Gadda, Beckett: Experimental Writing of the 1930s* can be profitably read in conjunction with other *Crosscurrents* studies as a continuous discourse, building on, say, Jean-Michel Rabaté's *The Ghosts of Modernity*; Albert Sbragia's study of Carlo Emilio Gadda, *The Modern Macaronic*; J. D. O'Hara's *Hidden Drives: Samuel Beckett's Structural Use of Depth Psychology*; and most recently, William Cloonan's *The Writing of War: French and German Novels and World War II*, to name just a few. Without abandoning traditional comparative methodology, the series remains receptive to the crosscurrents in critical, comparative, and performative theory, especially that generated by the renewed intellectual energy in post-Marxist Europe. It will, as well, take full cognizance of the cultural and political realignments of what, for the better part of the twentieth century, were two separated and isolated Europes. While Western Europe continues moving aggressively toward unification in the European Community—with the breakup of the twentieth century's last major, overtly colonial empire, the Soviet Union—Eastern Europe continues its subdivision into nationalistic and religious enclaves with the collapse of communist hegemony. The intellectual, cultural, and literary significance of such profound restructuring—how history will finally be rewritten—is difficult to anticipate. Having had a fertile period of modernism snuffed out in an ideological coup not long after the 1917 revolution, the nations of the former Soviet Union have, for instance, been denied (or spared) the age of Freud and Jung, most modernist experiments, and postmodern fragmentation. While Western Europe gropes beyond modernism, Eastern Europe may be struggling to reclaim it. Whether a new art can emerge in the absence—or from the absence—of such forces as shaped modernism is one of the intriguing questions of post–Cold War discourse.

Céline, Gadda, Beckett: Experimental Writings of the 1930s, then, forms another unit in the ongoing comparative social and literary study that the *Crosscurrents* series was designed to foster. The series henceforth will continue to critique the developing, often conflicting, currents of European thought through the prisms of literature, philosophy, and critical theory.

S. E. Gontarski
Series Editor

Acknowledgments

I have incurred many debts in the writing of this project. Carl Lemp's contribution is too vast to describe in detail. I will confine myself to thanking him for constant intellectual stimulation and personal support. I am also grateful to Peter Bondanella, Matei Calinescu, Andrea Ciccarelli, Wladimir Krysinski, and, last but not least, Breon Mitchell. His scholarly generosity and professional integrity have accompanied me in all stages of this work.

AN ARCHAEOLOGY OF THE 1930S

INTRODUCTION

Céline, Gadda, Beckett is a project of revision of our critical assumptions about the past. Informed by the methodological presuppositions of Foucaultian archaeology, it seeks to disclose a "discursive event";[1] a historically locatable moment of change that forces knowledge, along with its rhetorical formations, to enter into a new phase, or "positivity" (125).

Like all archaeological digs, this study is by necessity also polemical. Its main thrust is directed toward the prevalent account of the 1930s as the decade of engaged novelistic practices, and specifically toward the assumptions about language and its instrumental functioning that inform such accounts.[2] Broadly outlined, these assumptions are generally founded on the premise that the generation of the thirties' writers inherits the symbolist, *fin-de-siècle* aesthetics of modernist novelists by continuing to share a view of language as capable of providing order and finality to the contradictory and open-ended dimensions of life, to the temporal and spatial intricacies constitutive of the twentieth-century experience of the world. The prevalent thought, however, is that since the sociohistorical conditions of the thirties can no longer legitimize the modernist resolution of life within a subjective, private sphere of art, the thirties' writers engage reality directly by seeking to transform it ideologically and, ultimately, attempting to redeem it. More succinctly, this account assumes that the writers of the 1930s have a continued and sustained faith that language is capable of acting upon experience by finite and absolute words.

The implications of this account by literary historiography are manifold and far-reaching. From the vantage point of our problematic, postmodern linguistic consciousness at the dawn of the twenty-first century, the writers of the 1930s appear naive and generally lacking in interesting complexities, as witnessed by the paucity of current interest in the period. Writers who do exhibit a problematic relationship to language are often dismissed as "anomalous" and viewed as culturally isolated cases of the exhaustion of linguistic instrumentality assumed to have first blossomed in the years following World War II.

Without denying the widespread episteme of works informed by symbolist assumptions about language, or questioning the fact that a postmodern aesthetics has indeed established itself as the dominant mode of art after the Second World War, I argue that a number of texts produced during the 1930s, in the French, Italian, and English literary traditions, are already deeply permeated by an altered relationship to language and, by implication, literary subjectivity and artistic endeavor. Further, this new relationship is by no means confined to the abstract realm of theoretical reflection but is consistently revealed in a sustained experimentation with alternative economies of signification. Thus, these works collectively emerge as a "discursive event," which opens narrative to those different and less-masterful rhetorical practices prevalent in the second, postmodernist half of the century. In short, the focus of this archaeological inquiry, as with all projects of this kind, is to map the space of a dispersion and follow the genealogy of a development. In the words of Foucault, "the problem is no longer one of tradition, of tracing a line, but one of division, of limits; it is no longer one of lasting foundations, but one of transformations that serve as new foundations" (5).

Numerous steps have clearly led to the guiding intuition behind this work, but the critical assessments of Jean Paul Sartre's *What Is Literature?* and Alain Robbe-Grillet's *For a New Novel* have been most instrumental to the development of this idea. In 1947, the year *What Is Literature?* was composed, Jean-Paul Sartre discussed the literature that immediately preceded him. His assessment was close to that voiced, more than fifteen years later, by Alain Robbe-Grillet in his manifesto for the *nouveau roman*: 1963's *For a New Novel*. Sartre lamented that prose had lost its former, "regulating mission" of recovering the totality of life.[3] Some unnamed authors, he commented, had abandoned the finite and proper designations of a "language-instrument" (5) for a "poetic attitude" (7). As Sartre explained it, this was a language that no longer sought to give an order to a fleeting, contradictory reality but reflected that reality by figural, tropic modes of expression:

In short, all language is for him the mirror of the world. Its sonority, its length, its masculine or feminine endings, its visual aspect, compose for him a face of flesh which represents rather than expresses signification. As a result, important changes take place in the internal economy of the word. . . . The poet does not utilize the word . . . in each word he realizes . . . the metaphors which Picasso dreamed of when he wanted to do a matchbox which was completely a bat without ceasing to be a matchbox. Florence is city, flower, and woman. It is city-flower, city-woman, and girl-flower all at the same time. And the strange object which thus appears has the liquidity of the river . . . and finally . . . prolongs indefinitely its modest blossoming. (6–7)

However, the "poetic attitude" criticized by Sartre is precisely what Robbe-Grillet describes as providing the possibility for the renewal of narrative in the second, postmodern half of the century. Robbe-Grillet's *For a New Novel* is a collection of essays that traditionally has been taken to mark the shift from a modernist to a postmodernist novelistic practice. In it, Robbe-Grillet comments that the rejuvenation of fiction rests in a figural model of representation: in the presence of characters and stories so contradictory and ambiguous to elicit "many possible interpretations" (22). According to Robbe-Grillet, the significance of these figural procedures rests in the creation of a literature of "new realism,"[4] that is to say, in a novelistic practice capable of more adequately representing the complex reality of experience: "the world around us. We had thought to control it by assigning it a meaning, and the entire art of the novel, in particular, seemed dedicated to this enterprise. But this was merely an illusory simplification . . . the world has only, little by little, lost all its life. Since it is chiefly in its presence that the world's reality resides, our task now is to create a literature which takes that presence into account" (23).

Because Sartre's work, read through the lens of Robbe-Grillet's *For a New Novel*, raises such important questions about traditional accounts of the redemptive linguistic economy of 1930s fiction, it leads to the exploration of the period as a launching point for an already existing alternative writing.

Among the first authors of the thirties that come to mind is Nathalie Sarraute. Her *Tropismes*, which she completed in 1937, remained unnoticed until the fifties, when, in the context of the *nouveaux romans* penned by Robbe-Grillet, Claude Simon, Robert Pinget, and Michel Butor, it finally acquired its well-deserved success. This was a work that, beginning with its title, clearly pointed to a figural practice of language. As Sarraute was to explain in her preface to *L'Ere du soupçon* (1956), a preface that unfortunately was not included in the English version, *Tropismes* had been intended as a revision of symbolist aesthetics and for this reason was seeking to relate narrative to the experiential dimension of life by way of less well defined and generally more unstable representations. In Sarraute's words, "(t)he texts which composed this early work were the spontaneous expression of very real sensations, and their form was just as spontaneous . . . . They are indefinable movements, shifting very rapidly at the limits of our consciousness . . . . Now and then, they appear to me as the secret source of our existence."[5] Sarraute's alternative model of narration was by no means an isolated case in the 1930s and, in addition to *Tropismes*, an entire constellation of "anomalous" novels and short stories progressively emerged. These include, among others, Lawrence Durrell's *The Black Book* (1938); Flannery O'Brien's *At Swim-Two-Birds* (1939); Vladimir Nabokov's *Despair* (1934); Samuel Beckett's *Dream of Fair to Middling Women* (1932), *More Pricks than Kicks* (1934), and *Murphy* (1938); Carlo Emilio Gadda's *La cognizione del dolore* (1938–1941); Louis-Ferdinand Céline's *Voyage au bout de la nuit* (1932) and *Mort à crédit* (1936); Raymond Queneau's *Le Chiendent* (1933); Jorge Luis Borges' *El jardín de senderos que se bifurcan* (1941); Robert Musil's *Der Mann ohne Eigenschaften* (1930–1943); and Elias Canetti's *Die Blendung* (1935).

To demonstrate the parallel changes occurring in the French, Italian, and English literary traditions, a representative author from each of the three traditions was chosen. Louis-Ferdinand Céline was selected over Nathalie Sarraute because of the depth and vastness of his fictional production and essayistic reflection. Carlo Emilio Gadda, like Sarraute, made his name in the context of openness to alternative narratives during the late 1950s, despite the fact that his *oeuvre* was almost complete by the early forties. Samuel Beckett has increasingly become a staple in most discussions of postmodern aesthetics. Yet, it is important to learn how to trace Beckett backwards to understand that the origin of novels such as *Molloy* (1951), *Malone Meurt* (1952), and *L'Innomable* (1953) is located in his earlier and less discussed work of the thirties. As the voice of "the Unnamable" himself comments, Beckett's 1950s fiction is still haunted by "all these Murphys."[6] Further, my selection has been partially motivated by the possibility of establishing intertextual analogies between the work of Céline, Gadda, and Beckett. Gadda identifies, in Céline, an important precursor in terms of narrative and stylistic experimentation, and Beckett mentions him very early on, in a letter of 1933, where he complains that he has not been able to obtain a copy of *Voyage*. Concomitances between the work of Gadda and Beckett are also numerous, even if they reside not in a direct knowledge of each other's work but in a remarkably similar training in philosophy and literature.

The temptation to include the German novelists has been strong, since Elias Canetti and Robert Musil powerfully dismantle all attempts to enclose the chaotic and multiple aspects of experience. Moreover, in both discourse and style, they mount an important defense of life's metamorphic becoming. However, since both novels hark back to the work of Franz Kafka, their inclusion would have required a further exploration into that unique strand of German modernism represented by *The Trial* and *The Castle* and would have enlarged the argument to the point of unmanageability.

Because it is in the nature of limits that they are perceptible only in the transgression of what precedes them, the argument has been organized into two main sections: The first describes the broader paradigm of modernist narratives, and the second focuses on their displacement in works by Céline, Gadda, and Beckett.

Chapter 1, "Contextualizing Modernism," tries to avoid reductive visions of modernism—that is, modernism intended as an all-redemptive, affirmative practice but also modernism subsumed under the critical categories of postmodernism.[7] Drawing upon the insights developed by continental and poststructuralist theorists, this chapter argues that modernist art initially loses its *fin-de-siècle*, aestheticist distance from the temporality and spatial intricacies of life and reorients itself in a figural practice of ambiguity and regress, or more precisely, in that postmodern, "sublime" condition of rhetoric theorized by Lyotard as a phase preceding and antedating modernism. This condition not only is exemplified in the new art of film and in the practices of the historical avant-gardes but it is revealed in the regressive and ambiguous representations that inhabit the novels of writers crucial to the development of Céline, Gadda, and Beckett— notably Joyce, Proust, Woolf, Pirandello, and Svevo. However, after an excursion into the narratives of several of these authors, it can be seen that the condition of figurality is textualized as an intolerable state of corruption and entropy: a state that points to an anachronistic desire to restore art to its previous detachment from experience. This leads to a description of how different configurations start developing in early twentieth-century aesthetics. Taking what might be called an anti-de Manian approach,[8] I argue, via Walter Benjamin, that while the writers operating within the context of the Germanic *Sprachkrise* continue in their figural paths, other writers strive to transcend regress and ambiguity. Given the pioneering work of Auerbach, Spitzer, Lukács, and their numerous progeny, this modernist turn is a well-assessed condition within English and French literary traditions. However, the inclusion of Italian novels calls for deeper reflection. Prominent scholars have tended to place the work of Pirandello and Svevo in the context of the Germanic *Sprachkrise*, and therefore have emphasized the anomaly of Italian modernism within a Western European context. Nonetheless, by reexamining Pirandello's essay "L'Umorismo" [On humor] one can conclude that its promotion of narrative incoherence and open-endedness does not provide a theoretical justification for the author's longer novels, *Il fu Mattia Pascal* and *Uno, nessuno e centomila*, but only for the rhetorical experimentalism articulated in some of the short stories from *Novelle per un anno*. As for Svevo, the skepticism about symbolic premises of stability and order that are voiced through the character of Zeno Cosini paradoxically coincides with Zeno's cure following the psychoanalytical composition of the novel *La coscienza di Zeno*. The pharmacological authority of language at work here is confirmed intertextually by Svevo's *Il vecchione*, where an older version of Zeno comments that only narrative is capable of giving a measure of clarity and finality to lived experience. Because of this widespread instrumental view of language—a view that, albeit in different degrees, encompasses several literary traditions—it is perhaps to be expected that the creative imagination of modernism produced *Finnegans Wake*. While this novel is an epic of metamorphosis and change, it also embodies the ultimate dream of mastering figurality. It sets into place an abstract, complex machine of archetypal identity and circular history cast in "Wakese," the language of the novel and an idiom that attempts to contain plural and open-ended signs. Nonetheless, the *Wake* coincides with the end of redemptive narration, as a gulf opens inside and outside its structures. As Derrida has suggested, "Wakese" contains the seeds of its own undoing. Because, in the process of reading, difference and alterity are constantly foregrounded, an impossible double-bind opens between Joyce's will to erase spatialization and temporality, and the figures stubbornly haunting the novel. Moreover, and more significant to the purpose of this discussion, an unbridgeable gap occurs outside the narrative itself, where emerging superstructural developments undercut the possibility of a symbolic reconstruction of experience. In short, this is the time when Céline, Gadda, and Beckett, along with other writers of the 1930s, open a breach into the redemptive representational premises of modernism by revisiting the early legacy of the historical avant-gardes while beginning to experiment with less masterful economies of signification.

The discussion of thirties' writings begins with an analysis of Louis-Ferdinand Céline's work in the chapter "Turning the 'S' into the 'Z'." His *Voyage au bout de la nuit* (1932) and *Mort à crédit* (1936) are read, not so much as examples of tardive modernism, as the critical tradition suggests, but as *Bildungsromane*—that is, as apprenticeship novels into the inauthenticity of the modernist Name exemplified most particularly by the verbal behavior of the biological and spiritual fathers of the narrator, Ferdinand Bardamu. Yet the importance of Céline's novels of the thirties is by no means solely due to the presence of a counterdiscourse, but also resides in the alternative practice of representation that they exemplify. This is a practice that marks a departure from the reactionary linguistic ideality of modernist aesthetics and points to a realignment with the art of irreducible regress and ambiguity detected by Benjamin in the figural expressions of historical avant-gardisms. The affinities that Céline's aesthetics shares with some of the tenets of unanimism and with two of surrealism's rebel offshoots, Georges Bataille and Antonin Artaud, additionally suggest this filiation. Subsequent sections of the chapter describe how this practice reopens narrative to the radical ambiguity and temporality of experience—reopens it to the irreducible decay and anarchy of Western society and culture that modernism had confined to the limits of society, the body, and the text. However, because these novels are first-person autodiegetic narratives, the focus is on the character of Ferdinand. A compound of contradictory and ever-changing selves, Ferdinand explodes the frames of physical, social, and sexual containment. His voice mirrors his lack of boundaries and emerges as a compound of archaic and erudite forms, instinctual and argotic expressions, all coexisting in a state of relativization and open-endedness. Nonetheless, Céline's other thirties' writings, notably the three anti-Semitic pamphlets that immediately followed the publication of the novels, suggest that the absence of all eschatological dimensions of *Voyage* and *Mort* was too much to bear. Drawing upon the work of Julia Kristeva, I suggest that although the pamphlets do prolong some of the issues raised in the novels, they also degenerate into a dangerous paranoid fantasy. In fact, after journeying into the chaos of language, society, and the self, Céline will succumb to the modernist temptation of the ordering subject by seeking to absorb all contradiction and heterogeneity of experience in a single object: the Jew.

Whereas Céline's postnovelistic work falls back into modernist assumptions, Gadda's writing—which is discussed in "Meandering with Gadda's 'Heuristic' Words"—has its source in a modernist ideal, exemplified in the discourse of the author's war diaries, *Giornale di guerra e di prigionia 1915–1919*. The diaries, however, increasingly depart from their initial idealism, as the events surrounding World War I bring Gadda to the painful realizations not only that a gulf exists between ideal and empirical reality but that all dreams of personal and historical order are ultimately defeated by the chaos and messiness of the world. It is these realizations that will profoundly inform Gadda's subsequent endeavors: *Racconto italiano di ignoto del novecento* (1924), and *Meditazione milanese* (1928). While *Racconto* is a metaliterary commentary on the impossibility of an orderly, finite narrative in the modernist tradition, *Med-itazione* provides a philosophical underpinnning to the view that experi-ence is a space of irreducible temporality and heterogeneity. It accom-plishes this by drawing upon the metamorphic thought of the pre-Socratic and the antimetaphysical insights developed by Leibnitz, Spinoza, Kant, and Bergson. Further, *Meditazione*, along with other shorter intertextual pieces from the late 1920s up to the mid-1930s, also suggests how this condition calls for an alternative, "heuristic" mode of representation. This is a signifying practice willing to undo the violence of reductive oppositions and finality while promoting relations and con-tamination of borders, contingency and open-endedness. As in the case of Céline, Gadda's aesthetics certainly benefits from importing some of the avant-gardist tenets, particularly those voiced by the turn-of-the-cen-tury Italian *scapigliati*, the futurists and, in light of Gadda's praise for the cinematic medium, even the technique of montage in the new medium of film. Subsequent sections of this chapter, describe how Gadda's shorter fictions ("La madonna dei filosofi," "La casa," "San Giorgio in casa Brocchi") and novels (*La meccanica* and *La cognizione del dolore*), configure a space where modernist premises are parodically, and at times even tragically negated while seeds for change are sown. The discussion of Gadda is closed with an illustration of how Gadda's alternative signify-ing economy shapes the stylistic profile of his novels. Like Céline's *Voy-age* and *Mort*, *La meccanica* and *La cognizione* suggest the temporality and ambiguity of experience by using an unstructured idiomatic juxtapo-sition, or a "pastiche" of the elements contained in a vast linguistic patri-mony. This pastiche includes Italy's many dialects, Spanish, French, and Latin, and a variety of registers from the national idiom.

The third chapter, "Rite of Passage: The Early Beckett between 'Un-wording' and 'Linkwriting,'" suggests how the "English Beckett" shares Gadda's and Céline's understanding of experience as an irreducible con-tinuum in time and space and, much like them, parodies metaphysical ideals while striving toward alternative representations. The first point is illustrated by a reading of the early essay *Proust* (1931). Here Beckett fo-cuses on the figural passages of the Proustian A *la recherche du temps perdu* and praises those moments when the narrative no longer seeks re-lief from the equivocal and mutable condition of life, but registers it in images of excess and ambiguity. This is what Beckett quite aptly calls the "chain-figure of the metaphor." Other essayistic writings from this decade are also discussed, since they not only enlarge upon the issues raised in *Proust* but also reflect theoretically on a writing that intends to outdo, or in Beckett's term "unword," solacing symbols while taking steps toward the figural practices of a "linkwriting." The role of avant-gardism and film have been important to Beckett's development as well, and this chapter also recalls how, throughout the 1930s, he had extensive contacts with the unanimists, the surrealists, and the verticalists, whose manifesto he signed in 1932. It is against this background of tolerance for the ambiguity and temporality constitutive of experience that Beckett's fictions are situated. The discussion begins with *Dream of Fair to Middling Women*, which Beckett wrote in 1932 but which was not published until 1992. In this novel, parodic uncrowning of metaphysical questers is already at work, particularly in the description of Belacqua. Despite being a tumult of contradictory impulses, Belacqua is nonetheless affected by the same desire for identity and closure that informs some of Gadda's and Céline's parodied characters. Belacqua's emancipation, however, is shown by Beckett to be a quixotic remedy, and the narrative ironically dismantles the character's endeavors. The counterideology revealed in *Dream* shapes Beckett's other fictions as well, notably the collection of short stories *More Pricks than Kicks* (1934) and the novel *Murphy* (1938). In an increasing irony, the stories additionally undo the endeavor of an older version of Belacqua, Belacqua Shuah, and ultimately suggest the futility of damming the being of life. *Murphy* confirms the impossibility of governing anchors and perimeters by subjecting characters, events, and people to radical heterogeneity and becoming. The world at large however, is affected by Belacqua's syndrome and has little tolerance for this state of being. Even the character of Murphy ultimately succumbs to the lure of metaphysics and seeks to retreat from the phenomenal world at large. In a pattern of "return of the repressed" akin to that established in *Dream* and *More Pricks than Kicks*, the chaos and temporality of life make an important comeback.

More than in any other works by Beckett, the figural apprehension of reality is suggested by the novels' stylistic defiance, produced by the use of a combination of several registers of the English language and its geographical variants with a host of other idioms, including Italian, French, German, and Spanish. In one more attempt at relativization, Beckett also adds visual codes of abnormal typeface, italicization, and capitalization. In summary, then, Beckett's fictions of the 1930s, like those of Céline and Gadda, not only displace modernist ideals of emancipation from experience but, in both content and style, promote a narrative of irreducible plurality of signifieds and signifiers tending toward the horizon of postmodernity.

Céline, Gadda, Beckett: Experimental Writings of the 1930s concludes with a chapter entitled "Postponing a Conclusion . . . ," which provides a broad commentary on the field of dispersal established by these novelists. This is a dispersal that came about only after the Second World War, in the context of the renewal of fiction wished for by Alain Robbe-Grillet and other *nouveaux romanciers*. However, the origin of the dispersal, as Sartre might have intuited, already had been formulated in earlier, experimental prewar practices.

CONTEXTUALIZING MODERNISM

The emergence of early twentieth-century European art coincides with the dawn of the sense of relativity and impermanence of civilization and culture brought about by the experience of modernity. As James McFarlane has commented, modernist art

> is the art consequent on Heisenberg's 'Uncertainty Principle,' of the destruction of civilization and reason in the First World War, of the world changed and reinterpreted by Marx, Freud, and Darwin, of capitalism and constant industrial acceleration, of existential exposure to meaninglessness or absurdity. It is the literature of technology. It is the art consequent on the dis-establishing of communal reality and conventional notions of causality, on the destruction of traditional notions of the wholeness of individual character, on the linguistic chaos that ensues when public notions of language have been discredited and when all realities have become subjective fictions.[1]

As a correlative of the displacement of familiar frames of epistemic and socioeconomic reference outlined by McFarlane, during the first quarter of the twentieth century, both the artistic endeavor and the expressive possibilities of the modernist artist undergo important transformations. In

"The Work of Art in the Age of Mechanical Reproduction" (1936),[2] Walter Benjamin subsumes them under the defining proposition of the "decay of the aura." This implies the withering of late-nineteenth-century aestheticist notions of the artist as an isolated, individual genius and of the idea of art as a field endowed with a sacred, ritual-like detachment from the undecidabilities of life, from the temporality and the spatial intricacies constitutive of the daily-life world experience of modernity. In Benjamin's words, "The definition of the aura as a 'unique perception of a distance . . .' represents nothing but the formulation of the cult value of the work of art in categories of space and time perception. Distance is the opposite of closeness. . . . Unapproachability is indeed a major quality of the cult image" (243). Otherwise stated, the destabilization of cultural, social, and epistemological formations of the modern period coincides with art's departure from the paradigms of nineteenth-century mimesis. These are paradigms founded upon the notion of a self-identical Subject establishing difference and providing closure to the object in the mediating space of representation.

Two artistic phenomena are indicated by Benjamin as having been instrumental in the aesthetic reorientation of modernist art: the new art of film and the practices of the historical avant-gardes. Film displaces the paradigm of the artist as a demiurgic, monadic Subject by originating out of a cooperative effort and by finding completion in a collective model of reception. The compositional principle of the medium itself translates the evaporation of a solid, clearly definable reality into less stable symbolic mediations. In ways that will bring to mind a well-known essay by Erwin Panofsky on the "dynamization of space" and "spatialization of time" opened by the cinematic montage,[3] Benjamin writes that the contingency and opacity of the experience of modernity find expression in the heterogeneous, fast-moving shots of filmmakers: "Magician and surgeon compare to painter and cameraman. The painter maintains in his work a natural distance from reality, the cameraman penetrates deeply into its web. There is a tremendous difference between the pictures they obtain. . . . For contemporary man the representation of reality by film is incomparably more significant than that of the painter . . . since it offers . . . the thoroughgoing permeation of reality" (233–34). As for what regards the phenomenon of avant-gardism, Benjamin interprets it as a transposition of the withering effects brought about by film on traditional notions of art.[4] While the surrealists degrade individual talent and authorship by means of "automatic," passive creations, the dadaists do so through ephemeral collages of images. Formally, both avant-gardes tend toward the production of paradoxical juxtapositions of images, which for Benjamin are indicative of a more realistic representation—"a profane illumination"[5]—of the experiential dimension of modern life.

Writing in the Age of Film and the Avant-garde

Benjamin's observations on modernism are by no means confined to film and the avant-gardes, but foray into the transformations affecting verbal arts—narrative in particular. In the rhetorical practices of modernist novelists Benjamin locates the withering of a millenary culture founded on the prestige of the letter. Unlike the epic storytellers of time past, modern novelists[6] no longer can order experience in finite and totalizing symbols, but, like the writers of baroque dramas,[7] are engaging in "allegorical" writings of pluralization and regress. Franz Kafka's *The Trial* (1925) and *The Castle* (1926) are said to have "no definite symbolic meaning for the author from the outset,"[8] while "Die Verwandlung" (1915) and "Ein Hungerkünstler" (1924) offer only an array of "forms countless, uncertain, changing compounds, yielding a constant flow of new, strange products" (131).

Benjamin's discussion of the developmental tendencies of modernist art into nonauratic, "allegorical" processes of semiosis, falls short of a more extensive rhetorical analysis. Nonetheless, the latter has been a constant focus in poststructuralist theories of language and representation developed by Lyotard, Derrida, and Deleuze. Collectively considered, these provide additional clarification on the writing practices of cultural modernity.

Drawing upon Kant's *Critique of Judgment*, Jean-François Lyotard has argued that the presence of an "allegorical" language is indicative of a postmodern aesthetic of the "sublime." It should be noted, however, that in Lyotard's formulation the epithet "postmodern" is to be understood not only as the historical condition of late-twentieth-century art, but as a state that already exists in the first quarter of the twentieth century. For this reason, in *The Postmodern Condition* Lyotard has proposed the rather paradoxical definition of postmodernism as a phase preceding and antedating modernism: "A work can become modern only if it is first post-modern. Postmodernism thus understood is not modernism at its end but in the nascent state, and this state is constant."[9] Likewise, in *The Inhuman*, Lyotard has written that since the modern always includes and encompasses the postmodern, neither modernity nor postmodernity can be circumscribed as historical entities, that is to say, in terms of a chronological succession of before and after, "pre" and "post." He explains that "we have to say that the postmodern is always implied in the modern because of the fact that modernity, modern temporality comprises in itself an impulsion to exceed itself into a state other than itself. . . . Modernity is constitutionally and ceaselessly pregnant with its postmodernity."[10] More significantly to the purpose of this discussion, Lyotard has noted that a sublime, postmodern aesthetic emerges when the field of the visible no longer can be totalized in symbols of identity and closure, or precisely in what Kant called the harmonious, organic reconciliations of consensual "Beauty": "The sublime," he explains, "takes place . . . when the imagination fails to present an object which might, if only in principle, come to match a concept. We have the Idea of the world (the totality of what is), but we don't have the capacity to show an example of it. We have the Idea of the simple (that which cannot be broken down, decomposed), but we cannot illustrate it with a sensible object that would be a 'case' of it" (78). Thus, for Lyotard, the sublime originates where symbolic modes of representation fail and, like the account of "allegory" proposed by Benjamin, articulates the referent by means of contradictory and proliferating "figures."[11] These are metaphors partaking of more than one frame of reference, and metonymies and synecdoches of a nonrecoverable unity.

Like Lyotard, Gilles Deleuze has commented that in the absence of distance from the temporal and spatial continuum, or what he calls "the haptic, smooth space of close vision,"[12] writers become "nomadic." Akin to wandering tribesmen, they express themselves in "minor," deterritorialized words. Taking as a model Kafka's language,[13] Deleuze notes that "minor" words are rhetorical practices of dispersed and entangled meanings, figural processes of semiosis evoking the incommensurability and otherness of the phenomenal space: "Two conjoined tendencies in so-called minor languages have often been noted: an impoverishment of syntactical and lexical forms; but simultaneously a strange proliferation of shifting effects, a taste for overload and paraphrase" (149).

Arguably without fully sharing the materialistic intent that informs the work of Lyotard and Deleuze,[14] Derrida's account of rhetoric as *"différance"* provides a further description of figural, "minor" expressions. As its name suggests, *différance* has its source in phenomenal categories of temporal deferral and spatial differing. These categories are deployed in hybrid and regressive expressions, or what Derrida has variously named the "hymen," the *"supplément,"* the "graft," and the "sheaf," making up the fabric of the "text." As stated in *Of Grammatology:* "Origin of the experience of space and time, this writing of difference, this fabric of the trace, permits the difference between space and time to be articulated, to appear as such . . . This articulation therefore permits a graphic (. . . 'spatial') chain to be adapted, on occasion in a linear fashion, to a spoken (. . . 'temporal') chain. It is from the primary possibility of this articulation that one must begin. Difference is articulation" (65–66).[15]

Reading the Postmodern Condition of Modernism

"Allegorical" processes of semiosis, or, in poststructuralist terms, postmodern rhetorical practices, permeate many early-twentieth-century novels. Unlike the confident and omniscient representations of their nineteenth-century realist and naturalist predecessors, modernist works often exhibit an inability to order the referent in closed verbal structures, to organize the data of experience in coherent poetic wholes. In James Joyce's *Ulysses* (1922), for example, a single day in the metropolis of Dublin—June 16, 1904—is no longer narratable according to the stable, contained images provided, for instance, by Dickens's representation of London from *Bleak House,* or by Balzac's description of Paris from *Le Père Goriot.* Radically altered by modernity's unforeseen shifts of population and capitals, Dublin can only be textualized "allegorically," as a series, that is, of blurred and short-lived forms: "Cityful passing away, other cityful coming, passing away too: other coming on, passing on. Houses, lines of houses, streets, miles of pavements, piled up bricks, stones. Changing hands. This owner, that."[16] Like Joyce's Dublin, the Paris of the Proustian *Recherche* (1913–27), the London of Woolf's *Mrs. Dalloway* (1925), the Prague of Kafka's novels and short stories, the Trieste of Svevo's *La coscienza di Zeno* (1923), and many other metropolises of modernity emerge as "heterotopic" spaces. These are zones, as Michel Foucault has written, that can be narrated only by flowing and ebbing figures, "because they secretly undermine language, because they make it impossible to name this and that, because they shatter and tangle common names, because they destroy 'syntax' in advance . . . syntax which causes words and things to 'hold together'."[17]

Yet it is in the representation of the self and the self's relation to historical and cultural experience that the postmodern condition of figurality manifests itself most overtly. Because subjectivity depends upon the possibility of persisting over time and space—upon the internalization of stable relations, practices, and beliefs—amidst unstable formations the individual consciousness can emerge only as a flux of shifting, multiplying images or, more precisely, as the self as "*flâneur*." This is a subject, as Benjamin has cogently written in *Illuminations*, whose contours no longer generate the fullness of knowledge, the sense of "*Erkenntis*," but produce instead a shadow of individuality, the "quintessence of a passing moment [*Erlebnis*] that struts about in the borrowed garb of experience" (185).

The self as *flâneur* finds a clear exemplification in many of the characters from Joyce's *Ulysses*. The city dweller and twentieth-century man Leopold Bloom probes all representational grids by being an unfocused and paratactical assemblage of the most transient, heterogeneous thoughts and perceptions. As readers familiar with the novel well know, these may include a myriad of short-lived perceptions caused by a variety of external stimuli, but also casual recollections of the building blocks of his cultural heritage, fragments of his numerous existential concerns of time present and past, and so on. In the beginning of "Calypso," for example, as Bloom walks along Dorset Street on his way to purchase pork kidneys from Duglacz, the butcher, his thoughts wander from fantasies of oriental cities, complete with turbaned crowds and carpets, to perceptions of children reciting their lessons in a nearby school. Upon his arrival at the butcher's shop, additional thoughts crowd his already teaming consciousness. These thoughts comprise intimate sexual fantasies about a girl waiting in line as well as reflections about a model farm and its cattle on the lakeshore of Tiberias prompted by the newspapers' advertisements piled on the butcher's counter. Back on the road, Bloom's concerns with estranged Jewish friends of his youth and with the present unfaithfulness of his wife Molly alternate with passing references to a number of aspects of modernization. Bloom's thoughts now include the text of an advertisement about a systematic crop of citrus in Israel and the technical innovation of mechanized packaging of agricultural products: "Silvered powdered olivetrees. Quiet long days: pruning ripening. Olives are packed in jars, eh? I have a few left from Andrews. Molly spitting them out. Knows the taste of them now. Oranges in tissue paper packed in crates. Citrons too. Wonder is poor Citron still alive. . . . And Mastiansky. . . . Pleasant evenings we had then. Molly in Citron's basketchair. Nice to hold, cool waxen fruit, hold in the hand, lift it to the nostrils and smell the perfume" (60–1). A few passages later, recollections of his cultural heritage prompted by thoughts of plagued biblical cities and scattered Jewish people are succeeded by the sights of a poor woman crossing the street and of the surrounding houses, and the desire for a delicious breakfast. The entropy of this passage and of "Calypso" at large is repeated in virtually all sections of the novel.

Like a cinematic eye,[18] the narrative of "The Lotus Eaters" records additional fragments of Bloom's thoughts and visions as he continues to move across the city. Thus, the objects that he sees in the window of the Belfast and Oriental Tea Company in Westland Row give way to a reference to the Dead Sea, a casual meeting with the boring M'Coy, and a stylish woman waiting for a cab in front of the Grosvenor Hotel. In the sequence that follows, an advertisement about the play *Leah* and the reflections about Shakespeare's *Hamlet* that it spins off give way to the heterogeneous visions following Bloom's entrance into All Hallows' Church. These include images of conversions, rites in Latin, Catholic communion wine, and more prosaic recollections of Guinness porter.

Molly Bloom mirrors and perhaps even increases the sense of *Erlebnis* produced by the elusive and heterogeneous subjectivity of Leopold. As her monologue in "Penelope" confirms, she is a flowing, undammable river of perceptions. Her mind is a revolving sphere, and one that, in the language of Leo Spitzer,[19] "chaotically enumerates" the most disparate observations. These may include prosaic comments on the bedroom lamp, pork chops, and digestion, but also fragmented recollections of the milestones of literary history, including Defoe's *Moll Flanders*, medieval romances, and Rabelais' Renaissance novels. The figural redefinition of the self in relation to cultural and historical contexts suggested by the consciousness of Molly and Leopold is well captured in the comments of another character from *Ulysses*, Stephen Daedalus, for whom the modern experience expresses itself "allegorically," through the metaphors of one-thing-next-another, or *"nebeneinander"* (37), and the metonymies of one-thing-after-another, or *"nacheinander"* (37).

Figural representations like the one described above are by no means confined to Joyce's 1922 novel — even if, to be sure, *Ulysses* contains the largest and possibly best-known repertoire of this mode. As Lyotard reminds us, because the "sublime" is the condition of the artistic emergence of early-twentieth-century artworks, postmodern figurality informs a number of other modern narratives.

Marcel Proust's *A la recherche du temps perdu*, for example, opens with the description of an undecidable, postmodern subjectivity. Upon awakening from a brief sleep, the narrator Marcel finds that his identity is atomized in a variety of "real" as well as "imaginary" locations. Thus, if at first he identifies with the objects evoked in the pages of his latest bed-side reading — "il me semblait que j'étais moi-même ce dont parlait l'ouvrage: une église, un quatuor, la rivalité de François Ier et de Charles-Quint"[20] [I myself seemed to have become the subject of my book: a church, a quartet, the rivalry between François I and Charles V] — shortly thereafter he emerges as the child of time past, sleeping in the family's summer residence. In an additional metaphoric displacement, he is also the city dweller resting in a Parisian bedroom and the young tourist staying in Italian hotels: "à Combray chez ma tante, à Balbec, à Paris, à Doncières, à Venise, ailleurs encore" (16) [at Combray, with my great-aunt, at Balbec, Paris, Venice, and the rest]. The narrator's ontological frailty unfolds in the rest of the novel as well, where, in addition to his own subjectivity, other referents escape the defining grids of representation. This is particularly evident in the social space, where kaleidoscopic and enigmatic characters like the elusive Odette and Albertine multiply. In short, in Proust the self is an image that exists "amorphously and formlessly, indefinitely and weightily, the same way as the weight of his net tells a fisherman about his catch."[21]

An analogous inability to locate identity, to provide it with a stable grid of symbolic definitions, is the focus of Woolf's *Mrs. Dalloway* and *To the Lighthouse* (1927). In both novels, the central characters explode the boundaries of a single, absolute word and surface in the differential multiplication of perspectives voiced by all surrounding personae. Thus, in *To the Lighthouse,* if Mr. Ramsay is seen as autocratic and confident by his children, in Mrs. Ramsay's perceptions he is paradoxically frail and in dire need of assurances and sympathy. In one more chiastic inversion, Charles Tansley describes him as an accomplished scholar of philosophy, whereas in Mr. Bankes's words he is but a case of professional exhaustion. Mirroring the figurality of her husband, Mrs. Ramsay commands a clouded respect. "For always," as Mr. Bankes comments, "there was something incongruous to be worked into the harmony of her face."[22] Like Mrs. Ramsay, Clarissa Dalloway is the product of simultaneous and contradictory images, provided in part by the perception of her family and friends but also by Clarissa herself. In a passage that formulates quite clearly how the experience of modern life has a destabilizing effect on the ontological constitution of the Subject, Clarissa notes that she felt "not 'here, here, here' . . . but everywhere . . . some woman in the street, some man behind a counter—even trees, or barns."[23] Precisely for this reason, earlier in the narrative Clarissa had noted that "she would not say of Peter, she would not say of herself, I am this, I am that" (11).

Differential patterns of representation do not escape Italian modernist narratives, where they find expressions in Italo Svevo's *La coscienza di Zeno* (1923) and in Luigi Pirandello's *Il fu Mattia Pascal* (1904) and *Uno, nessuno e centomila* (1925–26). The main character of Svevo's novel, Zeno Cosini, epitomizes the definition of the human condition as a fluctuating ocean wave; "onda del mare, che dacché si forma, muta ad ogni istante finché non muore!"[24] [an ocean wave, which, from the moment it takes shape, continues to change till it dies]. Not only does Zeno's first-person voice waver between the opposite poles of truthfulness and overt unreliability, but it inscribes the drifting movement of the characters' personal existence and social integration in bourgeois culture. In the beginning of the novel, for example, Zeno ponders whether he should be a lawyer or a chemist. Then, toward the middle of the narrative, social and political changes fashion him into a quasi-businessman. His sentimental life follows a similar pattern of alternations, swinging as it does between the ugly Augusta, her more attractive sisters Ada and Alberta, Carla, and back to Ada and then Augusta. Sharing the mutability of Zeno are also the characters of Pirandello's *Mattia Pascal* and *Uno, nessuno e centomila.* Mattia's identity is no longer the result of deterministic and chronological categories, but the product of chance occurrences. His name records this instability, drifting as it does from "Mattia Pascal" to "Adriano Meis" and "Il fu Mattia Pascal"[25] [The late Mattia Pascal]. In this sense, Mattia's absence of a "proper" nomination anticipates the seriality of paradoxical images of Vitangelo Moscarda, the main character from Pirandello's second novel. Moscarda knows none of the certitude of the traditional Subject. His identity is defined according to the contradictory views of the Other, and therefore pluralized in a thousand images by the perceptions of his wife, lover, acquaintances, and even Moscarda himself. This is why, in the famous scene in front of the mirror, Moscarda no longer recognizes his own reflection or, more precisely, experiences it as that of an *"estraneo"*[26] [foreigner].

In summary then, there runs throughout these narrative a sense of undecidability and lack of difference. The Subject has lost the capability of ordering the external world in stable temporal and spatial grids. Representation of the self and the self's relation to the world has collapsed for a succession of images, for an undifferentiated, open-ended process of postmodern semiosis.

Figurality as Nietzschean Tragedy

And yet, despite these overt examples of figural modes of representation, despite the undeniable presence of a postmodern "sublime" informing many of these passages, modernist novels remain distinct from the developments of late-twentieth-century fiction. Because the fluctuating, contradictory space of personal and collective existence is embedded in a context of utter decay and entropy, these works bring to mind not so much the joyful shattering of totalizing concepts that inform the postmodern narratives of Nabokov, Barth, and Barthelme, but more a Nietzschean sense of tragedy as the space where bounded and finite being has been transgressed.[27] Joyce's *Ulysses,* for example, often expresses a problematic relation to the open-ended, heterogeneous configurations of historical and cultural modernity. In "The Wandering Rocks" section of the novel, the changing roads and buildings of Dublin are a frightful reminder of the frailty of humanity and its projects: "Piled up cities, worn away age after age. Pyramids in sand. Built on bread and onions. Slaves.

Chinese wall. Babylon. Big stones left. Round towers. Rest rubbles. . . .
No one is anything" (164). In the section "Scylla and Charybdis," the
disintegrating cultural homogeneity of Dublin is textualized as a threat to
the cohesiveness and purity of Western intellectual endeavors. Dublin's
National Library is no longer a monument to the Irish cultural heritage,
but has become the site of that useless, unstructured knowledge repre-
sented by the free-floating, fragmented allusions to Shakespeare, Plato,
Aristotle, Goethe, Hyde, Mallarmé, biblical narrative, and Greek and
Latin myths that traverse the conversations of A. E. the poet, John
Eglinton, Stephen Daedalus, Mr. Best, Buck Mulligan, and Lyster.

In *Ulysses* tragic visions are by no means confined to "The Wandering
Rocks" and "Scylla and Charybdis" but are prevalent in other chapters as
well. In the "Telemachus" section, for example, the sense of ephemerality of modern experience concretizes in the haunting figure of Stephen
Daedalus's dead mother, and, as its name suggests, the "Hades" chapter
of the novel is entirely focused on sepulchral visions. These include the
funeral of Patty Dignam, Bloom's painful memories of the brief childhood of his lost son Rudy, the suicide of his own father, and the death of
Stephen Daedalus's mother. The novel's *memento mori* and the anxieties
thus generated, find a verbal expression in "Nestor." As Stephen Daedalus gives a lesson on Pyrrhus, his mind is filled with thoughts about the
violently destructive forces of time. These are opposed to the theological
vision of temporal progress upheld by his headmaster and employer, Mr.
Deasy, and they ultimately explode in Stephen's famous affirmation that
"History . . . is a nightmare from which I am trying to awake" (34). The
pathos informing these sections of *Ulysses* crystallizes in that dramatic
explosion of figures making up the "Circe" session. In one of the brothels
of Dublin's night-town, Stephen becomes prey to life's "Dance of death"
(579). A series of grotesque and entangled images of beasts and humans,
comparable perhaps only to those hybrids of victims and assassins, insects
and humans in the "Zwischenwelt" of Franz Kafka, whirl around him:
"On nags, hogs, bellhorses, Gadarene swine, Corny in coffin. Steel shark
stone one-handled Nelson, two trickies Frauenzimmer plumstained
from pram falling bawling" (579). His dead mother returns, rises through
the floor, while uttering the following scream against the destructive
forces of time: "I was once the beautiful May Goulding. I am dead" (580).
In a scene that parallels Stephen's dance, a crowd of people who passed

through Bloom's conscious life returns to reproach his past actions. Shortly thereafter he encounters the whore-mistress Bella Cohen and is made to experience the wane of a stable, orderly definition of the self and of the self's relation to the world as a humiliating, even castrating condition: "(A sweat breaking out over him.) Not man. (He sniffs.) Woman" (535).

Like *Ulysses*, from first to last the Proustian *Recherche* represents the modern experience as a space of decay and chaos, a spectacle that lacks the former order and beauty of time past, as the following passage from "Nom du pays: le nom," [Place-names: The name], from *Du côté de Chez Swann*, suggests:

Et toutes ces parties nouvelles du spectacle, je n'avais plus de croyance à introduire pour leur donner la consistance, l'unité, l'existence; elles passaient éparses devant moi, au hasard, sans vérité, ne contenant en elles aucune beauté que mes yeux eussent pu essayer comme autrefois de composer. (501)

[And seeing all these new elements of the spectacle, I had no longer the faith that, applied to them, would have given them consistency, unity, life; they passed in scattered sequences before me, at random, without truth, containing in themselves no beauty that my eyes might have endeavored, as in the old days, to compose in a picture.]

The last section of the novel, *Le Temps retrouvé*, reiterates feelings analogous to the above-cited passage. The modern Parisian salon is a space where time and heterogeneity reign. The members of the old society are gone: "Hannibal de Bréauté, mort! Antoine de Mouchy, mort! Charles Swann, mort!"[28] [Hannibal de Bréauté, dead! Antoine de Mouchy, dead! Charles Swann, dead!]. Those who have survived, like M. de Charlus, have been transformed beyond recognition. "Il y avait d'ailleurs," comments the narrator, "deux M. de Charlus, sans compter les autres" (168) [Besides, there were at least two M. de Charlus, without counting the others]. The lack of social purity brought about by the new, sociopolitical configurations of modernity is now permeating the salon in its entirety, and it is exemplified in the character of Mme. Verdurin, a bourgeois, who has now become Princess of Guermantes. Thus, the narrator laments once more the absence of truth in the grotesque and fast-moving images of twentieth-century life, or what he suggestively calls the *"vision cinématographique"* (197) [filmic view] of experience.

As in the narratives of Proust and Joyce, in Virginia Woolf's *To the Lighthouse* and *Mrs. Dalloway*, modernity is textualized ultimately as a tragic experience. It is the zone where contradiction and transience reign, a force destroying all personal and historical order. In *Mrs. Dalloway* it takes the form of schizophrenic derangement and decay, affecting more directly the character of Septimus Ward Smith following World War I but functioning also as a covert reflection on the vicissitudes surrounding Clarissa Dalloway's life. In *To the Lighthouse*, life is a cosmic ravage, the upheaval destroying the European continent, two of the members of the Ramsay family, and their house on the Hebrides Islands.

These tragic sentiments permeate other novels as well. Through the character of Zeno, Svevo's *La coscienza di Zeno* introduces the notion of twentieth-century life and civilization as a disease. This is a disease that will end only in a final destruction, that is when a man will set off a bomb at the center of the earth, thus allowing the planet to return to a primordial state of purity: "Ci sarà un'esplosione enorme che nessuno udrà e la terra ritornata alla forma di nebulosa errerà nei cieli priva di parassiti e malattie" (480) [There will be a tremendous explosion, but no one will hear it, and the earth will return to its nebulous state and go wandering through the sky, free at last from parasite and disease]. Like Svevo's, Pirandello's novels do not escape tragic visions. *Uno, nessuno e centomila* is permeated by sentiments of dread and angst, beginning with the novel's title, whereby a one becomes "a hundred thousand" is in reality an entity devoid of all ontological consistency, or more precisely a "none." Analogous sentiments also shape many passages of *Il fu Mattia Pascal* and are voiced most explicitly in the *lanterninosofia* [philosophy of the lantern] of Anselmo Paleari. Dejectedly, this character laments the twilight of reason and notes that the loss of a cohesive force—the center formerly given by the brightness of the lanterns of scientific, philosophical, and religious systems (151)—has deeply affected the individual and the collective experience of modernity. In fact, like the somnambulists described in the final section of Hermann Broch's novel, *The Sleepwalkers*, twentieth-century people are doomed to a life of wandering and to the formation of ephemeral units at best: "Nell'improvviso bujo . . . chi va di qua, chi di là, chi torna indietro, chi si raggira; nessuno più trova la via: si urtano, si aggregano un momento in dieci, in venti . . . e tornano a sparpagliarsi in gran confusione, in furia angosciosa" (152) [In the sudden darkness . . . people go here and there, move back, turn around; they no longer find their way: they collide, form ephemeral groups of ten, twenty, then they scatter again in a great confusion, in an anguished fury].

These narratives' problematic relation to the cultural and historical contexts of modernity did not go unnoticed by early critics and theorists of the period. Eric Auerbach, for example, detects in the novels of Proust, Joyce, and Woolf "a certain atmosphere of universal doom . . . something hostile to the reality being represented."[29] Likewise, Lukács comments that in modernist narratives the totality of the historical process—the "concrete (in Hegel, 'real') potentiality"[30]—is either excluded or allowed to enter only in a discredited state of unstructured entropy. For this reason, Lukács notes that modernism no longer can achieve the representation of the "type"—an ideal synthesis of private and public man—but tends toward an excessively introspective mode, one capable of generating only a fragmentary, elusive depiction of selfhood. Walter Benjamin also, in a succinct and enlightening formulation from "On Some Motifs in Baudelaire," detects in the consciousness of the self-as-*flâneur* sentiments of "spleen" and "melancholy" provoked by the serial and fragmented images of modern life. "The spleen," he writes, "exposes the passing moment in all its nakedness. To his horror, the melancholy man sees the earth revert to a mere state of nature. No breadth of prehistory surrounds it: there is no aura" (185).

The Modernist Turn: The Novel in the Age of Husserl and Saussure

Benjamin, Lukács, and Auerbach also suggest that artistic modernity is a space of transcendence. For Auerbach, the narrative of *To the Lighthouse* illustrates a paradox. While it portrays experience as incongruent and incomplete—a "random fragment plucked from the course of a life" (547)—it also emanates the confidence that art and the artist might acquire an omnipotent role and ultimately portray the totality of life's fate. Like Auerbach, Lukács notices that to these novels' discrediting representation of historical and cultural reality corresponds a reemergence of nineteenth-century Platonic credos (68) of the Word as Genesis' *logos*, exemplified, among others, in the Goethian notion of "*Dichtung (as) Wahrheit*" and in Gustave Flaubert's conceptualization of literary language as an order above the contingency of life: "a book dependent on nothing external."[31]

Walter Benjamin's observations also touch upon the reactionary impulses of modernist narratives detected by Lukács and Auerbach. In "On Some Motifs in Baudelaire," from *Illuminations*, he writes that some modern writers do not simply mourn lost unities but, as a remedy to sentiments of "spleen" and "melancholia," develop "the protective eye" (191) of the person of contemplative stability. As a figure diametrically opposed to that of the *flâneur*, this is someone who no longer tolerates the "shocks" (161) of heterogeneous and swiftly moving images and therefore begins to gaze at the moving crowd in order to carve out self-contained, identical representation. In Benjamin's words, "His attitude towards the crowd is . . . one of superiority, inspired as it is by his observation post at the window of an apartment building. From this vantage point he scrutinizes the throng. . . . His opera glasses enable him to pick out individual genre scenes" (173). Translating the image of the man of contemplative stability in rhetorical terms, Benjamin notes that his gaze articulates itself in the restoration of a nineteenth-century language of Baudelairian "correspondances." These are expressions that not only enact the pluralization and regress of the "allegories," but, in a return to auratic modes of representation, seek to transform them into the finite and adequate "symbols" of the past: "*correspondances* may be described as an experience which seeks to establish itself in crisis-proof form. This is possible only in the realm of the ritual" (182). With these observations Benjamin points out how a different scenario occurs in early-twentieth-century art and how it bears upon the practices of avant-gardism and modern novelists. By the mid-1920s, writers operating outside the context of the Germanic "*Sprachkrise*"[32] start trusting in the possibility of containing in a totalizing order of language the complexity and transience of the phenomenal space, the sense of contingency and ambiguity inhabiting the sense of history and the self. To be more specific, while Dada's excessive practice of ephemerality and chaos causes the group to disappear,[33] both the surrealist avant-garde and the novelists retreat from their initial poetics of ephemerality and contradiction and move toward an ideology of progress and resolution. Quite possibly bearing in mind the surrealists' adherence to the hopeful messages of communism, in the essay "Surrealism," from *Illuminations*, Benjamin comments that the "profane illumination(s)" no longer find Breton and Aragon "equal to it or to themselves" (179). In "On Some Motifs in Baudelaire" he presents Proust's work as a desperate attempt to restore narrative to the position of the epic, that is to a former narration of symbolic unity: "Proust's eight-volume work conveys an idea of the efforts it took to restore the figure of the storyteller to the present generation."[34]

The reactionary linguistic ideality detected by Benjamin in some of the artistic practices of modernity has also occupied much of the attention of poststructuralist thinkers. In *The Postmodern Condition* Lyotard warns the critic against all easy assimilation of modernist narratives to avant-gardist and postmodernist practices. If the postmodern sublime is the condition of emergence of the modernist artwork, for Lyotard it is not its end point. Nostalgia brings modernity to "block"[35] figurality while questing for totalizing symbols in all spheres of culture. Indeed, Lyotard locates this gesture not only in our century's legitimizing "metanarratives" of political order and social progress but, along with Derrida,[36] also within the main developments of modernity's speculative and linguistic thought.

Broadly summarized through these theorists' frameworks, the modern episteme is seen as the culmination of Western culture's assumption that the human subject can ultimately rise above the temporal and spatial continuum in a totalizing order of representation. This logic, as Derrida has argued in *Of Grammatology*, is likely to have originated in the human experience of speech. As opposed to written communication, the words uttered by the speaker do not need graphic mediation and therefore foster the illusion of an absence of temporality and spacing (27–73). Otherwise stated, since in lived speech deferral and difference are reduced to a minimum, the speaker appears to be established as the Subject of an utterance capable of uniting univocally a signifier with a signified. Like Derrida, Lyotard also has commented in *The Postmodern Condition* that oral expressions, such as those made in the context of interviews and conversations, create a denotative illusion — one, that is, which seems to place the sender in a position of knowledge of an identifiable and representable referent (9). Despite the fact that these appropriative experiences are but lures, they nonetheless have structured entire epochs of thought. In *Dissemination* Derrida traces them to Plato and specifically to the "books"[37] of the *Dialogues* and *Timaeus*. He notes that whereas the pre-Socratic philosophies of Thales, Heraclitus, and Anaximander had partially tolerated the amorphousness and transitoriness of life, or the *"Khora"* (161), *Timaeus* firmly establishes symbolization as *"pharmakon"* (63–171), a semiotic remedy whereby a Subject can impose clarity and distinctness to the object of representation. Platonic ideality has not only established itself as the main frame of the Western mind, but has had illustrious progeny. Notwithstanding Kant's critique of the categories used by the speculative tradition to frame and structure experience, numerous metaphysical flowers have bloomed on European soil, particularly in the early decades of the last century. They are apparent for Derrida and Lyotard in the phenomenology of Husserl and in the structural linguistics of Saussure.[38] Starting with his *Logical Investigations* of 1900–1901 up to *Formal and Transcendental Logic* of 1929, Husserl rejects as logically invalid those laws that are acquired through perception alone. Whereas logic produces laws that are universal and necessary, perception is only capable of generalizations obtained by means of induction. Nonetheless, since for Husserl individual entities are contingent and temporal manifestations of universal, unchanging essences, the philosopher remains convinced that the perceiving consciousness can achieve logical "truths." Otherwise stated, when consciousness perceives the elements of the world of experience—the *"hic et nunc"*—it also has an immediate intuition of a particular case of an essence, or a *"quid."* Hence, Husserl's famous definition of the science of phenomenology as a universal philosophical system dependent upon evidence derived from the phenomenal experience. However, it is important to bear in mind that the inclusion of data obtained by experience is only a stepping stone toward idealist grounds. This is why the philosophical method of phenomenology is the *"epoché,"* or "phenomenological reduction." Indebted to the Cartesian philosophical doubt, *epoché* includes the temporal and spatial existence of particulars only to bracket them in order to establish that which remains unchanging and essential, or *"eidetic,"* in a Subject's perception of the world. In short, in Husserlian phenomenology, the open-ended, nonabsolute knowledge of the perceiving consciousness is transformed into an unambiguous intellectual dominion, a space of absolute, indubitable recognition: the *esse* of a *percipi*.

Structural linguistics mirrors the methodological idealism of phenomenology since, by way of a forceful reduction of semiosis and its processes of signification, it attempts to lend to the speaker the same certainty that Husserl sought for the perceiving self. In the 1915 *Cours*, a revival of romantic linguistic theories[39] allows Saussure to propose a restriction of the field of interpretative possibilities through the elimination of the historical and differential being of language—a being he describes as "many-sided and heterogeneous; straddling several areas simultaneously . . . a mass that lends itself to no other classification."[40] Upon this exclusion, Saussure also establishes how the semantic and grammatical value of a sign is to emerge only in a binary, closed opposition: "The entire mechanism of language . . . is based on oppositions . . . and on the phonic and conceptual differences that they imply" (121). To use a well-known description proposed by Roman Jakobson,[41] the propriety sought in the structuralist conception of language is achieved by a neutralization of figures, by the delimitation of metaphors and metonymies in privative oppositions and according to a linear unfolding toward closure.

It is precisely within the broader context of these foundational gestures of early-twentieth-century thought that one ought to recontextualize modernist novels. While it is undeniable that postmodernist elements do inhabit many of the narratives of the French, Anglo-Saxon, and Italian literary traditions, these are also works that resort to the abstraction of the aesthetic to recreate that order lost in the cultural and historical experience of modernity. Otherwise stated, without confining these narratives in a taxonomic, rigidly defined notion of modernism, it is also possible nonetheless to locate in them a shared desire to restore former paradigms of representation, to put together in totalizing symbols the fragments of the experience of modernity evoked by the figurality of the text.

The Return of the Symbol

The pursuit of a literary apparatus capable of countering the sense of a crumbling personal and cultural history finds its clearest expression in a passage of Joyce's *A Portrait of the Artist as a Young Man* (1916). A young

Stephen Daedalus lays bare the notion that the only worthy experience is the one created by the patterning power of art. In his words, pleasure does not reside in the expression of the sensible world by means of "a language manycolored and richly storied," but in "a lucid, supple periodic prose."[42] This belief in the primacy of "symbolic" over "allegorical" modes of representation is voiced in Stephen's often-quoted speech to Lynch. Stephen begins by sharply distinguishing between improper and proper art. The first, or "kinetic," foster both in the artists and in their audience a sense of instability and change (204). By contrast, proper practices tend toward the production of "an aesthetic stasis" (206) and do so in a tripartite movement of "*integritas*," "*consonantia*" and "*quidditas*" (212 ff.). While *integritas*, through the creation of a void around the object, allows the apprehension of the image "as self-bounded and self-contained upon the immensurable background of space or time which is not" (212), *consonantia* sums up all of the image's parts into an organic whole. Finally, from the synthesis of both *integritas* and *consonantia* the essence of the object, or the *quidditas* of its Being, can emerge without ambiguity and confusion: "You see that it is that thing which it is and no other thing . . . the whatness of a thing" (213). Subsequent passages of the novel confirm Stephen's aestheticist formulations, as art is consistently promoted to the means of rising above the contradictions of life at large, including those of Stephen's household, but also of Ireland, by then a country deeply fragmented in oppositional camps of nationality, language, and religion. The novel's ending confirms the ideology that informs the narrative. In the final entry of Stephen's diary, written on April 27, Stephen invokes his namesake, the mythical Daedalus—the artificer who built and escaped from Minos' labyrinth—to help him forge his artistic vocation and rise in a flight above the temporal and spatial elusiveness of the earth: "Old father, old artificer, stand by me now and ever in good stead" (253).

An analogous desire to recover from experience in the sanctuary of art is to be found in many other artist-stories of modernism. Considering the origin of this type of narrative, this is not surprising. As the work of Bakhtin in the typology of genres suggests, the artist-story, or "*Künstlerroman*," is part of "the novel of ordeal."[43] Unlike the "*Bildungsroman*," or apprenticeship novel, it conceptualizes the temporal and spatial dimension of existence, or what Bakhtin names the "chronotope" (27), as a state of Fall to be recovered in the course of the narrative. In Bakhtin's words, "the novel of ordeal always begins where a deviation from the normal social and biographical course of life begins, and ends where life resumes its normal course" (14). For this reason, the genre's antecedents are located in the Greek romances and the Christian hagiographies (12). These are narratives whose resolution is strictly dependent upon the feats of a heroic individuality. By implication, then, the *Künstlerroman* becomes modernity's favorite genre to reestablish the authority of the artist and his or her privileged function in a time of auratic decay.

Heroic recovery by the artist is precisely what occurs in Virginia Woolf's *To the Lighthouse*. In the beginning of the novel's final section, the narrative explicitly describes how the ravage of history cannot be ordered by the care of ordinary, "common" people. In fact, despite days of hard work, Mrs. McNab, Mrs. Bast, and Mrs. Bast's son have succeeded only in "stay(ing) the corruption and the rot" (209) of the Ramsays' house. Thus, the narrative shifts to a character endowed with an artistic sensibility, the painter Lily Briscoe. Lily is not only the one who has the most vivid recollections of Mrs. Ramsay, but she is the vessel chosen for an important understanding or, more precisely, for the "revelation" (241) that the writing pads on Mrs. Ramsay's knee were not simply an exercise in private correspondence. They were "little, daily miracles, illuminations, matches struck unexpectedly in the dark" (240). Their function, as Lily and the reader come to learn, was to transform "allegories" into "symbols," to endow the "this and that and then this" (240) of the phenomenal experience with permanence: "In the midst of chaos there was shape; this eternal passing and flowing (she looked at the clouds going and the leaves shaking) was struck into stability" (241). Thereby, Lily proceeds to take steps to raise her medium to the same omnipotence of Mrs. Ramsay's writing. She auratically retreats from the world at large— "drawn out of gossip, out of living, out of community" (236)—and strives to sketch a drawing. Despite many difficulties and an occasional ironic commentary on the abstract, "fictional" nature of her endeavor—"it would be hung in the attics, she thought" (267)—she nonetheless proceeds in her quest; "it would be rolled up and flung under a sofa; yet even so, it was true" (267). Toward the end of the narrative, Lily achieves her goal: "With a sudden intensity, as if she saw it clear for a second, she drew a line there, in the center. It was done, it was finished. Yes, she thought

. . . I have had my vision" (310). Meanwhile, Mr. Ramsay and his children, James and Cam, land at the lighthouse. As an icon of towering permanency, the building emerges as a symbol of the omnipotence of art and of the artist's endeavor in the midst of the fluctuating and ever-changing movement of experience: "The Lighthouse became immovable, and the light on the distant shore became fixed" (272).

A promotion of artistic symbolization analogous to that of Woolf's *To the Lighthouse* is to be found in Marcel Proust's *A la Recherche du temps perdu*. If, as the first book of the novel suggests, subjectivity and experience are a space of utter figurality, the narrative also establishes a powerful antidote in involuntary acts of memory. These are privileged moments of respite from fragmentation and confusion and are exemplified in the famous episode of the madeleine, where a familiar taste allows the main protagonist Marcel to give wholeness and identity to an entire period of his life. The full significance of this revelation, however, is disclosed in the last section of the novel, *Le Temps retrouvé*. In the course of the *"matinée Guermantes,"* and upon experiencing three epiphanies analogous to that of the madeleine, Marcel realizes that they are the key to achieving an absolute form of knowledge:

au vrai, l'être qui alors goûtait en moi cette impression la goûtait en ce qu'elle avait de commun dans un jour ancien et maintenant ce qu'elle avait d'extra-temporel, un être qui n'apparaissait que quand, par une de ces identité entre le présent et le passé, il pouvait se trouver dans le seul milieu où il pût vivre, jouir de l'essence des choses, c'est-à-dire en dehors du temps. (179)

[In truth, the person within me who was at that moment enjoying this impression, enjoyed it in the qualities it possessed that were common to both an earlier day and the present moment, qualities that were independent of all considerations of time; and this person came into play only when, by this process of identifying the past with the present, he could find himself in the only environment in which he could live and enjoy the essence of things, that is to say, entirely outside time.]

Nonetheless, these privileged moments of cognition depend on chance occurrences and acts of voluntary recollection remain powerless before the utter *"défilé cinématographique des choses"* (189) [the filmic parade of things]. It is precisely at this juncture that Marcel introduces the redemptive power of art. This is a power that resides in a "bared"[44] model of iteration, in the rewriting of lived life in the pages of a book. As Marcel comments, because "true" life exists only in literary transposition—"La vrai vie, la vie enfin découverte et éclaircie, la seule vie par conséquent pleinement vécue, c'est la littérature" (202) [true life, life discovered at last and made clear, consequently the only life that is really lived, is literature]—he retreats from phenomenality at large into the sanctuary of his room, from where he promises to create a literary monument of order and eternality for himself and for future generations. In an analogy to that "house of fiction" described by Henry James as a way to order "The spreading field, the human scene,"[45] he sketches his book project as a cathedral. Despite a momentary, ironic awareness that such endeavor might not last more than one hundred years (348–49), this nonetheless is presented as a symbol of harmony and order spanning several generations:

Moi je dis que la loi cruelle de l'art est que les êtres meurent et que nous-mêmes mourions . . . pour que pousse l'herbe non de l'oubli mais de la vie éternelle, l'herbe drue des oeuvres fécondes, sur laquelles les générations futures viendront faire gaiement . . . leurs "déjeuner sur l'herbe" (343)

[I say that it is the cruel law of art that human beings should die and that we ourselves must die after exhausting the gamut of suffering, so that the grass, not of oblivion but of eternal life may grow, the thick grass of fecund works of art, on which future generations will come and . . . gaily have their "picnic lunch."]

The teleological, ideal visions that inform this as well as other passages of modernist novels are by no means confined to discursive levels but often unfold in stylistic patterns. Here they create a variety of structuring devices that, as Derrida has commented in *Writing and Difference*, should be interpreted as additional tools to repossess the fragments of history and culture: "The concept of centered structure is in fact the concept of a play based on a fundamental ground, a play constituted on the basis of a fundamental immobility and a reassuring certitude, which itself is beyond the reach of play" (278).

In Joyce's *Ulysses*, for example, the disquieting multiplication of differences is neutralized by a number of strategies. Not only did Joyce collaborate on the novel's first guidebooks,[46] but his revival of medieval and epic structuring devices are but additional means to create a symbolic order out of the figurality of the text. To be more specific, while the epic, or "mythic method" allows him to connect each of the chapters to one of the Homeric episodes, the medieval spatial order institutes organization by making each of the novel's sections correspond to arts, hours of the day, colors, parts of the human body, and so forth.[47] Further, and because "in Joyce. . . . The utilization of English . . . brings about all sort of worldwide reterritorializations,"[48] *Ulysses'* newfound stability in language is also reflected in much smaller units of the narrative. The tone for many of these semiotic recoveries is set in the "Proteus" chapter. Stephen's realization that experience reaches the perceiver within the shifting dimensions of time and space—the figures of the "*nebeneinander*" and the "*nacheinander*"—is followed by the important corrective provided by the rhythmic linguistic patterns of an aesthetic language: "Shut your eyes and see. Stephen closed his eyes to hear his boots crush crackling wrack and shells. You are walking through it howsomever. I am, a stride at a time . . . I am getting on nicely in the dark . . . Sounds solid . . . Rhythm begins, you see. I hear" (37). Shortly after this revelation, two cocklepickers approach. Wandering gypsies, they speak a mixture of different languages. Yet, out of their opaque and cacophonous sounds, the possibility that meaning can be fixed is also foregrounded. Stephen tears a piece of paper from a letter and begins to write: "Paper . . . Old Deasy' letter. Here . . . Signs on white field . . . Hold hard . . . Coloured on a flat: yes, that's right" (48).

Stephen's realization that language is a provider of stability is also shared by Bloom. As Franco Moretti has suggested in his recent *Opere Mondo*, Bloom's stream of consciousness is not merely an outstanding achievement of the modernist presentation of narrative consciousness, but it is also a powerful semiotic weapon to restore the modern self to a position of mastery of both inner and outer experience. In Moretti's words, Leopold's stream represents the modernist equivalent of the epic shield of Heracles, the means for "allowing vertical meaning to emerge from the horizontal world of prose."[49] In "The Lestrygonians" section of the novel, for example, as Bloom walks along Grafton Street, a proliferation of external stimuli are entering his consciousness and preventing him from focusing on his main existential concern, namely Molly's unfaithfulness. Leopold's initial statement that "Molly looks out of plumb" (168) recedes in a horizontal succession of details, initially provoked by the "China silks" (168) in the window of Brown Thomas's store and later by the fragments of an advertisement for a company selling land in Turkey. However, in and by language, Bloom arrests the dislocating effects of external stimuli of modern life. Through the repetition of the word "plumb" and its variations, he is able to create an isotopic grid of meaning, a system of semantic analogies allowing him to complete his reflection concerning Molly: "A warm human plumpness settled down on his brain. . . . With hungered flesh obscurely, he mutely craved to adore" (168). A few paragraphs later, the word "plumb" reemerges from the figurality of the background and denotes the passage in its entire clarity. Leopold, now restored to the position of Subject of the enunciation, can finally objectify the feelings of his pain in an utterance of symbolic stability: "What is home without Plumtree's potted meat? Incomplete" (171).

There are, however, other recovering strategies that Leopold's stream puts in place. As Moretti again suggests, these are sets of commonplaces whose function is to reduce alterity to a more familiar range of explanation, to a scenario in which the modern Subject and the bearer of Western culture can recover former frames of reference, including that sense of sociopolitical and cultural centrality lost by the advent of modernity. In "The Lotus Eaters," for instance, the threat to cultural purity suggested by the hybrid images of European "family tea" (71) and tropical vegetation of the Orient that cross Bloom's mind as he stands before the window of the hybrid Belfast *and* Oriental Tea Company, are immediately followed by a verbal reduction of exotic components to a prosaic—and Western—familiarity: "The far East. Lovely spot it must be: the garden of the world, big lazy leaves to float about on, cactuses, flowery meads, snaky lianas they call them. . . . Those Cinghalese lobbing around in the sun, in dolce far niente. Not doing a hand's turn all day. Sleep six months out of twelve." (71) Likewise, in "Calypso" the aporias of modern capitalism suggested by the juxtaposition of the German enterprise to grow citrus in Israel with the old, desolate Irish woman crossing the street, are cast off by another banality and ultimately neutralized by farcical, deflating statements. The horrifying contradiction, the lack of social rationality lurking at the center of modern society is attributed to "Morning mouth bad images. Got up wrong side of the bed" (61). In short, at the level of the sentence also, language becomes the tool to order the labyrinths of civilization and culture of twentieth-century life and the displacing effects that these have on the constitution of the self. Not surprisingly, then, even that flowing river of threatening figurality that Molly and her monologue represent comes to be contained and won over by Leopold in one last reconciliation. Despite her recent unfaithfulness, at the very end of "Penelope" Molly is again willing to give herself to her husband and decides to allow Leopold to end his nomadic wandering and return home. Her voice inscribes the conciliatory movement of the novel as a whole since, after much drifting, it settles in the affirmative, and repeated utterance of "yes I said yes I will Yes" (783). Since Molly's many utterances of "yes" join the beginning phoneme of *Ulysses*—the letter "S" of "Telemachus"— they also provide an iconic representation of language as the "*omphalos*"; the semiotic chord of the modernist episteme, linking together in a literary structure the regressive and contradictory images of modernity. Further as Derrida has commented, in the sibilant sound of the "S" might also be contained Joyce's authorial voice of triumph and jubilation over difference; the "yes-laughter of encircling reappropriation, of all-powerful odyssean recapitulation . . . the encyclopedic reappropriation of absolute knowledge which gathers itself up close to itself, as Life of the Logos."[50]

Without approaching the levels of complexity and sophistication of *Ulysses'* appropriative devices, other novels of modernism also tend to a structural ordering. Moretti, for example, has cogently commented that the "book" promised by Marcel at the end of *Le Temps retrouvé* might very well be present embryonically as early as *Du Côté de chez Swann*, in the syntax shaping the description of the famous episode of the madeleine. This often-quoted scene occurs on a gray, winter day. Marcel has been attempting to remember his childhood at Combray, but only the images "tournoyantes et confuses" (14) [twirling and confusing] of his bedtime kiss and childhood readings have emerged. However, in the paragraph that follows, the figural movement is brought to a close and order begins to emerge. The regressive accumulation of adverbs and tenses in the sentence "Et bientôt, machinalement, accablé par la morne journée . . . je portai à mes lèvres une cuillerée de thé où j'avais laissé s'ammollir un morceau de madeleine" (59) [And soon, mechanically, weary after a dull day . . . I raised to my lips a spoonful of the tea in which I had soaked a morsel of the cake] is brought to a close and a hypotactical organization rises. The meaningless details are reduced, a void is created, and denotative order begins:

Et tout d'un coup le souvenir m'est apparu. Ce goût c'était celui du petit morceau de la madeleine . . . . Et dès que j'eus reconnu le goût du morceau de madeleine . . . aussitôt la vieille maison sur la rue, où était sa chambre, vint comme un décor de théâtre . . . et avec la maison, la ville. (60–61)

[And suddenly, the memory returned. The taste was that of the little crumb of madeleine. . . . And once I had recognized the taste of the crumb of the madeleine . . . immediately the old gray house upon the street, where her room was, rose up like the scenery of a theater . . . and with the house, the town.]

From this point onwards, Marcel describes an entire section of his life by way of what he calls "les anneaux nécessaires d'un beau style" (196) [the necessary rings of a beautiful style]. As Leo Spitzer has written,[51] this is nothing but a complex hypotactical construction, a rhetorical device suggesting that the formerly fragmented self has given way to a Subject capable of defining the objects of representation in a properly ordered system of grammatical syntax. Otherwise stated, the Proustian *beau style* is a symbolic process whereby difference and temporality are organized in a hierarchical phrase.

Also in Virginia Woolf's *To the Lighthouse* and *Mrs. Dalloway*, it is style that offers the meaning lost in heterogeneous, open-ended representations. In *To the Lighthouse*, the notion that life can be perfected by art is expressed not only in the tripartite, almost Hegelian symmetry of its chapters "The Window," "Time Passes," and "To the Lighthouse" but permeates the sentence-level as well, where connotative regress is generally erased by the emergence of denotative symbols akin to the isotopic grids of meaning found in Bloom's "stream of consciousness." In *Mrs. Dalloway*, the presence of redemptive rhetorical devices is suggested by a diegesis that depends upon an extensive use of similes. As Auerbach has noted in a section of *Mimesis* that discusses the Homeric style, the simile captures the seriality of images of the object of representation within spatial and temporal relationships (6). The following passage from *Mrs. Dalloway* confirms Auerbach's observations. The regressive details embedded in the voice of Peter Walsh are brought to an end by being equated to the final term of comparison provided by the epic "simile": "Then, just as happens on a terrace in the moonlight, when one person begins to feel ashamed that he is already bored . . . very quiet, sadly looking at the moon, does not like to speak, moves his foot, clears his throat, notices some iron scroll on a table leg, stir a leaf, but says nothing—so Peter Walsh did now" (63). As in the case of Joyce's novels, then, the organization of Woolf's *To the Lighthouse* and *Mrs. Dalloway* confirms Lily Briscoe's conceptualization of the modern artwork as an object "on the surface, feathery and evanescent, one color melting into another . . . but beneath . . . clamped together with bolts of iron" (255).

In Italian modernism, a metaphysical functioning of language might be harder to assess. In fact, despite the undertakings of scholars such as Gian Paolo Biasin, Robert Dombroski, and Gregory Lucente, many critics focus on the high degree of tolerance for figurality present in Pirandello's and Svevo's novels. For this reason, Pirandello and Svevo have at times been discussed as writers of the *Sprachkrise*.[52] In the case of Pirandello this critical assessment has been legitimated by the essay "L'umorismo" [On humor], which Pirandello wrote in 1908. The piece not only engages polemically with the neo-Hegelian idealism of Benedetto Croce's *Estetica* (1902) but, in the vein of Heraclitus, Democritus, and Giordano Bruno, puts forward a conceptualization of experience as a state of boundless transformation and process.[53] More significantly, the essay outlines two different models of representing this condition of being. On one hand stand the practices of the epic and the tragic poets. Informed by an idealistic logic, they contain life in the stability of form: "la logica . . . tende appunto a fissare quel che é mobile, mutabile, fluido, tende a dare un valore assoluto a ciò che é relativo" (154–55) [now logic tends precisely to fix what is changeable and fluid; it tends to give an absolute value to what is relative]. On the other hand, there are the writers of *umorismo*. Respectful of the "materialità della vita . . . cosí varia e complessa" (159) [the materiality of life, so varied and complex], they dismantle identity and evolve representational models capable of inscribing the incongruity and variability of being. In Pirandello's words, "Di qui, nell'umorismo . . . quella ricerca dei contrasti e delle contraddizioni, su cui l'opera sua si fonda, in opposizione alla coerenza cercata dagli altri" (159) [Hence, comes in the art of humor . . . a search for contrasts and contradictions, which is the basis of the art of the humorist as opposed to the coherency sought by others]. Because the first published version of this essay was dedicated by Pirandello to the character of Mattia Pascal "Alla buon'anima di Mattia Pascal bibliotecario" [To the good soul of the late Mattia Pascal] — the piece as a whole often has been interpreted as Pirandello's poetic manifesto and as a document to distinguish his narratives from those of other novelists operating in the French and English literary traditions.

Suggestive as the essay might be for a study of the spatial dispersion of the theoretical *Sprachkrise* and for future developments in the tradition of the Italian novel, it nonetheless can be granted only local validity in Pirandello's production. More specifically, whereas the essay "On Humor" certainly can be interpreted as a justification of the stylistic expressionism deployed in a number of Pirandello's short stories, the discursive structures of *Il fu Mattia Pascal* and *Uno, nessuno e centomila* are situated within the boundaries of more traditional forms.

As Pirandello comments in the section "L'umorismo e la retorica" (46–59) [Humor and rhetoric], the primary rhetorical manifestations of "umorismo" are to be found in styles that dislocate symbolic representation through a variety of means, including the use of dialects, linguistic variants, pastiche, and other macaronic practices.[54] "E l'umorismo," he writes, "lo troveremo—ripeto—nelle espressioni dialettali, nella poesia macaronica e negli scrittori ribelli alla retorica" (53) [Humor—I repeat— will be found in dialects, in macaronic poetry and in those writers who are opposed to rhetoric]. Significantly, among the foreign practitioners of *umorismo*, Pirandello mentions Rabelais and Sterne, while he considers Meli, Folengo, Porta, Bersezio, and Lombardy's nineteenth-century *pasticheurs*, or *scapigliati*, as Italian authors who have departed from the formal stability of traditional rhetoric.

It is certainly possible to locate in several of Pirandello's short stories from *Novelle per un anno* a model of representation akin to the one discussed in the essay "On Humor." As Benvenuto Terracini and, more recently, Romano Luperini have noted,[55] *Novelle* articulate a vision of life as a space of incommunicability and alienation unredeemable by symbolic correspondences. This vision brings Pirandello to experiment with a variety of narrative techniques, ranging from expressionistic devices to surreal representations. Thus, for example, the narratives of "Rondone e Rondinella," "Lontano," and "Nenia"[56] translate the incommunicability of language by textualizing the incomprehensible, defamiliarizing idiom of foreign speakers. Other stories achieve the same effect by juxtaposing standard Italian to entire fragments of vernacular expressions drawn from central and northern dialects. The absence of proper, single nomination, is suggested by Pirandello even in stories narrated within the boundaries of a single language. This is the case of "Ciàula scopre la luna,"[57] where the finality and closure sought in traditional models of representation are unsettled by an extensive use of indefinite expressions and nominal sentences produced by paradigmatic enumerations of nouns, verbs, and adjectives. Yet, as Benvenuto Terracini has commented (360 ff.), the key to assess the depth of Pirandello's experimentalism is to be found in the stories' unstable point of view—that is to say, in the stylistic device of free indirect discourse. This device, which is present in the majority of the tales, is the product of a fusion of the contradictory voices and perspectives of both narrators and characters. Its effect is one of disorientation and chaos, of loss of epistemological integrity and cognitive rationality.

However, if *Novelle* emphasize (in and by language) failure and discordance, Pirandello's *Il fu Mattia Pascal* and *Uno, nessuno e centomila* strike the reader for their departure from an original condition of dualism as well as for their final dependence upon a homogenous, at times even traditional style. In this sense, then, these are works that illustrate the symbolic utopian compensation that Fredric Jameson in his *The Political Unconscious* not only uncovers in the "framing and containment strategies"[58] of the early modernist practices of Henry James and Joseph Conrad but ultimately comes to praise as a worthy means to counter the derealized experience brought about by the advent of modernization. More specifically, in Pirandello's novels, the radical temporality and ambiguity that Mattia and Vitangelo have experienced as characters do not engender a corresponding mode of narration. On the contrary, in the process of narrating their own story, Mattia and Vitangelo are relocated to the position of Subjects of representation, domesticating their displaced and postmodern selves[59] in a space of identity and closure. Like a nineteenth-century narrative, *Il fu Mattia Pascal* is composed of eighteen chronological chapters and is prefaced by two introductory sessions, while *Uno, nessuno e centomila* follows a rigid division of eight causal, consecutive books, all including corresponding subsections. This stylistic reappropriation is confirmed in the epilogues of both novels, which disclose how a reconstruction of the self has occurred in the fictional, abstract space of the aesthetic—in a zone, that is, ideally divorced from the contaminating forces of history and the displacing effects of the Other. As we might recall, the first novel begins with a preterite tense suggesting the loss, or even the absence of a "proper" authoritative name: "mi chiamavo Mattia Pascal" (3) [my name *was* Mattia Pascal]. Yet, as a result of a process of literary self-creation, it ends with the present tense of "to be"; in the affirmation, that is, of an ontological recovery: "Io sono il fu Mattia Pascal" (233) [I *am* the late Mattia Pascal]. This also explains why the novel as a whole is framed by the "Boccamazza" library. Initially presented as a heterogeneous and dusty collection of books that Mattia has been hired to order and restore, the Boccamazza emerges as a spatial icon of the enabling use of symbolization that both Mattia—and partially the library itself—will undergo in the course of the narrative. Vitangelo's narration in *Uno, nessuno e centomila* parallels the metaphysical intent of Mattia's, as in the diegetic process Vitangelo's narrating "I" objectifies the experience of Vitangelo-the-character into a cohesive image. The epilogue confirms the aesthetic recovery of the novel by transforming the past tense of the initial ontological crisis—"credevo d'essere per tutti un Moscarda" (12) [I thought I was for everybody the same Moscarda]—into the affirmative proposition of "io credo" (222) [I believe]. It is precisely for this reason that, as Robert Dombroski has recently argued in *Properties of Writing*, the closure of *Uno, nessuno e centomila* bears striking analogies with some of the texts of our philosophical modernity. Vitangelo's lifeworld experience is not only akin to the Husserlian notion of being-in-the-world of undifferentiated vision, but his decision to abandon the city and retreat in a hospice for the mentally ill also doubles Husserl's notion of a transcendental, self-sufficient Subjectivity. As the novel tells us, thanks to his retreat, Vitangelo is able to fashion a mythical identity, one no longer dependent upon the forces of history and society but endlessly produced as artifice: "Sono quest'albero. Albero, nuvola; domani libro o vento: il libro che leggo, il vento che bevo. Tutto fuori, vagabondo" (224) [I am this tree. Tree, cloud; tomorrow book or wind; the book that I read, the wind that I drink. All outside, all vagrant]. Such mythical identity,

Dombroski reminds us in his *Properties* (91), is ultimately to be interpreted not so much as a critique of capitalistic logic and modernization in the sense outlined by Jameson, but more as a choice that endorses the position of the Right. More specifically, it is a choice that dangerously approaches the D'Annunzian mythological machine as well as aestheticization of the self and the self's relation to the world that occurred in Italy after the consolidation of the fascist regime.

As in the case of Pirandello, Italo Svevo's narratives have also been interpreted within the context of the *Sprachkrise*. In part, this has occurred for biographical reasons, since Svevo was from the city of Trieste, which historically has been under the repeated influence of the culture of *Mitteleuropa*. More subtle arguments however, have focused on the undeniable undercurrent of skepticism about the authority of language running through *La coscienza di Zeno*. The narrative is allegedly part of a psychoanalytical cure that has been suggested to Zeno by "Dottor S." in order to give stability and continuity to his displaced subjectivity: "Scriva! Scriva! Vedrà come arriverà a vedersi intero" (26) [Write away! And you will see how you will get a clear picture of yourself]. Zeno, however, does not seem to receive any immediate benefits from his writing. He comments that his words are diseased, incapable of recovering the people and the events of his past and present life. He also notes that, as a dialect speaker of an idiom halfway between German and Croatian, his choice of writing in standard Italian will impair a truthful representation of his consciousness. Other statements extend the ineffectuality and powerlessness of verbal language to affect symbolization in general. For example, in order to stop smoking, Zeno attempts to impose a pattern on time by writing numbers. His endeavor, however, not only results in a covering of walls with ever-receding dates but is obliterated by the landlord's request to replace the defaced paper. Another example of skepticism is provided by the novel's comments on music. Zeno believes that health, for him a metaphor of existential order and logical development, can be achieved by musical rhythmic patterns: "Per mettere al posto giusto le note, io devo battermi il tempo coi piedi e con la testa . . . . La musica che proviene da un organismo equilibrato è lei stessa il tempo ch'essa crea ed esaurisce. Quando lo farò cosí sarò guarito" (139) [If I am to play the notes right, I am compelled to beat time. . . . The music that is produced by a well-balanced physique is identical with the rhythm it creates and exploits; it is rhythm itself. When I can play music like that I shall be cured]. Zeno, of course, cannot play, and his inability is set against the brilliant musical execution of Bach's D Minor *Chaconne* performed by his rival Guido Speier. These skeptical comments finally add themselves to Zeno's awareness of the "fictionality" of all aestheticist endeavors voiced in his notion of "i colori complementari" (453) [the complementary colors]. As he explains it, complementary colors are an imaginary construct, the product of a literary artifice that renders written life (in this case, the colors of the sky, which a book tells about), much more intense than it really is. Nonetheless, despite the repeated emphasis on the limitations of various symbolic forms and overt examples of ironic consciousness, several passages in the narrative suggest that, in and by literary language, Zeno will achieve the order that he sought in numbers and music. At one point, for example, he recalls how poetry became the means to compensate for the death of his mother. At another point, he notes that the epistolary act, in this case a letter to his lover Carla, gave him relief: "Scrissi e riscrissi . . . era un grande conforto per me; era lo sfogo di cui abbisognavo" (300–301) [I wrote and rewrote . . . it was a great comfort; it was the release that I needed]. Considering the above statements, it comes as no surprise that, toward the end of the novel, he comes to refer to his memoirs as "miei cari fogli" (443) [my dear papers]. But, as in the case of Pirandello, it is the epilogue of the novel itself that discloses Svevo's reliance on a literary order. As Gian-Paolo Biasin has noted,[60] the end of the writing of La coscienza does coincide with Zeno's cure. This cure is exemplified in the character's newfound integration within the mediating systems of bourgeois society, notably in his successes as businessman happily married to the robust and healthy Augusta. Svevo's faith in the literary order is confirmed in Svevo's other novel, *Il vecchione*, which the author composed in 1928. An older version of Zeno begins his recollections by describing graphic representation as a pharmacological substance: "una misura di igiene cui attenderò ogni sera"[61] [a hygienic measure to which I will attend every evening]. In subsequent paragraphs, the ideality of this initial statement is expanded and language is clearly promoted to a position of epistemological superiority. Mirroring the "bare" repetition of Proust, literary transposition of lived life, or what the narrator calls "La vita . . . letteraturizzata" (372) [Life . . . made into literature], becomes the means to neutralize regress and ambiguity by allowing the modern self to persist in a single, self-contained subjectivity: "Ma io qui nella mia stanzetta posso subito essere in salvo e raccogliermi su queste carte" (136) [But here, in this small room, I can be safe and collect myself on these papers]. In an act of retrospective completion, the narrator also comments that an analogously redemptive use of symbolization was already at work in the earlier novel *La coscienza di Zeno*. For this reason, the segments of narrativized life contained in the pages of the book now appear as the only truthful moments of his past existence:

Un'altra volta io scrissi . . . anche allora si trattava di una pratica di igiene perché quell'esercizio doveva prepararmi ad una cura psicanalitica. La cura non riuscí, ma le carte restarono. Come sono preziose! Mi pare di non aver vissuto altro che quella parte di vita che descrissi. (137)

[Another time I wrote . . . even then it was a question of hygienic practice, because I was preparing myself for a psychoanalytical cure. The cure failed, but the writings remain. How precious they are! It seems to me that the only life that I have lived is the one that I have described.]

In light of these aestheticist affirmations, it is perhaps not surprising that in his essays Svevo came to express much admiration for the work of Proust and Joyce. In his "Scritti su Joyce," for example, he highly praised the cohesive structure of the Proustian's *beau style*.[62] Concerning Joyce, who had been his English teacher in Trieste in 1907, Svevo significantly wrote that the narrative of *Ulysses* was "una cosa tanto intera da sostituire la realtà" (742) [something so complete as to substitute for reality]. It may very well be that the substitution sought by *Ulysses* was precisely what Svevo was attempting to recreate as early as *La coscienza*, whose composition might have been inspired by an early reading of *Ulysses*' last chapter in 1921, when Svevo took Joyce's manuscript from Trieste to Paris (706).

Thus, without forcing that unique strand of modernism represented by the Italian novel in a too-rigid taxonomy, it is undeniable that the restoration of the "symbol" remains a conspicuous presence in this tradition also, and one that Dombroski's *Properties of Writing* correctly associates with the older, nineteenth-century endeavors of Manzoni, Verga, and

D'Annunzio as regards their shared dependency on art as the means to find a refuge for the self in the face of a troubled reality.

The *Wake* and Beyond

Given the widespread dispersal of semiotic recoveries in the first quarter of the twentieth century, it is not coincidental that the modernist imagination produced and yet attempted to depart from that epic of ambiguity and regress that is Joyce's *Finnegans Wake* (1923–39). As the most (post)modern of all modernist novels, this is a narrative that expands, to macroscopic proportions, the explosion of grotesque and fast-moving cinematic images present in *Ulysses:* the "Moviefigure(s) on in scenic section."[63] The mercurial HCE, for example, is a spreading geography of city, land, and mountain. Further, "under veerious persons" (373), he also emerges as Humphrey Chimpden Earwicker, the legendary Finn McCool, Jarl van Hoother, Persse O'Reilly, Parnell, and many others. Like HCE, ALP is an amalgam of figures: wife, mistress, Penelope, Eve, and the river flow. Nonetheless, *Finnegans Wake* is also profoundly informed by totalizing impulses. As Breon Mitchell has acutely noted, to see in *Finnegans Wake* an embodiment of a shift in Joyce's poetics runs counter to an entire apparatus of intertextual evidence and textual exhibits:

Joyce's constant enterprise from *Dubliners* on remained one which could reasonably be called modernist: to stretch the limits of his art as far as he could, to recreate the world in language, to fulfill Flaubert's dream of a book spinning like a world in the emptiness of space. *Finnegans Wake* is the logical continuation of the Joycean aesthetic, an expanding universe of language. Certainly no shift or reversal was ever implied by Joyce. He called *Ulysses* his day book, *Finnegans Wake* his night book. One led logically, in terms of the Joycean aesthetic, into the other, the seeds of the *Wake* being clearly present in *Ulysses*.[64]

Indeed, on closer inspection, the *Wake*, like *Ulysses*, puts in place a complex machinery to act upon its figures—"The Key to. Given!" (628)—and ultimately strives toward a transcendence akin to that romantic, Coleridgian aesthetics of the symbol as a "multeity-in-unity."[65]

Hence, the fluctuating borders of the characters are contained in the universality of an ontological archetype through a pattern of eternal return, or what Joyce called the "trellis" given to him by Vico's philosophy of recurrent history.[66] According to Vico, from a primitive-divine age, humanity passes through a heroic-patriarchal to a human-democratic stage. Following a period of silence, the thunder of God, which the *Wake* expresses in a 100-letter word, marks the return of the divine age and with it another beginning of the historical cycle. In short, regress is contained in the eternality of the circle; a form the novel suggests through a perfect congruity between its beginning and ending sentence: "A way a lone a last a loved a long the . . . riverrun, past Eve and Adam's, from swerve of shore to bend of bay, brings us by a commodius vicus of recirculation back to Howth Castle and Environs" (628; 3).

However, Joyce's attempts to reduce difference does not rest solely in the structures of ontological universality and cyclic history, but comes to acquire the macroscopic physiognomy of "Wakese"; the language of the novel. As a multivalent idiom based on English but composed of over forty other tongues, this is a Word that seeks to destroy the pluralization and regress of the cosmic heteroglossia in some sort of Esperanto. In the words of Anna Livia's letter, the *Wake* "is told in sounds in utter that, in signs so adds to, in universal, in polygluttural, in each auxiliary neutral idiom" (117).

Yet, and despite Joyce's intent, this novel seals the fate of the modernist, all-empowering Name, as a gulf begins to open inside and outside its structure. As Derrida has argued, "Joyce's revenge with respect to the God of Babel"[67] only partially succeeds. Because, in the process of reading, difference and alterity are constantly foregrounded, an impossible double bind opens between the master's will to erase spatialization and temporality, and the figurality haunting the novel. In Derrida's words, "Of course this hegemony remains indisputable . . . a war through which English tries to erase the other language or languages . . . to present them for reading from one angle. But one must also read the resistance to this commonwealth. . . . What matters is the contamination of the language of the master by the language he claims to subjugate, on which he has declared war. In doing so he locks himself in a double bind from which YHWH [God] himself will not have escaped" (156).

Announcing Other Voices

In addition to the unbridgeable hiatus detected by Derrida within the narrative of the *Wake*, radical developments in society and thought paralyzed claims for the redemptive power of art, for the abstraction of all aestheticist endeavors. The *Wake's* publication, which stretched from the late 1920s to 1939, coincided with a time when the pressures of history were becoming increasingly strong. As we might recall, following such events as Wall Street's 1929 collapse, Europe began witnessing a widespread economic depression and, shortly thereafter, experienced the consolidation of right-wing parties. From the mid-twenties, for example, Italy had been under the grip of Mussolini, Hitler seized power in 1933, and by 1936 Spain was a country ravaged by civil war. If those sociohistorical events invalidated metanarratives of progress and development, emerging superstructural developments further undercut the possibility of ordering experience either speculatively or aesthetically. Throughout Europe, a number of writers began to depart from the premises of methodological idealism. In 1927 Heidegger published *Being and Time* and, upon revisiting the pre-Socratic patrimony, mounted a challenge to the Western intellectual tradition from Plato onwards. He reopened the question of ontological difference and argued that being's radical temporality and spatialization precluded the positing of a Subject to an object of perception and representation, sought, as we might recall, by Husserl and Saussure. The Heideggerian critique of the epistemes informing modernity found a new impetus in the work of Wittgenstein. In the preliminary study to *The Philosophical Investigations*, *The Blue and Brown Books* (1934–35), Wittgenstein demolished his own *Tractatus Logico-Philosophicus* of 1921 by arguing that in language there are always elements of ambiguity and regress, residues of meaning ultimately irreducible to Saussurean relations of closed and binary oppositions.[68] Otherwise put, Wittgenstein displaced the paradigms of modernist representation by (re)foregrounding the limits of our language. The unsettling effects coming from the German context found a counterpart in the French intellectual milieu. In 1930 the Parisian printer Alcan published *La théorie de l'intuition dans la phénoménologie de Husserl* by Emmanuel Levinas, who had been one of Husserl's students in Freiburg. Levinas's work, however, was more than simply a bright student's introduction to his teacher's philosophy. It represented an indictment of phenomenology as a violence performed on otherness, a forceful reduction of the ontological alterity of being to a Being for a consciousness. Further, it also timidly began to lay the groundwork for an alternative theory of perception and ethics based on an openness to the infinity and alterity of the other. The animation of the French intellectual scene was enriched by the emergence of a group of founding-fathers of the tradition of counterthought. This group included Lacan and Bataille, both active participants of Kojève's rereading of Hegel conducted at La Sorbonne in the early thirties.[69] It is at this time that Georges Bataille began to formulate his theory of "sovereignty"; a description of the material negativity, the "residue" contained in the physical, political, and social body, and which remains heterogeneous to all intellectual order and dominion.[70] Another thinker, Jacques Lacan, who in 1937 published "The Mirror Stage" in *The International Journal of Psychoanalysis,* also participated in Bataille's anti-Hegelianism. Combining the insights of Freudian psychoanalysis with a differential understanding of the linguistic sign, Lacan not only demolished the idea of finite and self-identical images as the product of an "Imaginary" (mis)recognition—"the function of a méconnaissance"[71] originating in the child's reflection in the mirror—but conceptualized the space of language as a process of endless figural displacement, an incessant sliding of the signified of meaning under the signifier of language.

It is at this intersection of historical pressures coupled with new fermentation in thought that alternative artworks emerge.[72] No longer founded on the paradigms of modernist representation, they will be more akin to the Greek temples described in 1936 by Martin Heidegger.[73] Precarious, failing constructions, these temples record the forces of time in their defaced facade of stones, while the alternation of their inner chambers suggests the contradictory, confusing movements of experience. In short, this is the time when, in the French, Italian, and Anglo-Saxon literary traditions, Louis-Ferdinand Céline, Carlo Emilio Gadda, and Samuel Beckett reflect on the unrepeatability of nineteenth-century auratic notions carried out by their modernist predecessors. They do so through a more or less overt revisitation of the early legacy of the historical avant-garde, including the unanimist, the futurist, and the surrealist avant-gardes.[74] As a consequence, these three first-time novelists, encounter, like Oedipus, the elderly Laius on the path to Delphi, and at the 1930s' crossroads where the representational assumptions of our heroic cultural modernity are no longer dominant, but are beginning to succumb to the weaker configurations of an emerging postmodern aesthetics.

TURNING THE "S" INTO THE "Z"
Céline's *Voyage au bout de la nuit* and *Mort à crédit*

Moi, c'est parler qui me fatigue . . . j'aime pas parler . . .
je hais la parole . . . rien m'exténue plus.
Louis-Ferdinand Céline, *Entretiens avec le Professeur Y*[1]

[Speaking does me in . . . I don't like to talk . . .
I hate speech . . . nothing tires me more.]

Because of their thematic and chronological proximity to
the narratives of Proust, Joyce, and Woolf, Louis-Ferdinand
Céline's novels of the 1930s, *Voyage au bout de la nuit* (1932)
and *Mort à crédit* (1936), generally have been interpreted as
examples of tardive modernism.[2] In this chapter I would like
to suggest that, on the contrary, Céline's novels represent a
departure from modernist figurations of language, literary
subjectivity, and narrative representation. In order to argue
this position, I will begin by describing how *Voyage* and *Mort*
narrativize an apprenticeship into the inauthenticity of in-
herited language. Because this apprenticeship is recounted
in an "autofictional"[3] mode of diegesis—that is, in a writing
that consciously blurs the identity of fictional narrator and
historical author—*Voyage* and *Mort* also textualize a critique
of modernist literary fathers and their rhetorical practices.
However, Céline's countervision is by no means confined to
the discursive structures of his novels, but unfolds in a rhe-

torical practice of instability and ambiguity. Associated with a "feminine" mode of writing and indebted to the darker lines of developments within the French surrealist avant-garde, this practice discloses an experience of modernity till now confined at the limits of society, the self, and—ultimately—the modernist text itself. I will conclude this chapter by discussing Céline's anti-Semitic pamphlets, which were published between 1937 and 1941. Drawing upon the current reformulation of the postmodern turn, I will argue that Céline's rewriting of the most dangerous tropes of modernity should not disqualify him from the pantheon of readable novelists. On the contrary, it ought to be accepted for the valuable message it offers to harness facile celebrations of unbounded relativism of values and knowledge.

The *Bildungsroman* of Ferdinand's *Sprachkrise*: The Early Years of *Mort à crédit* (1936)

As in Joyce's *A Portrait* and Proust's *A la recherche, Mort à crédit* begins on a linguistic recollection. Ferdinand, the novel's narrator and bearer of the same first name as the historical author Destouches, nostalgically recalls how his old aunt Armide only spoke in the imperfect subjunctive.[4] Unlike Joyce's Stephen Daedalus and Proust's Marcel, however, for Ferdinand the charm of bygone speech is quickly replaced by an apprenticeship into the bankruptcy affecting language, particularly that of Auguste and Courtial des Pereires. Ferdinand's biological and spiritual fathers respectively, Auguste and Courtial, also emerge as symbols of Céline's modernist antecedents.

Like a modernist father, Auguste is obsessed with temporal and spatial ordering or, as Leblanc has put it, he is a character deeply affected by "chronomania" and "*Ordentlichkeit.*"[5] These traits are not only revealed in his frantic cleaning activities and compulsive collection of all kind of timepieces but, more significantly, they manifest themselves in his verbal behavior. The son of a "professeur de 'Rhéthorique'" (60) and a man of artistic temperament (55), Auguste uses tales to redeem his own existential distress. Throughout the narrative, he verbalizes bourgeois values of morality and hard work as the keys to achieve economic success: "Abnégation? Oui! Renoncement? Oui! Privations? Ah! Ah! Tout! Encore!" (82) [Self-sacrifice? Yes! Abnegation? Yes! Yes! Parsimony? All of it—and more!]. Nonetheless, *Mort* emphasizes how Auguste's speech is an inauthentic, phantasmagoric discourse, one intended to "animate the ghosts . . . to transform momentarily the victims into the victors."[6] The context surrounding Auguste's description of his visits to the "Exposition Universelle" (82–84) and Brighton (127–34) are cases in point. While Auguste presents them as marvelous experiences, Ferdinand notes that in reality they were miserable, catastrophic adventures in the underworld (131). The sabotaging maneuvers of another character, the neighboring lady Madame Méhon, corroborate the lack of credibility of Auguste's voice. On the occasion of Auguste's first tale, she waves a paper with "MENTEUR" [liar] written on it, while during his retelling of the English trip, she causes an explosion to end all imaginary flights (85). Likewise, Auguste's repeated verbalizations of modern capitalistic credos is shown to be empty ideological rhetoric. Not only does Auguste's life record a progressive descent into financial hardship, but Ferdinand often strays away from the "proper" course indicated by Auguste's language. In this sense, then, Auguste's life exemplifies the workings of the ideological apparatus as defined by Althusser: "all ideology represents in its necessarily imaginary distortion not the existing relation of production . . . but above all the (imaginary) relationships of individuals to the relations of production and the relations that derive from them."[7]

The discrepancy between symbols and their referents, the failure of a world-words relationship suggested thus far is, on occasion, shared by other characters in the novel. Madame Divonne, for example, trusts that Donizetti's "Lucie de Lammermoor" and Beethoven's "Clair de la lune" (113) will provide her with a refuge from her misery. Madame Pinaise and Monsieur Dorange attempt to resolve in melodramatic performances of lovers' quarrels-cum-romantic reconciliations the abusive relationships that they witness every day among the workers and tenants of the squalid city block of "le Passage." At the end of a socially alienating week, the working classes of the Parisian suburbs console themselves with another model of phantasmagoric symbolization—the mass-produced Hollywood movies that were being imported into France in the first quarter of the twentieth century.[8] Formulating something akin to the earlier critique of the bourgeois cultural industry developed in the context of the Frankfurt School,[9] *Mort* presents them as systems of subjection, fostering quiescence in the viewers and, ultimately, interpellating them as additional subjects to "suture"[10] with the dominant ideology. In short, to use a more Lacanian formulation, the narrative explains that in order to challenge a derealized, fragmented experience, Auguste and other characters engage in "Imaginary" quests for stability and closure, in mythical searches for an impossible *"plénitude."*

Besides undoing the father's name by way of foregrounding the incredibility of discourse, the discrepancy between symbols and reality, the narrative also does so by connecting language to the crisis points of Ferdinand's life. Virtually all of Ferdinand's failures in the workplace are occasioned by speech-acts. The malicious words of Monsieur Lavelongue terminate his employment at Berlope (149), while his apprenticeship at Gorloge is put to an end by the seductive voice of Gorloge's wife. As a result, Auguste engages in repeated examples of verbal domination. At times he shames Ferdinand into accepting his values by evoking an illustrious, intimidating canon of humanistic—and Western—intellectuals:

Il faisait des phrases entières latines . . . il me jetait l'anathème, il déclamait à l'antique. Il s'interrompait pour des pauses . . . pour m'expliquer . . . parce que j'avais pas d'instruction, le sens des 'humanités' . . . Lui, il savait tout . . . J'étais méprisé de partout, même par la morale des Romains, par Cicéron, par tout l'Empire et les Anciens . . . Il savait tout ça mon papa. (198)

[He used to throw off entire phrases in Latin . . . hurling his anathemas at me, perorating in the classical manner . . . to explain to me, I was so uneducated, what the humanities meant . . . As for him, he knew everything . . . I was condemned from all sides by Roman moral standards, by Cicero, by the Empire, by the whole antique world . . . My Papa knew it all.]

Other times language becomes the space of the father's totalizing explanations, as in the following sections, where a number of minority groups are identified as the source of his existential distress and are then subjected to the violence of his racial slurs:

Il déconnait à pleine bourre. . . . Il en avait pour tous les goûts. . . . Des juifs . . . des intrigants . . . les Arrivistes . . . Et puis surtout des Francs-

Maçons. . . . Je ne sais pas ce qu'ils venaient faire par là . . . Il traquait partout des dadas. (158)

[He had shivering fits. . . . He railed against everything. . . . The Jews . . . confidence tricksters . . . plotters . . . social climbers and, above all, the Freemasons. . . . I don't know how they came into it . . . He raved on.]

Mon père . . . Il s'en allait en monologues. Il vituperait, il arrêtait pas . . . Tout le bataclan des maléfices . . . Le Destin . . . Les Juifs . . . La Poisse . . . L'Exposition . . . La Providence . . . Les Francs-Maçons. (196)

[My father . . . drifted off into monologues. He fumed, he wouldn't stop. . . . The whole evil hooroosh . . . Fate . . . The Jews . . . Poverty . . . The Exhibition . . . Providence . . . The Freemasons.]

And precisely because language is experienced as either a space of illocutionary violence and/or of Utopian—and therefore—inauthentic compensation, in a turn that certainly echoes some of the sentiments expressed in the context of the German *Sprachkrise*, Ferdinand becomes increasingly attracted to silence. To be sure, this attraction was present earlier in the narrative, particularly in those passages evoking the memory of Caroline and Edouard.[11] Yet, in the chapters dealing with his permanence in England, silence becomes a dominant feature of Ferdinand's *Bildungsroman*. Not surprisingly, Nicholas Hewitt's *The Golden Age of Louis-Ferdinand Céline* has described them as examples of fictionalized "autism" (112).[12] Whereas, upon his arrival in Folkestone, he is enchanted with the English language because of its unknown, "silent" words—"C'est bien agréable une langue dont on ne comprend rien" (214) [It's nice listening to a language you don't know a word of]—by the time of the Rochester's fair, the foreign tongue has become all too familiar. For this reason, he now feels compelled to reject the company of a girl to whom he is attracted as soon as she attempts to speak to him: "Elle me parle . . . Alors là je me sens tout rétif! Je fais affreux dès qu'on me cause! . . . J'en veux plus moi des parlotes. Je sais où ça mène" (218–219) [She speaks to me . . . Whereupon, dammit, I begin to get restive! I grow foul as soon as anyone talks to me! . . . I've had enough of words. I know where that sort of things leads to]. This mutism continues throughout his stay at the British "Meanwell College," where Ferdinand will not speak for three entire months, till the owner of the school, concerned about the pupil's academic failures, informs Auguste. The latter puts an end to Ferdinand's protective enclosure by way of another violent speech-act; three letters overflowing with a thousand threats and horrible oaths, coupled with insults in Latin and Greek (244).

Back in France, at "le Passage," Ferdinand spends a summer only half-heartedly seeking new employment. Failing over and over again to live up to the ideals of bourgeois integration upheld by Auguste, the latter increases his verbal abuse. Auguste, however, also encounters Ferdinand's resistance. In what is perhaps one of the most semantically charged scenes of the novel, Ferdinand breaks the glass face of one of Auguste's clocks and then throws a typewriter at him. The machine, an objective correlative to an act of silencing in and by language the father's name, is a *"mise en abîme,"* a part reproducing the narrativized critique of language which informs the novel as well as the implication of the novel's critique for future developments in literary tradition. As a result of the incident, Ferdinand is expelled from Auguste's house and enters at the service of Roger-Marin Courtial des Pereires.

A twentieth-century man full of nineteenth-century ideals, Courtial is but an extension of Ferdinand's biological father, as suggested by the French word for "father" inscribed in the first phonemes of his last name and by his obstinacy to order space and time. For example, mirroring Auguste's desire to control the forces of time, Courtial composes an opuscule on a house, "Le 'Chalet Polyvalent,'" that is so adaptable it can survive the wear of age and weather (382). Later on, he organizes a contest to measure the perpetual movement (402 ff.) of the earth. The project represents the ultimate humanistic and modernist ideal, the dream of temporal mastery and control that already informed some of Courtial's intellectual models: "Michel-Ange! Aristote! et Léonard de Vinci! . . . Le Pic de la Mirandole!" (440). At Blême-le-Petit, a farm in the French countryside, Courtial solidifies another one of Auguste's fantasies: the control of space. By way of magnetic energy, he sets out to produce large crops of potatoes despite inclement weather and poor soil conditions. Courtial's leisure activities are but additional manifestations of his desire to defy matter and contingency. In the company of his pigeons, like Daedalus Icarus, Courtial often ascends the sky with a balloon, the "Zélé." From the heights, he then releases the birds in a symbolic flight above the earth. Yet, just as in the case of Auguste, it is in his verbal practices that Courtial emerges most visibly as a modernist father. Convinced that in and by language—"dans le résumé, l'article, la conférence, en prose, en vers et quelquefois . . . en calembours" (348) [in reviews, essays, public speeches, in prose or verse and sometimes . . . in acrostics]—the contingency and opaque materiality of life can be redeemed, Courtial engages in a frantic writing activity. His pieces, mostly published in a journal of his own creation, Le Génitron, seek to stabilize in a redemptive totality the ever-evolving and complex fields of modernization. Comparable only to the encyclopedic breadth and scope of Ulysses' retotalization of the ruins of culture, they range from agriculture, astrology, and botany, to astronomy, education, physics, architecture, mechanics, and more. Yet again, as in the case of Auguste, the narrative of Mort emphasizes the precariousness of Courtial's desire to restore unity and permanency. To tell it with Oswald Spengler, no act of "Zivilization" is capable of restoring wholeness to a dying, fragmented "Kultur": "The Civilization is the inevitable destiny of the Culture, and in this principle we obtain the viewpoint from which the deepest and gravest problems of historical morphology become capable of a solution. Civilizations are the most external states of which a species of developed humanity is capable. They are a conclusion, the thing-become succeeding the thing-becoming, death following life, rigidity following expansion."[13]

In a manner similar to Elias Canetti's Die Blendung (published in Germany a year earlier, 1935), the narrative of Mort proceeds to recount how Courtial, like Canetti's Kien, is dazzled and ultimately blinded by the dream of order offered by language. In an epilogue inserted in the tradition of parody of the "virus encyclopédique"[14] initiated by Flaubert's Bouvard et Pécuchet (1880) and followed, more recently, by the postmodernist practices of Umberto Eco,[15] Mort illustrates the ultimate irreducibility of irrationality and disorder. Ferdinand recalls how, despite Courtial's desires, chaos persists, beginning with the offices of the Génitron: "en fait de terrible désordre, de capharnaüm absolu, de pagaye totale, on pouvait pas voire beaucoup pire . . . un ouragan de poussière . . . un volcan foireux d'immondices" (357) [for appalling disorder, for absolute anarchy, for total chaos, it would have been impossible to find the equal . . . a deluge of dust . . . a floating mass of rubbish].[16] The fate of the projects designed or supported by Courtial participates in an analogously futile quest for harmony and synthesis. The "Chalet Polyvalent" is never given a chance to withstand weather and time and is destroyed by the first visitors to the "Exposition" (382). The contest to measure perpetual movement is unmasked as a symptom of paranoia. As a judge observes, since humans and their creations participate in the endless change of forms, no instrument of measurement can provide absolute knowledge of the movement's dynamics. The person who thinks otherwise is deluded by impossible dreams of omnipotence: "Vous vous sentez éternel? . . . Il faut l'être, vous entendez bien, pour juger ça valablement" (440) [You feel yourself eternal, eh? . . . You'd have to be that, mark you, to judge this competition of yours properly]. In a disquieting progression, the agricultural experiment fails, too, and promotes an unprecedented growth of parasites. Even Courtial's ascensions are doomed. In an ironic commentary on a subject who had voiced metanarratives of progress and rationality, Courtial's balloon loses the competition to airplanes (403). Its cloth, too old to be replaced, begins to leak air (421), while its pigeons are first drowned and then eaten to feed the hungry molecules of human bodies. The *Génitron*, an icon of the symbolic library erected by Courtial's writings, disappears. As in Canetti, the modernist project to order and classify the phenomenal world is undermined in a symbolic *auto-da-fé* when a "horde" (474) of two-thousand inventors storms the office of the journal (473). Projects are destroyed, shelves are shaken, books fall in a "cataracte de paperasses" (476) [in a waterfall of bad papers] and explode in a great cloud of dust. Faced with such ostensible failures, Courtial commits suicide. Like Jorge de Burgos in Eco's *The Name of the Rose* and Canetti's Kien—burned in the fires of the Athenaum and the Theresianum libraries, respectively—the novel's description of Courtial's death and cadaver ratifies once more the futility of totalizing projects. In what is perhaps a belated realization of his excessive faith in language, Courtial shoots himself without leaving a letter of farewell. His mouth explodes in a myriad of fragments while the shards of his head remain stuck to the earth: "C'était pris comme un seul bloc avec les graviers et la glace . . . ça faisait un pavé compact avec les cailloux de la route" (558) [The whole thing formed a solid mass with the frozen gravel . . . it was a hash mix with the stones of the road]. This horrifying fall into unsublimated materiality is followed by the dispersal of the cadaver. In a scene Beckett will recall through the character of Cooper in *Murphy*, the priest Fleury dismembers Courtial's body and then scatters its fragments in the surrounding areas (594). Ferdinand's last memory of Courtial is of a skeleton frozen in the position of the end-letter of the alphabet: "Il restait en Z" (560) [He was left in the shape of a Z]. A powerful symbol of the failure of meta-narratives to redeem the opacity of the cultural and historical experience of modernity, the visual iconicity of the letter is also a commentary on the mythos of redemptive symbolization, a horizontal slash across the affir-mative "S" of modernist fathers and their empowering narrations.

Newly unemployed, Ferdinand seeks shelter at his uncle's house and, after a short stay, leaves to join the army (616). It is precisely at this junc-ture that Céline's 1932 novel, *Voyage au bout de la nuit*, begins. This narrative not only validates *Mort's Bildungsroman* into the bankruptcy of language, but expands to universal proportions the critique of the mod-ernist name already exemplified in the characterization of Auguste and Courtial. Indeed, in a process of "*Abschattungen*," or what Latin has called the novel's "*palimpseste verbal*,"[17] Ferdinand becomes acquainted with additional examples of semiotic fall and realizes that the fallen state of language is by no means confined to his own childhood and youth, but reproduces itself across classes, genders, and continents.

The Cosmic Pitfalls of the Name: *Voyage au bout de la nuit* (1932)

Voyage opens in Place Clichy, where Ferdinand is discussing the col-umns of the newspaper *Le Temps* with his friend Arthur Ganate. While Ganate believes in their truthful representation of reality, Ferdinand ap-pears to have been rendered skeptical by his upbringing. He comments that they are only a tool at the service of the dominant order, official examples of an "imaginary" language. The columns' assessments of eco-nomic progress, he argues, hide the real conditions of the vast majority of the French population: "la faim, la peste, les tumeurs et le froid . . . C'est ça la France et puis c'est ça les Français" (16)[18] [hunger, illness, pestilence and cold . . . That's your France, and those are your Frenchmen]. Like-wise, the columns' report of the Gallic heroism on the battlefields is but an example of propaganda, since "la race . . . c'est seulement ce grand ramassis de miteaux . . . chassieux, puceux, transis" (16) [the race . . . is only that great heap of worm-eaten sods . . . bleary, shivering, and lousy]. The defiant tone of this initial paragraph, however, is surprisingly reversed as the dialog between Ferdinand and Ganate progresses. Foregrounding how language is a terrain of instability and illocutionary violence, the words of Ganate move from a declared belief in symbolic referentiality to occupy Ferdinand's enunciative space: "C'est tout à fait comme ça!" que m'approuva Arthur, décidément devenu facile à convaincre" (18) ["You've just hit it!" agreed Arthur, who'd certainly become very easy to convince]. Conversely, Ferdinand sheds his protective shields and decides to enroll in a regiment leaving for World War I to determine if the newspaper's words correspond indeed to referents, if language is perhaps truly ideologically neutral. Upon his arrival in Flanders, however, Ferdinand quickly and painfully realizes that the connection between the name and the state of things—"Les Mots et les choses" to use Foucault's best-known title[19]—has receded. Despite being a fluent German speaker, Ferdinand cannot understand the actions of the enemy. More significantly, even the words of the French language have no referential correlatives on the battlefields. Neither the beauty nor the heroism of the Gallic race described by the French newspaper *Le Temps* (16) correspond to the reality of the war and the behavior of the militia.

The disjunction between words and their referents that informs these pages of the novel is by no means confined to the war-fields but, as Ferdinand discovers during a period of convalescence, it affects the verbal practices of the civilians laboring in Paris during the conflict. Like many characters from *Mort*, these attempt to find solace from the reality of experience, and do so by engaging in inauthentic, phantasmagoric production of images. Some, for example, search in language the confirmation that the French race is indeed one of heroic and courageous beings. For this reason, they applaud approvingly when presented with propagandist types of art, such as the epic poems about the military exploits of the French troops produced by the Comédie Française. Even foreign volunteers are not immune from the lure of phantasmagoric tales. For example, an American nurse from New York, named Lola, asks Ferdinand for an idealized description of the "Bois the Boulogne," now in an utter state of decay. Lola is unable to accept the ravages of history and temporality: "le temps, ce tableau de nous" (103) [time, this portrait of ourselves]. In what is a clear allusion to the Proustian narrator of *Le Temps retrouvé*, she trusts that language will allow her to transcend the melancholy of the evanescent, to give her the Proustian confidence that "le temps perdu! Elle le rattraperait sans dommage" (78) [lost time was nothing! She would recapture it as easily as anything]. Ferdinand, however, cannot transform "time lost" in "time regained." He can only parody the Proustian *beau style* in a rhyming portrait of the elegant and beautiful women of time past: "Les robes . . . Les élégantes . . . Les coupés étincelantes . . . Les trompes allègres et volontaires . . . Le saut de la rivière" (77) [The dresses . . . The elegant women . . . The glittering cut carriages . . . The happy and voluntary horns . . . The river falls].[20]

Additional confirmations of the inauthenticity of language lay in wait for Ferdinand at the end of the conflict, notably in the course of his travels across Africa and France. On his journey toward the African colonial outpost of Fort Gono to seek employment with the "*Compagnie Pordurière*," Ferdinand relives one of his experiences of childhood—that is, the connection of crisis-point to language. Aboard the ship *Amiral Bragueton*, he risks being executed. Unfounded and malicious rumors are circulating on his regard among the other passengers. Upon his arrival, his initial beliefs in the myths of "L'Afrique, la vraie, la grande" (148) [Africa, the real, vast Africa!]—quite possibly in an allusion to the French procolonial rhetoric—are quickly shattered. The only "poetry" of the tropics is the one produced by the aggressive and fake voices of the white colonialists (172). And, mirroring the episode of the English "Meanwell College" from *Mort*, in *Voyage* the inauthenticity of discourse increasingly fosters a desire for silence. Thus, when Ferdinand is sent to the trading-post of Topo to prepare an inventory for the *Compagnie Pordurière*, he sees no point in informing his superior of the theft of the company's profits. Language has indeed become so opaque as to render all attempts at communication futile.

Back in France after a brief period in the United States, Ferdinand completes his medical studies and begins to practice in the Parisian suburbs and, later on, in the mental hospital of Vigny-sur-Seine. His work allows him to observe daily how language is increasingly implicated in the most violent exchanges. These range from the "*séances ménagères*" (337) [family scenes] of working-class couples who can achieve sexual arousal only by verbally (and physically) abusing their children (338 ff.), to the episodes related to the Henrouilles. This is a couple who is offering a large sum of money in exchange for the murder of their elderly mother and an alibi to cover up the murder. Against this background the vision of language as a space irreducibly connected to chaos and disorder—in one word, to madness—begins to gain in substance. To be sure, this vision had been present in an embryonic form as early as Céline's 1924 doctoral dissertation. In this work, entitled *La Vie et l'oeuvre de Ignace Semmelweis*, Céline had recounted the story of the Hungarian doctor Semmelweis (1818–65) whose discovery of very simple hygienic procedures to end the spread of puerperal fever was totally disregarded by the European scientific establishment of the Napoleonic period. Faced with the unreasonableness and stubbornness of the scientific community, Semmelweis lost his sanity. In the course of an autopsy at the Faculty of Anatomy, he began to scatter parts of the cadaver while screaming illogical phrases. He died of a self-inflicted wound while continuing to rant madly: "il entra dans une sorte de verbiage incessant, dans une réminescence interminable, au cours de laquelle sa tête brisée parut se vider en longues phrase mortes" [he entered into a sort of endless verbiage and interminable reminiscences, during which his shattered head seemed to empty itself in long dead phrases].[21]

In *Voyage* the theme of madness returns and concretizes itself in the events surrounding another doctor, the psychiatrist Baryton. In the mental hospital of Vigny-sur-Seine, the well-known scientist gradually begins to lose his French identity while studying the English language. Finally, he fashions himself as an Englishman and departs from France, leaving both his family and the clinic behind. To no one's surprise, Ferdinand voices one of the novel's most powerful indictment of words:

Quand on s'arrête à la façon par exemple dont sont proférés les mots, elles ne résistent guère nos phrases au désastre de leur décor baveux. C'est plus compliqué et pénible que la défécation notre effort mécanique de la conversation. Cette corolle de chair bouffie, la bouche, qui se convulse à siffler, aspire et se démène, pousse toutes espèces de sons visqueux à travers le barrage puant de la carie dentaire, quelle punition! Voilà pourtant ce qu'on nous adjure de transposer en idéal. C'est difficile. (426–27)

[When you consider the way in which words are formed and uttered, they fail to stand up to the test of all these appalling trappings of spittle. The mechanical effort we make in speaking is more complicated and harder than defecation. The mouth, that corolla of puffed flesh, which

convulses when it whistles; sucks in breath and labors, and ejects all sort
of viscous sounds past a barrier of dental decay—what a punishment it
is! Yet, this is what we are urged to consider ideal. It isn't easy.]

As Ferdinand's *Bildung* approaches its conclusion, the discredited state of
language articulated so powerfully by this passage comes full circle.
Lured by the words of the Henrouilles, Ferdinand's friend Robinson
agrees to kill their elderly mother, but he is severely wounded while setting off the explosives. Sent to Toulouse to recover and find employment,
he becomes engaged but, shortly thereafter, is shot to death following
another speech-act: a violent verbal exchange with his fiancée Madelon.
Faced with the cosmic profusion of fallen names that he has experienced
across classes, genders, and continents, Ferdinand puts an abrupt conclusion to his apprenticeship. As the narrative of *Voyage* comes to an end,
Ferdinand evokes a sound capable of sweeping away the people and all
their words:

De loin, le remorqueur a sifflé; son appel a passé le pont, encore une
arche, une autre, l'écluse, un autre pont, loin, plus loin . . . Il appelait
vers lui toutes les péniches du fleuve toutes, et la ville entière, et le ciel
et la campagne et nous, tout qu'il emmenait, la Seine aussi, tout, qu'on
n'en parle plus. (635)

[From far away, the tugboat hooted; calling across the bridge, the arches
one by one, a lock, another bridge, further, further away . . . It was calling to itself every boat on the river, every one, the whole town, and the
sky, and the country and us, all of it was being called away, and the
Seine too, everything—let's hear no more of all this.]

The Beginning of Writing

This epilog is crucial and merits further reflection. While the *Bildungsroman* of Ferdinand through the narratives of *Mort* and *Voyage* has come
full circle, the presence of a sound carrying with it the amalgam of people
and words, announces the emergence of a new writing practice. This
practice is that alternative rhetorical economy that is revealed in the
diegesis of Ferdinand-as-narrator of his own, first-person novels. Indeed,

both the authorial signature and the titles of Ferdinand's narratives textualize a departure from the father's name. Ferdinand-as-narrator chooses to write as "Céline"—that is, he adopts the name of Destouches' mother, Marguerite Louise Céline Destouches Guilloux. As for the novels' titles, unlike Proust's resonant *Le Temps retrouvé*, Virginia Woolf's *To the Lighthouse*, and Joyce's *Ulysses*, *Voyage* and *Mort* are but "journey(s) at the end of night" and "death(s) on the installment plan." Hence, through the choice of the mother's name as signature for titles that neither arrest nor order experience, Céline inscribes his work within (an)other's genealogy. This genealogy is both "feminine"[22] (and therefore removed from the father's name) and avant-gardist, because it is aligned with those darker lines of development represented by two of surrealism's apostates: Georges Bataille and Antonin Artaud.[23] The novels' marginalia and pre-texts provide additional confirmation of Céline's departure from the modernist symbolic name and teleological passageway. *Voyage* opens with an epigraph comparing writing to an endless journey[24] into the undifferentiated and opaque materiality of life:

> Notre vie est un voyage
> Dans l'hiver et dans la Nuit,
> Nous cherchons notre passage
> Dans le Ciel où rien ne luit. (9)

> [Our life is a voyage
> In the winter and in the Night
> We search our passage
> In the Sky where nothing shines.]

The prolog that follows introduces the novel as the endeavor of a literary Subject no more endowed with talents than the rest of his readers,[25] and capable only of repeating the contradiction and temporality of our darkest life-world experience:

Il va de la vie à la mort. Hommes, bêtes, villes et choses, tout est imaginé. C'est un roman, rien qu'une histoire fictive, Littré le dit, qui ne se trompe jamais.

Et puis d'abord tout le monde peut en faire autant. Il suffit de fermer les yeux.

C'est de l'autre côté de la vie.

[It goes from life to death. All is imagined: People, towns, and things. It is a novel, nothing but a fictional story, as Littré says, and it is never wrong.

And besides, everybody can do just as much. All that is needed is to shut one's eyes

It is on the other side of life.]

Like *Voyage*'s marginalia, the ironic epigraph of *Mort* presents experience as a predicament. In five rhythmic verses, it announces a merry journey around the world—"Le tour du Monde" (11)—and yet undermines all teleological progress by disclosing the source of the verses in a prisoner's chant of lamentation—a *Chanson de prison*. The impossibility of a redemptive practice as well as the need for alternative representations is further articulated in the long prologue that follows the epigraph. A delirious Ferdinand begins by lamenting the loss of an idealized narrative that he had composed about the battles of Christendom and the tournaments of the knights in Vendée: "de très beaux rêves . . . Des véritables merveilles . . . de la pure extase" (18) [beautiful dreams . . . True marvels . . . pure ecstasy]. Yet, when after much searching a portion of the romance is found under the bed of Mireille, Ferdinand comes to the realization that the work's "aura" has all but disappeared. Not only does the romance disappoint him—"J'étais bien deçu de la relire. Elle avait pas gagné au temps ma romance" (24) [I was disappointed when I read it again. Time had not improved it]—but its tales are so detached from reality as to be incapable of interesting the audience. While Gustin, a doctor of the poor Parisian suburbs is dozing, the other listener, Mireille, cannot rise above the reality of her experience to identify with it. At sixteen, she has already worked in seven factories, and her desire to find a husband has recently pushed her to a mercantile bartering of her body (34). Thus, Ferdinand concludes that time has come to introduce other, nonredemptive stories: "J'aime mieux raconter des histoires. J'en raconterai de telles qu'ils reviendront, exprès, pour me tuer, des quatre coins du monde. Alors ce sera fini et je serai bien content" (14) [I prefer to tell a few stories. And I will, too—such tales that they'll come back on purpose to kill me, from the four corners of the earth. Then, that'll be over, and I shall be pleased].

Confirming the intent of their marginalia, both *Voyage* and *Mort* set out to disclose the darker underside of the modern experience. Theorized by Bataille as the "heterological excess,"[26] it will be narrativized in Ferdinand's tales as the irreducible residue confined at the limits of society, the subject and—ultimately—the modernist text itself.

Disclosing the Residues: Modern Society

In a clear actualization of that book, as Artaud put it in *The Umbilicus of Limbo* (1925) "which would be like an open door leading (men) where they would never have consented to go, in short, a door that opens into reality,"[27] *Mort* shatters modernist myths of economic progress and social rationality. Page after page, it discloses how the disestablishing of past, slower-paced economic organizations not only has brought about efficient cars and buses, electricity, and better roads, but also has created an ever-growing population of brutal and diseased human beings. Exploited by the paradoxical models of capitalistic production, the working classes have become the sick hordes of the Chapelle-Jonction who daily storm the medical office of Gustin Sabayot to seek a cure for their many ailments:

Toute la crasse, l'envie, la rogne d'un canton s'était exercée sur sa pomme. . . . L'aigreur au réveil des 14000 alcooliques de l'arrondissement . . . les rétentions extenuantes des 6422 blennorrhées . . . l'angoisse questionneuse de 2266 hypertendus, le mépris inconciliable de 722 biliaires à migraine, l'obsession soupçonneuse des 47 porteurs de taenias . . . la horde trouble, la grande tourbe des masochistes de toutes lubies. (31–2)

[All the squalor, the mange and venom of the neighborhood had taken pot-shots at his hapless mug. . . . The hangover of the 14,000 alcoholics of the district, the exhausting retentions of 6,422 cases of clap . . . the querulous torment of 2,266 nervous wrecks, the inveterate scorn of 722 sufferers from bilious headaches, the suspicious obsession of 47 owners of tapeworms . . . the seething throng, the hordes of masochists with phobias of every kind.]

Next to the workers, other groups are also sharing the devastating effects of modern economic organization.[28] As Nicholas Hewitt has noted,[29] *Mort* reveals the disappearance of countless artisans and small-store owners brought about by the advent of capitalistic rationality. Ferdinand's mother, Clémence, is a case in point. Her modest store in Courbevoie for the retail and repair of handmade laces has lost the competition with machine-made fabrics. As a result, she has had to declare bankruptcy:

D'abord maman se rendait bien compte, elle se l'avouait dans les larmes . . . c'était un courant pas remontable . . . Plus de délicatesse . . . Ni d'estime pour les choses du fin travail, pour les ouvrages tout à la main . . . . Plus que des engouements dépravés pour les saloperies mécaniques . . . La belle dentelle était morte. (286)

[And anyhow Mamma realized it full well, she had to admit with tears in her eyes . . . it was a current you could not check . . . No longer any refinement . . . No appreciation of craftsmanship, of fine work done by hand . . . Only a depraved infatuation with messy machine-made stuff . . . The day of the exquisite lace was over.]

Clémence's two other business ventures, in the Passage des Bérésinas and Rue de Babylone respectively, also fail, as the constant restocking of merchandise required by a consumerist economy is clearly beyond the reach of small entrepreneurs like herself. In one last business attempt, Clémence tries to sell in the Parisian open markets of Cligancourt, La Porte, and "aux Puces," only to find out that here, too, exchange is ruled by the customers' desire for the latest merchandise. Clémence's case is by no means an isolated phenomenon, as it is shared by the woodworkers, like the Alsacian Wurzems; the smiths, like Gorloge; and numerous others: "Des sertisseurs, des lapidaires, des petits chaînistes . . . qu'ont disparu comme des orfèvres dans le vermeil et des ciseleurs sur agates" (162) [Jewel-setters, stonemasons, fancy-chain makers, glass cutters . . . who have disappeared like the silver-gilders and the agate-engravers].

Even intellectual workers are not immune from the disastrous effects of modern economic organizations. Small and privately run schools, like the "Meanwell College" of Nora Merrywin and her husband are unable to compete with corporate institutions like "The Hopeful Academy." Funded by large sums of money, these lure students by boasting large sports complexes and luxurious living quarters. Ferdinand's father, Auguste, is experiencing the disappearance of his profession. After having worked for twenty-two years as a calligrapher for the insurance company, the "Coccinelle-Incendie," he risks losing his job. His boss prefers to employ people trained in the new technology of the typewriter or, in Auguste's words, "très forts . . . de leur formation très 'moderne'" (271) [very proud of their very "modern" background]. It comes as no surprise, then, that faced with an uncertain future and an impending threat of poverty, the members of the lower middle-class start engaging in brutal forms of behavior. Auguste, for example, becomes an abusive father and husband. Madame Gorloge gets involved in numerous acts of sexual perversion. Nora Merrywin chooses suicide, while her husband seeks relief in whisky and brandy.

The shattering of modern myths of progress and economic well-being that informs the narrative of *Mort* is pursued in *Voyage*'s exploration of "la grande pagaye" (533) [the great mess] of Western civilization and culture between 1915 and the years immediately following World War I. Europe's entrance into the conflict is presented as the "necessary" and horrifying outcome of a dying civilization:

Avec casques, sans casques, sans chevaux, sur motos, hurlants, en autos, sifflants, tirailleurs, comploteurs, volants, à genoux, creusant, se défilant, caracolant, dans les sentiers, pétaradant, enfermés sur la terre comme dans un cabanon, pour tout y détruire, Allemagne, France et Continents, tout ce qui respire, détruire, plus enragés que les chiens . . . et tellement plus vicieux. (24)

[With or without helmets, without horses, on motor bicycles, screeching, in cars, whistling, sniping, plotting, flying, kneeling, digging, taking cover, wheeling, detonating, shut in on earth as in an asylum cell; intending to wreck everything in it, Germany, France, the whole world, every breathing thing; destroying, more ferocious than a pack of dogs . . . and so infinitely more vicious.]

Trench warfare is divested of all heroism and described as a space of absurdity and decay by endless recollections of dismembered, putrefying bodies, and of confused, directionless soldiers.[30] This state of madness is perhaps best exemplified in Ferdinand's mission to the village of

"Noirceur-sur-la-Lys," or "Darkness-on-the-Lily" (53 ff.). Confused by the orders of his superiors and forced to carry a set of conspicuously noisy armaments, Ferdinand describes the mission as a human sacrifice, a rite not too different from the puzzling customs of the Aztec Indians. On the path toward the village, the absurdity of the war is further emphasized by the words of a group of French civilians who comment that, since plenty of Germans also speak fluent French, they remain incapable of distinguishing between enemies and national militias. The episode culminates with the encounter with the city's mayor, who sends Ferdinand back to his post, explaining to him how he would rather give up the town to the Germans that to allow a member of the French troops to help.

Absurdity and decay, however, extend far beyond Ferdinand's experience on the war-fields. During his permanence among the civilians, he finds out that while soldiers are dying on the front or in military hospitals, in the urban space of Paris, women such as Madame Hérote, Musyne, and Olympia are enriching themselves by opening lucrative taverns and whorehouses. More blows at Western civilization and culture, however, lie in wait, particularly in the decade following the war—namely, in the course of Ferdinand's travels to Africa, America, and France.

Confirming Michel Beaujour's description of Céline's novels as masterpieces of the repulsive,[31] Ferdinand describes how in Africa capitalistic wealth is implicated in the most brutal exploitation of the indigenous masses. In the outposts of Fort-Gono, Bikobimbo, and Topo, Ferdinand has a firsthand experience of the physical and moral decay of European colonialists. While most of them are wasting away under the effects of tropical diseases, the few who have preserved their strength are brutally exploiting the indigenous population. In theaters of organized robbery, they force the African peasants to exchange large amounts of unrefined rubber for old handkerchiefs: "Toi y en a pas parler 'francé' dis? Toi y en a gorille encore hein? . . . Toi y en a parler quoi hein! . . . Bushman! Plein couillon! . . . Il lui reprit l'argent d'autorité et à la place des pièces lui chiffonna dans le creux de la main un grand mouchoir très vert" (180) [You don't parly French, do you? Still a gorilla, are you? . . . What do you savy then, tell me? A bush ape! A damn great clod! . . . He snatched the money away from him and in its place shoved into the palm of his hand a large, bright green handkerchief].

As in the African outposts, in the United States the last vestiges of humanity also have been erased under the laws of capitalist production.[32] In its place, two new Gods have emerged: the dollar and the machine. In Manhattan, people enter their banks as if they were sanctuaries and speak to the new Gods' priests with the same reverence of former confessionals. In Detroit, the machine has erased all need for thought and imagination. The assembly line of Ford Industries requires a total abolition of life, or admits of it only as the potential for the creation of one more object: "Il faut abolir la vie du dehors, en faire aussi d'elle de l'acier, quelque chose d'utile. . . . Faut en faire un objet donc, du solide, c'est la Règle" (288–89) [Life outside, you must abolish; it must be turned into steel, too; into something useful. . . . It must be made into a thing, something solid. It's the Rule].

But since, as Ferdinand comments, "On ne sera tranquille que lorsque tout aura été dit" (415) [We shall never be at peace until everything has been said], more examples of irrationality and decay break through the metanarratives of modernity when Ferdinand returns to France. The four last episodes of the novel, set in Rancy, Paris, Toulouse, and Vigny-sur-Seine, respectively, are but additional and even deeper travels into the mud, into that Bataillean *"part maudite"* repressed by the Platonic sun. As Ferdinand begins to practice medicine among the working classes, he further explores the diseased state of modern society. The suburb of Garenne-Rancy, formerly in the Parisian countryside, has been taken over by urban growth. Transformed into a compound of smelly dwellings, it is inhabited by alcoholics, child abusers, and sexual perverts. And it is through the observation of the people of Garenne-Rancy that Ferdinand comes to displace the bedrocks of Western civilization: the institutions of family, morality, science, and religion. In Rancy, next to the Henrouilles—who, as we might recall, are seeking to end the life of their elderly mother for fear of having to support her financially—Ferdinand witnesses the death of a woman, following her parents' refusal to hospitalize her in order to hide her abortion. He also recalls meeting a husband who would rather lose his wife and the mother of his five children than spend 100 francs for her hospitalization. This powerful debunking of the myth of the family is succeeded by an episode that shakes the institution of science. Since one of his patients, Bébert, is dying of typhus, Ferdinand decides to seek the help of the experts working at the famous Bioduret Institute. What he discovers, however, is that this monument of Western scientific progress is but a place of chaos and waste, a site sharing numerous affinities with Courtial's "Génitron":

rien que des objects bousculés en grand désordre, des petits cadavres d'animaux éventrés, des bouts de mégots, des becs de gaz ébréchés, des cages et des bocaux avec des souris dedans en train d'étouffer . . . des livres et de la poussière, encore et toujours des mégots, leur odeur et celle de la pissotière, dominantes. (355)

[just a litter of things in no sort of order, carcasses of little animals cut open, cigarette butts, twisted gas brackets, boxes and glass jars with mice inside quietly suffocating . . . books and dust, still more cigarette butts, and the smell of them, and of latrines, predominating.]

More significantly, Ferdinand realizes that the Institute's foremost scholars, like Parapine, are but perverted old men, occasionally spattering a bit of ink on paper, but, more often, voyeuristic admirers of the adolescent girls studying in a nearby school. Finally, even the last institution of French society—religion—becomes implicated in this dissolution, as Ferdinand recalls the visit of the Abbé Protiste. More interested in the pleasure of the flesh and in materialist comfort than in the spiritual uplifting of souls, Protiste offers Ferdinand a large sum of money to send both the elderly Henrouille and Robinson to Toulouse. Here they will work as tour guides for the church of Saint-Eponime, transformed into a lucrative source of income following the discovery of catacombs.

The (Post)modern Subject

Yet, and perhaps expectedly considering these novels' chronological proximity to modernist representations, it is in the subjectivity of Ferdinand that the debunking of modernist myths is at its strongest point. In *Voyage*'s words, this is where the farce of self-identity is unveiled: "Tout notre malheur vient de ce qu'il nous faut demeurer Jean, Pierre ou Gaston coûte que coûte pendant toutes sortes d'années" (427) [All of our unhappiness is due to having to remain John, Peter, or Gaston, cost what it may, through a whole series of years]. Otherwise stated, it is in the representation of consciousness that Ferdinand's narratives record the collapse of the modern Subject and the advent of an utterly undecidable postmodern self. This condition has been theorized by Kristeva's *Powers of Horror* as the "abjection," or that which "disturbs identity, system, order. What does not respect borders, positions, rules" (4). As such, it implies a total breakdown of the paradigms of representation, of the separation of subject from object, inside from outside, male from female. Pervasive in the narrative of *Mort* and *Voyage*, it is manifested beginning with Ferdinand's material, physical existence, but extends to encompass his social and cognitive selves as well.

Ferdinand's body is a grotesque vessel, a mass of molecules tending toward a centrifugal dispersion and often rupturing toward the outside, as illustrated by the numerous examples of *"expenditure"*[33]—that is, of defecation and vomit—that litter the page. The body's sexuality is just as uncontained. Despite Ferdinand's recollections of numerous female lovers, several passages intimate a more fluid sexual identity. Finally, in Africa he emerges from the closet by mentioning his refusal of homosexual acts with which he seems to be well acquainted: "le petit nègre . . . revenait sur ses pas pour m'offrir ses services intimes . . . je n'étais pas en train ce soir-là" (173)[34] [the black boy came back to offer me his intimate services. . . . That evening, I wasn't in the mood]. An analogous lack of boundaries characterizes Ferdinand's social and cognitive being as well, and confirms the appropriateness of his name "Bardamu." This is an epithet that indicates a shifting and contradictory speaker, or, more precisely, a "Bard(a)mu," from the verb *"mouvoir,"* "to set in motion," or "to stir." Never confined within one social position, Ferdinand endlessly shifts from one role to the next, and emerges as a *"personne-groupe,"*[35] a soldier turned colonialist, an immigrant, a factory worker, and a medical doctor. Significantly, in this open series of identities, he also becomes an actor for the Tarapout company, and therefore a player of many personae: "tantôt prince, centurion par deux fois, aviateur un autre jour . . . la nuit le policeman" (457) [sometimes a prince, twice a Roman centurion, an aviator after that . . . at night a policeman]. Ferdinand's cognitive self is equally fluctuating and, as numerous critics have noted, deploys itself in a generalized inability to settle within stable frames of time and space.[36] In the openings of *Mort* and *Voyage*, for example, Ferdinand initially establishes a chronological frame from which to recount the events of his past, younger self. *Voyage* begins with the recollection, cast in past tenses, of Ferdinand's meeting with Ganate: "Ça a débuté . . . Moi, j'avais jamais rien dit . . . Ganate . . . m'a fait parler" (15) [It all began just like that. . . . I hadn't said anything. . . . It was Ganate . . . who started me off]. Likewise, an analepsis introduces the narrative of *Mort*: "Le siècle dernier je peux en parler, je l'ai vu finir . . . Il est parti sur la route après Orly" (47) [I know something about the last century, I saw it depart. It disappeared along the road beyond Orly]. Nonetheless, as Ferdinand's narrative progresses, all differentiation is lost in a chronotopic labyrinth of time past and present. Ultimately, as Charles Krance has stated in *The I of the Storm*, the "I" that tells the world is no longer kept distinct from the "Eye" that was experiencing it (28).

This inability to order time is accompanied by a spatial confusion, which is particularly evident in the novels' coexistence of the antithetical orders of reality and fiction. In *Voyage*,[37] for example, Ferdinand's rational assessment of the absurdity and chaos of the Flanders carnage of war gives way to endless declarations of his own, personal delirium, or more precisely of "la pagaye dans mon esprit, tout comme dans la vie" (344) [the chaos in my soul, as in life]. These declarations are concretized in the course of his journey to Africa and France. In one of the colonial outposts, Ferdinand experiences a long period of sickness culminating in a confused state of consciousness: "je n'essayais même plus de reconnaître le réel parmi les choses absurdes de la fièvre qui entraient dans ma tête les unes dans les autres en même temps que des morceaux de gens et puis des bouts de résolution et des désespoirs qui n'en finissaient pas" (230) [I didn't even try to make out what was real amid the absurd things that the fever sent coursing through my head, one thing telescoping into another and bits of people and tail ends of good resolutions and despair— an endless stream]. Back in France, he is again prey to delirium, and in the Place de Tertre (462 ff.) lucidity recedes for ghostly visions of people he could not possibly have met. These include cadavers from the cemetery of Saint-Pierre, built in 1305, the "communards" (463) of 1871, the "Cosaques" (464) of 1820, and even the voyagers drowned in the many shipwrecks of the Pacific Ocean. Delirium is also a prominent feature of the narrative of *Mort*. It is revealed in the vision of a giant woman with planet-sized breasts (91 ff.) heading an unruly omnibus to a rampage across Paris, and in the episode of the Bois the Boulogne (37 ff.). Here the entire crowd of the park, transformed into phantasms of Ferdinand, entices him to abuse his companion Mireille. Considering the overt examples of temporal and spatial instability suggested by these narratives, it comes perhaps as no surprise that in 1932, in a letter addressed to Léon Daudet, Céline compared his work to the grotesque and delirious portraits of madmen, which were emerging in the transition from the Middle Ages to the Renaissance:

Vous connaissez certainenement, Maître, l'énorme fête des Fous de Brueghel. Elle est à Vienne. Tout le problème n'est pas ailleurs pour moi. Je voudrais bien comprendre autre chose — je ne comprends pas autre chose. Je ne peux pas. Tout mon délire est dans ce sens et je n'ai guère d'autres délires.[38]

[You certainly know, Sir, the great celebration of the madmen by Brueghel. It is in Vienna. Nothing else concerns me. I would like to understand other things — but I don't. I can't. My delirium is in this sense and I have no other deliriums.]

The Language of Abjection

The condition of physical, social, and cognitive "abjection" that permeates Ferdinand's subjectivity unfolds, by necessity, also in his language. Here it gives rise to a generalized faltering of definite, absolute words. This faltering is reflected not only in the macroscopic presence of aposiopesis, that is the famous Célinian "three dots," but also in various forms of linguistic hesitation. Leo Spitzer has described these forms as stylistic procedures of "rappel." As a mode of expression "belonging to someone who does not feel certain at all about his enunciation,"[39] "rappel" comprises pleonasms and retouching of speech. However, in addition to the rhetorical devices suggested by Spitzer, there are also other, perhaps subtler, linguistic strategies put in place by the narrative discourse to reveal the presence of nonabsolute words. In ways that certainly recall Artaud's invitation, in "The Activity of the Surrealist Research Bureau" (1925), to "all coproloquists . . . all aphasics, and in general all the disinherited of language and of the word" (107) to embark in "an absolute and perpetual confusion of languages" (105), Ferdinand's speech emerges as an unstructured montage of numerous registers contained in the French language. In *Voyage*'s description of the Flanders carnage of war, for example, highly erudite and archaic verbal forms[40] coexist with typical expressions of the spoken idiom.[41] Thus, next to the correct inversions of pronouns in interrogative sentences, one finds the idiosyncratic forms of the demotic. These are reflected in the omission of the double negative of normative French or in the use of the particle "*que*" as conjunction and relative pronoun. A variety of other idioms drawn from the heteroglossia add to the relativizing effect that the juxtaposition of normative and demotic has on the sentence. Confirming what Catherine Vigneau-Rouayrenc has baptized the Célinian "*entrecroisement,*"[42] or "the crossing of voices," both *Mort* and *Voyage* make extensive use of specialized terminologies, particularly those drawn form the dictionary of the sciences. Instinctual expressions[43] also emerge as a favorite tool to confuse language, and not surprisingly in view of Céline's self-representation as a lyrical-emotive writer. In the words of *Entretiens*, "le 'rendu émotif' est lyrique . . . l'auteur lyrique, et j'en suis un, se fout toute la masse à dos" (20) [the "emotive yield" is lyrical . . . the lyrical author, and I am one of them, tosses the whole mass up on his back]. In both *Voyage* and *Mort*, for instance, affectivity is intimated in the deformation of words through addition of beginning prefixes and ending syllables.[44] Yet it can also be reflected by scatological expressions, obscenities, and even markings such as exclamatory points, all intended to suggest that irrational howlings and moanings of the physical body lurk beneath the logical propositions and beauty of the Cartesian mind. At times, the language of the Other is revealed in an associative, dreamlike logic. In *Voyage*, for example, Ferdinand's lucid assessments of the war often give way to passages structured according to musical,[45] rhythmic repetitions of ending phonemes. A good example is provided by the following passage, where the elements of the sentence appear to be chosen and combined according to sound patterns rather than cognitive, instrumental reference: "Avec casques, sans casques, sans chevaux, sur motos, hurlants, en autos, sifflants, tirailleurs, comploteurs, volants . . . (24)[With or without helmets, without horses, on motor bicycles, screaming, in cars, whistling, sniping, plotting, flying . . .]. More sophisticated associations lift the reader's attention away from the referent to writing itself. The name of "Noirceur-sur-la-Lys," for example, fails to produce the denotative illu-

sion, or what Roland Barthes once called *"l'effet de réel,"*[46] by being excessively close to the context it promises to represent. Similar strategies are at
work in the attribution of the patronymic "Mr. Mischief" to one of the
immigration officers from Ellis Island, or "Musyne" to a female artist.
Likewise, in *Mort*, the English college attended by Ferdinand is too aptly
called "Meanwell," while the names of Ferdinand's parents, Auguste and
Clémence, are inordinately congruous with the characters' psychologi-
cal traits of severity and mercy respectively.[47] It comes as no surprise that
Céline described this profoundly syncretic, non-Saussurean language —
in a 1932 letter to the *Nouvelle Revue Française*, just recently collected in
Lettres à la N.R.F. 1931–1961[48] — as a "symphonie littéraire, emotive." This
musical metaphor will also be crucial to the multilingualism of Gadda and
Beckett.

Symbolic Failures

At this juncture, it could be argued that Céline's novels of the 1930s do
not represent a substantial departure from the rhetorical manifestations
of modernism. Like Joyce's *Ulysses*, Proust's *Recherche*, and Woolf's *To
the Lighthouse*, *Voyage* and *Mort* do articulate the modern experience by
means of contradictory, open-ended allegorical practices. To reprise the
comments of Lyotard and other theorists discussed in the previous chapter, modernist novels appear incapable of enclosing the referent in coherent poetic wholes. However, whereas in modernism allegories are textualized only to be transcended in closed verbal structures, in the Célinian
sentence there are no consoling, integrating symbols. Unlike Bloom's
"stream of consciousness" or Marcel's *beau style*, Ferdinand's speech does
not block figurality. To tell it with Annie Montaut, it is a speech that does
not rest in any forms of apodictical, symbolic stability, but "makes the
paradigm play in and against the syntagm."[49] Many passages illustrate this
point; in this context, suffice it to recall just a few representative examples
from both novels. In *Mort*, for instance, the narrator's portrait of Clémence and Ferdinand's return from the open markets is irreducibly projected on the paradigmatic, vertical axis of past participles: "on rentrait
. . . Ahuris, pantelants, croulants, trempés . . . mouillées . . . " (163) [we
returned . . . Dumbfounded, panting, weak, sticky, soaked . . . drenched].
Like the description of Clémence's and Ferdinand's homecoming, the

content of the store of one of Ferdinand's many employers, Monsieur Berlope, is expanded to the storehouse of common nouns for fabric and qualified by a connotative drift of verbs coordinated by parataxis only: "Toutes les largeurs, les métrages, les échantillons, les entamés qui s'épar-pillent, s'emberlificotent, se retortillent à l'infini . . . " (143) [All sorts of widths and lengths, snippets and pieces get scattered, mixed up, twisted all over the place . . .].

Similar phenomena are also noticeable in *Voyage*. Ferdinand never encloses the dominant classes in a proper name but describes them as "Allemand ou Français, ou Anglais, ou Chinois" (73) [German or French, or English, or Chinese]. Likewise, in Flanders he gives the location of the Germans through a drift of spatial adverbs: "Par devant . . . Par derrière . . . partout . . . " (63) [In front . . . behind . . . everywhere].[50] A quotation from *Entretiens* summarizes well the effect of this rhetorical practice by comparing it to a subway, always installing additional rails but never finding a point to rest: "mon métro s'arrête nulle part" (106) [my subway stops nowhere]. Otherwise stated, in sharp contrast to modernist texts, the Célinian sentence lacks semiotic strategies to organize and reduce the dissemination of phonemes. It does not include isotopic grids of meaning, hypotactical structuring, extensive use of simile, and other rhetorical devices to arrest the productivity of language. By way of a multiple selection of elements contained in the storehouse of language(s), it remains open-ended and—ultimately—suggests how words fail to enclose objects in the stability of traditional representation.

And given the absence of "proper" nomination that affects Ferdinand's language, it is perhaps not surprising that even the status of his narrative remains undecidable. "C'est un roman" [It is a novel], states Ferdinand in the beginning of *Voyage*, but then he attempts another definition using the entries provided by the official dictionary of the French language; "rien qu'une histoire fictive, Littré le dit, qui ne se trompe jamais" (11) [nothing but a fictional story, as Littré says, and it is never wrong]. *Voyage* is also a "neither/nor," the unnamable "*ça*" [it], by which the diegesis opens and closes: "Ça a débuté comme ça" (15) [It began like this] and "qu'on n'en parle plus" (636) [let's hear no more of it].

Nevertheless, and from today's vantage point, it is possible to attribute a clearer specification to Céline's endeavors. Because *Voyage* and *Mort* are no longer books of *Zivilization*, but creations that unsettle the mythos of the Word in the retotalization of the modern experience, their status is one of a "discursive event," a performance promoting change and transition toward alternative figurations of language, literary subjectivity and novelistic representation.

Paranoia, or the Modernist Return

And yet, was the absence of all eschatological dimensions of this novelistic experience too much to bear? Was the demystification of the modernist order carried out by *Voyage* and *Mort* too unsettling to tolerate? This certainly seems to have been the case when we consider Céline's other writings of the thirties—namely, the three anti-Semitic pamphlets that immediately followed the publication of the novels: *Bagatelles pour un massacre* (1937), *L'Ecole des cadavres* (1938), and *Les Beaux draps* (1941). To be sure, in many respects the pamphlets do prolong some of the issues raised by the novels, particularly in their unveiling of what lurks beneath the images of order, rationality, and progress of the social and cultural institutions of Western civilization. *Bagatelles pour un massacre,* for example, explores the inauthenticity of discourse that runs through Ferdinand's *Bildungsroman.* Foraying into literary history, it criticizes numerous French authors, including Descartes, Pascal, Zola, Balzac, Claudel, Girardoux, Gide, Mallarmé, and Valéry for having disseminated throughout their writings an idealized notion of language. Outside the French context, the writings of "Virginie Woolf" are said to be "sentencieux" (152) [sententious] while D. H. Lawrence is accused of creating "un roman anglais très prétentieusement littéraire" (163) [an English novel full of literary pretensions] and "prémonitions mondiorénovatrices" (150) [and advice for a worldwide renewal].[51] Yet, it is the French modernist novelist Marcel Proust who is the object of the pamphlet's most sustained and severe critique. Described as the writer of a Spitzerian, caterpillarlike proposition which forgets nothing and orders hierarchically whatever is being represented (106, 141),[52] the author of *A la recherche* is said to service the French literary establishment by "Le 'Livre'" (137). In what is perhaps one of the most lucid critiques of the redemptive practices of narrative modernism, the pamphlet also notes that the style employed in Proust's "Livre" and in the writings of other, lesser contemporaries or "proustophile(s)" (184), is a "cuirasse luisante" [a shining armor] protecting authors from their descents into the open-ended temporality and spatial contradiction of the modern experience. And mirroring the outcomes of the novels, the pamphlet suggests that symbolic compensation is losing its edge. On one hand, the sense of philosophical and existential stability that it affords is "Imaginary"—a "point de capiton"—as Lacan would say, produced in the artificiality of representation. On the other hand, symbolic compensation is further displaced by the unveiling of what lurks beneath images of order, rationality, and progress. Page after page, *Bagatelles* discloses how European democracies hide a widespread, dangerous desire to engage in one more world conflict, to send those who have survived the slaughter of World War I to the final massacre. Communism does not represent a viable alternative to capitalistic models of production, but rests upon the same brutal exploitation of the masses. The European population is a mass of alcoholic and diseased beings, with France leading the statistics. The spiritual center of the libraries has been replaced by the whorehouses, the "bistrots," and the movie theaters. La Sorbonne and the Academy of French Medicine are crumbling institutions, headed by a group of pseudo-intellectuals and scientists. Yet, if *Bagatelles* does strike words of truth concerning the cultural and social experience of modernity, it also degenerates into a paranoid fantasy. As Kristeva has noted in *Powers of Horror*, it does so "from the moment when reason attempts to globalize, unify, or totalize" (178). Otherwise stated, after journeying into the chaos of language, society, and the self, Ferdinand succumbs to the modernist temptation of the ordering Subject by seeking to reabsorb all heterogeneity and contradiction in a single Object: the Jew. This turn is announced in the portrait of Yubelblatt, whose name—a neologism of the German "*jübel*," or "rejoice," and "*Blatt*," or "paper"[53]—is a prelude to dangerous equations to come. Ferdinand begins by recalling how Yubelblatt prided himself with being able to resolve the aporias of the General Assemblies of the League of Nations by waving his piece of paper:

Je donne à tout ce bavardage une sorte d'"éjaculation" . . . Je leur sors mon petit texte . . . je déplie mon petit bout de papier, une "Résolution" . . . retenez ce nom . . . une "Résolution" . . . Je la glisse au président . . . Il a plus qu'à lire, ânnoner . . . C'est fait (89).

[I provide a sort of "climax" to all this chatter . . . I take out my small text . . . I unfold my piece of paper, a "Resolution" . . . remember this name . . . a "Resolution" . . . I pass it to the president . . . he has nothing to do but read, to repeat . . . It's done.]

Then, he recalls the time when Yubclblatt coerced him into writing a letter about a deceptive social rationality, about an economic order that did not exist: "Ces précisions sont inutiles . . . Laissez-les donc . . . ils imagineront beaucoup mieux . . . demeurez assez vague . . . toujours dans la note élégante . . . " (93) [These precisions are useless . . . leave them out . . . they will imagine much better . . . be sufficiently vague . . . always in an elegant style]. From this point onwards, paranoid explanations take the upper hand. Not only does the identification of the inauthenticity of discourse with Judaism come to inform entire sections of *Bagatelles*,[54] but the Jew is also posited as the cause of all absurdity and chaos of the modern experience. In Ian Noble's words, the Jew becomes the very essence of an ideological construct: "a figure which precisely enables the text to negotiate, to fix in a single entity, a multiplicity of contradictions" (176). Thus, in a paranoia[55] of metonymies, the First World War and the upcoming Second, the "robotization" of humanity following the advent of capitalism, the exploitation of the masses by communism, the horror of the French colonial policy, and even the decay of its cultural institutions, are all explained as a Jewish conspiracy to end Western society:

Les Juifs sont nos maîtres-ici, là-bas, en Russie, en Angleterre, en Amérique, partout! . . . . Le juif est le roi de l'or et de la banque et de la Justice . . . Il possède tout . . . Presse . . . Théâtre . . . Radio . . . Chambre . . . Sénat . . . Police . . . ici ou là-bas. (*Bagatelles* 41)

[The Jews are our masters, here and there, in Russia, in England, in America, everywhere! . . . The Jew is the king of gold, of the bank and of Justice . . . He has it all . . . Publishing . . . Theater . . . Radio . . . The Chamber . . . The Senate . . . The Police . . . here and there.]

Toutes les doctrines humanitaires, égalisatrices, justicières, libératrices de Progrès par la Science, de Vérité Maçonnique, de Démocratie Universelle, etc . . . ne sont en définitive qu'autant d'affublant pompeux

stratagèmes de la même entreprise juive: L'Asservissement total.
(*Ecole* 220)

[All of humanitarian doctrines, of equal rights, justice, freedom, Scientific Progress, Mason's Truth, Universal Democracy, etc. . . . . are nothing but high-flown, pompous strategies of the same Jewish enterprise: The total Enslavement.]

And traveling even further into the terrain of totalizing explanations, Ferdinand becomes easy prey to a dangerous optimism, to that redemptive vision for which our modernity has paid one of the heaviest prices known to humanity. In *Bagatelles*, he endorses the organized massacre of the Jews promoted by the Aryan myths and carried out in the Nazi atrocities. Likewise, in both *L'Ecole des cadavres* and in *Les Beaux draps*, he argues that the retotalization of European culture can come about only if the Jews are totally suppressed. In short, after having dwelt at length in the unrepeatability of all redemptive visions, Ferdinand rejoins the meta-narratives of modernity. These include also those of his father, Auguste, whom, as we might recall, often exorcised his own distress by identifying in other races the origin of the world's existential anguish and absurdity. It is perhaps for this reason that the pamphlets are no longer signed with the "feminine" name of Céline, but bear the patrilineal appellation of Destouches. And yet, even if Céline's horrifying return cannot be justified by claiming, as Gide did, that the pamphlets were nothing but anti-Semitic spoofs,[56] one also need not repeat the other extremity. This is an extremity that has been exemplified by Sartre[57] and, more recently, by other critics[58] for whom the publication of *Bagatelles*, *L'Ecole des cadavres*, and *Les Beaux draps* disqualifies Céline from the pantheon of readable novelists. It is important to keep in mind that a radical difference exists between the novels and the pamphlets. The pamphlets not only seek resolution in a genre traditionally tending toward assertion and demonstration, but are an overt renunciation of that vision of unbounded, undifferentiated experience disclosed by the novels. More fundamentally perhaps, the existence of the pamphlets forces the contemporary reader to consider how, after the wane of modernist certainties and order, the celebration of ambiguity and instability might have a dark underside. Stated in other words, the violent rhetoric of *Bagatelles*, *L'Ecole des cadavres,* and *Les Beaux draps* should be valued precisely because it is a reminder that the collapse of Western metaphysical values might not always result in a positive embracing of difference and alterity. On the contrary, it might engender a negative, anarchist kind of freedom or even a reactionary desire to restore former monolithic orders. As John O'Neill has commented recently in a poignant critique of the contemporary euphoric celebration of knowledge and value relativism, the danger resides in the fact that "postmodern celebrants . . . will have to dance the dance of difference, breakdown and discontinuity with nothing to hold on to—no tradition, no text, no subject and no story to remember."[59] Some celebrants will of course adjust to these dimmer lights of pluralism and heterogeneity, contenting themselves with those "local," more "provisional" truths afforded by common-sense values and dialogic rationality. Others, however, might follow the path of the historical author Destouches and rewrite, once again, the dangerous tropes of our modernity[60] by choosing the wrong signifiers as anchoring devices for a world bereft of sense.

MEANDERING WITH GADDA'S "HEURISTIC" WORDS

MORALUZZA:
E' bene rimettere alle parole e alle favole un mandato provvi-
sorio e, direi, una limitata procura . . . incastonar le parole nella
necessità del momento, sì con un certo senso del limite loro . . . .
Carlo Emilio Gadda, *I viaggi la morte*[1]

[A SMALL ADVICE:
It is best to return to words and fables their provisional mandate
and, if I am allowed to say so, their limited proxy . . . it is best to
set words in the necessity of the moment, yes, and with a certain
sense of their limits.]

Italian critics traditionally have interpreted the writings of
Carlo Emilio Gadda as the practice of a belated modernist
whose totalizing projects of noumenal, absolute knowledge
have tragically run amuck.[2] This assessment has been legitimated not only by the idealism that informs Gadda's war diaries, *Giornale di guerra e di prigionia 1915–1919*, but also by
the unavailability, till 1974 and 1983 respectively, of two of
Gadda's major writings: *Racconto italiano di ignoto del novecento* (1924) and *Meditazione milanese* (1928). In this chapter, I propose a more comprehensive account of Gadda's
work by taking into consideration not only the parabola of
the war diaries but also the writings that follow. My intent is
to suggest how, as early as the mid-1920s, Gadda was questioning the premises of idealism while patterning that profoundly nonmodernist economy of signification that informs
his novelistic production of the thirties.

Gadda and the Modernist Ideal: The War Diaries

Between August 24, 1915, and December 31, 1919, Gadda kept a diary covering the events surrounding his participation in World War I and recounting his arrival on the front, his capture at Caporetto, his imprisonment in Germany and, finally, his return home to the news of the death of his younger brother, the beloved Enrico. Available in print as early as 1955, Gadda's war diaries have been correctly interpreted as the endeavor of a young man full of modernist ideals.[3] Unlike Céline, for whom the war represented the horrifying outcome of a dying Western civilization and culture, Gadda believed that a conflict was needed to restore Italy to the sociopolitical and moral values of the nineteenth century, now undermined by internal divisions and external aggressions. Moreover, as Manuela Bertone has acutely noted in her "I diari del 'tempo perduto'" (41 ff.), it is quite likely that Gadda saw the war as the perfect opportunity for him to restore his family's name to the prestige it had enjoyed during the period of the kingdom of Italy under the direction of the *"destra storica."* Readers familiar with the author's biography will recall that his ancestors had included aristocrats, such as Paola Ripamonti, who had married Gadda's grandfather, and rather prominent politicians like Carlo Emilio's uncle Giuseppe Gadda. An active participant in the Risorgimento, the movement for Italian independence and unification, Giuseppe Gadda had been a successful minister of public works in the Gabinetto Lanza-Sella between 1869 and 1873. Despite such glorious ancestry, however, by the turn of the century, the prestige of the Gadda family had been seriously weakened. The failure of Gadda's father, Francesco Ippolito, in a silk-business venture coupled with the construction of a villa well beyond the family's means, had seriously diminished the family's affluence. With the death of Gadda's father in 1909, his mother, Adele Lehr, took over the family's finances. Her poor administrative skills only resulted in sending the family into even more difficult years of financial hardship.

The opening pages of the first volume of Gadda's diaries, titled *Anno 1915 giornale di campagna*, and dating from August 24 to February 15, 1916, seem to confirm the compound of feelings and motivations that pushed Gadda toward an active support of the conflict. The preface of the volume, signed in Latin with the name "Gaddus. —1915," discloses the possibility of individual heroism offered by the war, the potential for

individual epic deeds. The orderly, legal-sounding prose that immediately follows the Latinate signature reveals the "public" origin of the
diary:

24 Agosto 1915.
Il bollettino del Ministero della Guerra del giorno 5 agosto 1915 mi
nominava, dietro mia richiesta del 27 marzo u.s., sotto-tenente ufficiale
della milizia territoriale, arma di fanteria, con destinazione al 5 Alpini.-
Il comando reggimentale di Milano a cui mi presentai il 17 agosto mi
destinò al magazzino di Edolo.-Il 18 sera ero a Edolo, dopo aver prestato
il giuramento a Milano.
Edolo, 24 agosto, 1915.
CE Gadda.-
-Carlo Emilio Gadda.-[4]

[August 24th, 1915.
Following my request of March 27, on August 5, 1915, the bulletin of the
Ministry of War nominated me to the position of official second lieuten-
ant of the territorial militia, regiment of infantry, with destination the
Fifth Alpine battalion.-On August 17th, I reported to the regimental
command, and was destined to the warehouse of Edolo.-On the evening
of the eighteenth, after taking my oath in Milan, I reached the town of
Edolo.
Edolo, August 24th, 1915
C. E. Gadda.]

Within the text itself, the presence of words of intolerance for the present
state of Italy and of long passages recollecting painful moments of childhood and youth confirm once more the plurality of motives that brought
Gadda to support the war as a corrective to a derealized personal and
public history. Yet Gadda's ambitions are quickly put to the test. His days
in Edolo are spent in the boredom of useless tasks and in the company of
soldiers lacking the discipline and the organization that Gadda deemed
necessary to achieve heroic feats. Nonetheless, armed with what the second section of the diary, entitled *Giornale di guerra per l'anno 1916*, calls
"la mia dose di idealismo, di pazienza, di speranza, di fede inalterabile"
(567) [my dose of idealism, of patience, of hope, of unalterable faith],
Gadda continues to await his chance to participate in history, while la-

menting the decay of the Italian nations and of its soldiers. The following passage is a case in point. The page departs from the orderly, controlled prose of the preface to become a space to vent sentiments of anger, frustrations, and rage: "Ma io devo e voglio combattere. Lascio che i porci, i ladri, i cani, gli impostori sgavazzino e faccio il mio dovere" (481) [But I must and I want to fight. I leave the pigs, the dogs, the impostors to debauch and I fulfill my duty]. Then, at the beginning of October 1917, his *Diario di guerra per l'anno 1917* announces the long-awaited transfer to the main Isonzo front. The possibility of heroic deeds finally seems to realize itself when, on October 25 of the same year, Gadda is defeated at Caporetto. The event not only marks the beginning of a long period of imprisonment in the camps of Rastatt and Cellelager—events that Gadda will describe in the last volume of his diary, *Vita notata. Storia*— but represents the wane of the young Gadda's dreams: "La tragica fine" (663) [The tragic ending]. After the armistice, Gadda returns home. To the embitterment of Caporetto is now added the pain of a tragic loss: the death of his brother Enrico during a test flight. Prey to feelings of total disillusionment, Gadda comes to the realization that not only does a gulf exist between ideal and empirical reality but that all dreams of personal and historical order are ultimately defeated by the chaos and messiness of the world:

Se la realtà avesse avuto minor forza sopra di me, oppure se la realtà fosse di quelle che consentono la grandezza (Roma, Germania), io sarei un uomo che vale qualcosa. Ma la realtà di questi anni . . . è merdosa; e in essa mi sento immedesimare e annegare. (863)

[If reality had less hold on me, or if it had been one of these realities that allow greatness (Rome, Germany), I would be a man worth something. But the reality of these years . . . is shitty; and in it I feel myself identifying and drowning.]

And precisely because the diary was intended as the record of heroic deeds, to the wane of all dreams of personal and historical order corresponds the end of textuality itself. By the author's own admission, the diary has become a pointless endeavor, a writing unworthy even of private memory:

Non noterò più nulla, poiché nulla di me è degno di ricordo anche
davanti a me solo. Finisco così questo libro di note.-
Milano, 31 dicembre 1919. Ore 22. In casa.-
Qui finiscono le note autobiografiche del periodo post-bellico; e non ne
incominciano altre né qui né altrove.
   Carlo Emilio Gadda
   Milano, 31 dicembre 1919
Fine delle mie note autobiografiche e di tutte le note raccolte in questo
libro. CEG
   Milano, 31–12–1919.-(867)

[I will no longer record anything, because nothing in my life is worthy
of memory, even before myself alone. I end here this book of memoirs.-
Milan, December 31, 1919. 10.00 P.M. At home.-
The autobiographical notes of the postwar period end here and will not
be resumed—either here or elsewhere.
   Carlo Emilio Gadda
   Milan, December 31, 1919
This is the end of my autobiographical notes and of all the notes col-
lected in this book. C.E.G
   Milan, 12–31–1919.]

Back among the civilians, Gadda completes his university degree and
begins working as an engineer. In 1924, upon returning from Argentina,
where he had been employed by La Compañia General de Phosphoros,
he abandons momentarily his career to dedicate himself to the composition of *Racconto italiano di ignoto del novecento,* to which will follow the
1928 *Meditazione milanese.* Available in print only in 1974 and 1983, respectively, these texts not only bid farewell to the idealism of the diaries
but announce the author's pivotal role in the context of twentieth-century narrative. While *Racconto* translates the experience of World War I
into the failed account of an orderly, finite narrative, *Meditazione* seeks to
give a philosophical underpinning to the chaos and messiness of the
world. It also lays the groundwork for that poetics of metamorphic representation that will shape Gadda's future novelistic production.

The Unrepresentability of the Real: *Racconto* (1924)

Composed in 1924 in response to a 10,000-lire literary prize for a novel offered by the publisher Mondadori, *Racconto* is Gadda's first attempt at a major creative endeavor.[5] Originally intended as the story of the fall of a good character in the troubled society of postwar Italy, today *Racconto* is little more than a "Cahier d'études," alternating "*studi*,"[6] or attempts at fictional composition, with a series of metafictional commentaries, or "*note*" (393), on the *studi* themselves. Despite their looseness and fragmentation, Gadda's *note* are most important for the purpose of this discussion, as they articulate with great clarity the author's awareness of the impossibility of translating a messy, chaotic reality in a traditional model of representation. Indeed, after having announced, in the first note, the subject matter and the main lines of development of his tale, by the second note, Gadda declares to be unable to decide the general tone to be assumed by his story. On one hand, his individuality is pluralized in five voices, which correspond to just as many worldviews and perspectives:[7]

Nota Cr 2.—(24 marzo 1924—ore 16.30)
Tonalità generale del lavoro. E' una grossa questione. Le maniere che mi sono più famigliari sono la (a) *logico-razionalistica*, paretiana, seria, celebrale—E la (b) *umoristico-ironica* . . . la (c) umoristico seria manzoniana . . . . Posseggo anche una quarta maniera (d) enfatica tragica, 'meravigliosa 600' . . . . Finalmente posso elencare una quinta maniera (e), che chiamerò la maniera cretina, che è fresca, puerile, mitica omerica . . . . (396)

[Note Cr 2.—(March 24, 1924—4:30 p.m.
General tone of the work. It is a big question. The manners that are more familiar to me are the manner (a); *logico-rationalistic*, Paretolike, serious, cerebral—And the manner (b); humoristic-ironic . . . the manner (c); serious, Manzonilike humor . . . . I even have a fourth manner, the manner (d); emphatic, tragic, "marvelously 1600s." . . . Finally, I can mention a fifth manner, the manner (e), which I will call the naive manner. It is fresh, puerile, mythic, and Homeric.]

On the other hand, the objects of his intended representation cannot be defined according to the antithetical—and therefore unambiguous—attributes of "a, b, c" (464) but, like Gadda's kaleidoscopic subjectivity, are open to permutation and change of roles. In Gadda's words, characters are becoming "*a* e *b*" (464) and are revealing their nature as "omnipotenziali" (463) [omnipotential]. Even the setting of the novel comes to be implicated in this open-ended state of being. Despite Gadda's intention to represent postwar Italian society, his extant attempts at fictional composition reveal that the original fabula was expanded to embrace a number of other, often unrelated narrative topics, including stories of convoluted murders and melodramatic romances. In short, as one of Gadda's notes puts it, the narrative plot is becoming a complex tangle, "e quale ingarbugliato intreccio!" (460) [and what a complex tangle!], subject to the open-ended movement of reality: "il comporsi e il ridecomporsi, il continuo trasformarsi" (493) [the composition and the decomposition, the continuous transformation].

The representational impasse revealed in these theoretical notes and fictional fragments of *Racconto*—an impasse that has been described felicitously as "the impossibility for the twentieth-century novel to propose, once more . . . a global, comprehensive representation of life"[8]—brings Gadda to lay the groundwork for an alternative model of narration.[9] Toward the end of *Racconto*, he timidly suggests that perhaps it would be better to abandon the will to order phenomena in stable verbal structures and begin instead to write by a *"Mischung"* of expressions and through the colliding superimposition of discourse and counterdiscourse, thesis and antithesis, point and counterpoint. The result of this synthetic writing would be "un romanzo psicopatico e caravaggesco" (411) [a psychopathic, Caravaggio-like novel]. An almost Bakhtinian[10] example of grotesque and polyphonic representations, Gadda's "psychopathic novel" would be more suitable to articulate the baroque[11] reality of life: "Pensavo stamane di dividere il poema in tre parti, di cui la prima *La Norma, (o il normale)*—seconda l'Abnorme . . . terza La Comprensione o Lo Sguardo sopra la vita (o Lo sguardo sopra l'essere)" (415) [This morning I thought about dividing the poem in three parts: The first part would be the Norm (or that which is normal); the second part the Abnormal, . . . and the third part, the Comprehension or the Look upon life (the Look upon being)].

Despite these suggestive commentaries, however, *Racconto* falls short of actualizing such a work. Since the novel's fluctuating point of view would engender accusations of "variabilità, eterogeneità, mancanza di fusione, mancanza di armonia, et similia" (461) [variations, heterogeneity, lack of integration, lack of harmony, and so on], and its plot "'contraddizione!, incoerenza!, incertezza!, ecc.'" (472) [contradiction!, incoherence!, uncertainty!, etc.], fear of criticism prevents Gadda from transforming *Racconto* into more than an early and yet crucial reflection on the impossibility of a metaphysical mode of representation. In short, Gadda foresees the possibility of an alternative model of narration, intuits the future of a novel unwilling to confine existence in the rigidity of traditional form and discourse, but cannot yet commit to a corresponding writing practice. Instead, Gadda chooses to turn to the terrain of philosophical speculation—namely, to the pages of *Meditazione milanese*, from where he will further explore the elusive, baroque nature of experience.

From Being to Beings: *Meditazione milanese* (1928)

Written in 1928 as a dissertation for a degree in philosophy, which Gadda had begun in 1922, *Meditazione* emerges out of an intellectual climate profoundly influenced by the neo-Hegelianism of Benedetto Croce. However, instead of reflecting this climate, *Meditazione* mounts an important critique to the ideality informing modernist epistemic figurations. These include Croce's endeavor, but also transcendental phenomenology and structural linguistics.[12]

Introduced by a title and a preface that disclaim the absoluteness of traditional philosophical discourse—*Meditazione* being from the lesser, more provincial city of Milan and a work reputedly tainted by "limiti" and "deficienze,"[13] [limits and "deficiencies"], the text suggests a larger revisionary context by aligning itself with those thinkers who have questioned the main frames of the Western mind: "Come i lettori avvertiranno, di queste idee una buona parte già si affacciarono qua e là, sia pure in contesti diversi, allo spirito umano" (622) [As readers will notice, several of these ideas have emerged, albeit in different contexts, throughout the human spirit]. The first section of the work, aptly titled "Critica del concetto di metodo di alcune posizioni ermeneutiche tradizionali" (625) [Critique of the concept of method in some traditional hermeneutic positions], fulfills the reader's horizon of expectations. The section harks back[14] to the metamorphic thought of the pre-Socratics and also draws upon the antimetaphysical insights of Bruno, Leibnitz, Spinoza, Kant, and Bergson to unsettle the structures of ideality: "dissolverò li eroi e le armi loro . . . le loro armi dedalee" (675) [I will dissolve the heroes and their arms . . . their Daedaluslike arms]. Thus, in "Il dato e l'inizio della attività relatrice (627 ff.) [The datum and the beginning of relational activity], Gadda resumes the Kantian critique of apodictical categories and argues that the frames of inquiry that are supposedly indubitable and first in themselves are in fact historical and contextual, subject to further mutation and definition (628). For this reason, what is conceived today as infinitely small or great, be it the atom or the infinite, will be displaced tomorrow, just as the Ptolemaic system was supplanted by the Copernican (712–19).

Next to the dissolution of a priori and absolute categories, Gadda demolishes another myth, notably the idea of a stable, self-identical substance. In the section "La grama sostanza" (631) [The false substance] Gadda inserts his argument in the line of the radically temporal differentiation and spatial coimplication of being proposed by the pre-Socratics, Bruno, Spinoza, and Bergson. He writes that the concept of substantiality depends upon a perceptual illusion whereby a quantitative decrease in mobility and complexity has been taken as a mark of stability and self-sameness. This illusion, he adds, is akin to what one experiences during a game of chess, when the move of certain pieces creates the optical illusion of the fixity of the remaining ones. And precisely because the concept of a self-identical substance is a mythopoetic creation, Gadda suggests to preface the term "substance" with the epithet of "*grama*" (633) [false], so as to avoid all future confusion.

The dissolution of apodixis and substantiality illustrated thus far, is followed by the demolition of the equation of existential well-being with sameness and closure. Gadda argues that, from the Platonic struggle to impose form on the "*Khora*" of matter, or what he calls "la lotta platonica fra üle e morfé" (637) [the platonic struggle between matter and form], to the epistemologies informing "il cervello pleistocenico della borghesuccia" (666) [the pleistocenic brain of the petit bourgeois], happiness has been associated with a static experience of life. In reality, however, such experience is only conducive to an imperfect, illusory condition of well-being. In Gadda's words, "questa immagine della felicità è assolutamente fittizia . . . la felicità . . . è tutta consegnata al compito, all'azione,

al divenire. . . . Il concetto statico di felicità ripugna con tutte le mani-
festazioni della vita" (643) [this image of happiness is absolutely false.
. . . happiness is given by duty, action, becoming. . . . The static concept
of happiness goes against all manifestations of life].

In subsequent sections of Gadda's dissertation, the corollaries of these
arguments unfold to encompass traditional definitions of subject, object,
and occurrence. Echoing here, as Beckett will, Spinoza's idea of the "affect," Gadda suggests that since the human self participates in the complexity and temporality of the real, it cannot be thought as a centripetal
monad, but is composed of molecules that combine and recombine in
multiple figurations: "un insieme di relazioni non perennemente unite"
(649) [a compound of relations never perennially unified]. Like the subject, the object does not escape chronotopic differentiation—that is,
change in time and space. In one of the many wonderfully prosaic examples that function as mirrors to reflect the materialistic intent of the
work, Gadda writes that the object is like a *"gnocco"* (655), the Italian
potato noodle whose contours become gradually coimplicated with the
sauce, the cheese, and the other *gnocchi* served on a plate. As for what
regards occurrences, Gadda observes that the "ipotiposi della catena
delle cause" [the hypotiposis of the chain of causes] is the result of an
artificially imposed conceptual category. For this reason, he proposes to
replace the line of *ananke*—"de(la) curva della ananche" (407)—with
that of the rhizomatous network (650); a figure, that is, better suited to
articulate occurrences as the product of molecular relations and becoming.

After this Rabelaisian meal, "una spiacevole agape" (675) [a displeasing banquet], the author moves to the "pars construens" of *Meditazione*.
Under the umbrella-concept of *"euresi"* [heuresis], he patterns an alternative relation to the baroque nature of the visible. Broadly summarized,
euresi is a provisional and extensional configuration. Because it originates
as a critique of the identity-thinking of the speculative tradition, and in a
deep respect for substance's complexity and immanence, it undoes the
violence of reductive structures of opposition and finality. Further, it also
promotes relations and contaminations of borders, contingency and
open-endedness. In Gadda's words, the practitioners of *euresi* seek "il
maggior numero di relazioni" (713) [the greatest number of relations] and
the amplification of the "$n + 1$" (695). Nonetheless, these same practitio-

ners are conscious that all amplifications are but "paus(e)" (702) [pause(s)], Lyotardian local "stations" of knowledge, rather than final, absolute destinations. In other words, the relational increase of *euresi* does not tend toward the exhaustiveness and totality of an hyperintegrative system, or what Gian Carlo Roscioni in *La disarmonia prestabilita* has called Gadda's totalizing desire of "Omnia circumspicere" (63 ff.). On the contrary, every step of the *euresi* is always subject to further displacement. As Jacqueline Risset has written compellingly in "Carlo Emilio Gadda ou la philosophie à l'envers," Gadda's *Meditazione* reverses traditional philosophical premises since "it can never become a system, precisely because it strives towards the impossibility—of the system itself."[15] A number of comments voiced by Gadda further illustrate this crucial point and show how Gadda's encyclopedia remains open, a monadology whose extension is unchecked by the Leibnitzian central monad. Anticipating critical observations that *euresi* seeks to enclose the totality of knowledge—"nella biologia, nella sociologia, nel diritto, nella botanica, nella economia umana, ecc." [in biology, sociology, law, botany, human economy, etc.]—Gadda replies that "Troppo enorme sarebbe il lavoro e dieci volumi non basterebbero" (784) [The work would be too extensive, and ten volumes would not suffice]. In another passage, he notes that neither superstructures nor "*Ersätze*" exist (783), but only systems of relations whose limits are "provvisori o removibili" (677) [provisional and removable].[16] Moreover, the text also provides several icons to emphasize the open-endedness of the *euresi*. It includes a drawing of a source of light that becomes increasingly weaker as its rays move from the center to the periphery (700), an open bookshelf whose outer right-and left-side volumes are leaning diagonally (679) and, mirroring the geometries of Samuel Beckett's essays of the 1930s, even a polygon with one side left open (799).

Given these premises, it follows that, unlike metaphysical idealism, *euresi* presupposes a weaker epistemic subjectivity. To reprise one of Gadda's example, it is a subjectivity ready to drift across oceanic waters aboard an unstable boat: "Io parto dal traballante ponte della mia caravella . . . per osservare: e non sono il celigena disceso dall'assoluto . . . ma un grumo di relazioni . . . un groviglio di maglie del reale" (676) [I leave from the unstable bridge of my boat to observe: and I am not the celestial being who has descended from the absolute . . . but I am a compound of relations, a tangle in reality's web].

The implications of this epistemic model are far-reaching since, as Guido Guglielmi has suggested, following the Spinozian extension of *"ordo rerum"* into *"ordo idearum,"*[17] Gadda derives from his self-proclaimed *"arzigogolata filosofia"* (696) [convoluted philosophy] both an ethics and an aesthetics. Good and evil, happiness and pain in all their social and cultural manifestations, are in fact defined in *Meditazione* according to their degree of relation and open-endedness. Echoing here, as Musil had done in *Der Mann ohne Eigenschaften* (1930–43),[18] the Machian view of dissolution of truths into values, Gadda argues that neither "Il Male" (744 ff.) [evil] nor "Il Bene" (756 ff.) [good] can be framed by a corpus of fixed, static attributes, but are categories relative to contextual interpretation. Moreover, additionally implicating ethics within the larger frame of *euresi*, Gadda argues that "Il bene: o realtà" (689) [good: or reality] occurs when no relations and convergences have been excluded, when no selection and reduction have been imposed on life. Conversely, evil emerges with the decomposition of life's relations, with the rigidity of simplicity and finality of the "non-vita" (802) [nonlife]. Elsewhere in *Meditazione*, he again stresses this point by commenting that the greatest extensionality has "la massima eticità" (691) [maximum ethical value], whereas evil is "il regresso dal significato $n + 1$ ad n o il non accedere ad $n + 1$ durante l'attività euristica o creativa" (763) [the reduction of the meaning of $n + 1$ to n, or the failure to achieve $n + 1$ during the heuristic or creative activity].

Even more significant to the purpose of this discussion is the unfolding of *euresi* in the field of artistic practice, which might have been influenced by Gadda's interest in the Kantian theory of the sublime and in Schopenhauer's notion of aesthetic will-lessness and *"pietas."*[19] Quite possibly bearing in mind the failure of *Racconto* in the actualization of an alternative novel, Gadda writes that "heuristic" artists not only do not fear the coordinates of "tempo-spazio" (707) [time-space] but, equipped with their weaker attitude of "sentimento" (795 ff.) [feeling], are willing to follow the baroque meandering of the world. They do so by a rhetorical practice that is diametrically opposed to the Cartesian and structuralist axis of opposition and closure. In a passage that brings to mind the famous example of the "8:25 P.M. Geneva-to-Paris" train described by Saussure's *Course in General Linguistics*, Gadda inaugurates his departure from the structuralist model of language and the idealism that it implies.[20] Indeed, Gadda comments that those who use words according to ideals of logic and finality—"freddamente e antistoricamente astraendole dal vivente e vissuto e raggiunto contesto di una lingua" (844) [coldly and ahistorically abstracting words from the living, lived, and achieved context of a language] are not artists but apprentice telegraphers in a train station (845). As a possible alternative, Gadda proposes (839) a linguistic model closer to Gianbattista Vico's theory of heroic metaphors from *Scienza Nuova*. These are figures built extensionally and analogically. As such they are removed from the abstractions and generalizations of philosophical language and are closer to the metamorphic, ever-changing nature of being.[21]

A Poetics of "Heuristic" Words: Gadda's Essays (1927–29)

The poetics of "heuristic" words that has emerged from the final pages of *Meditazione* was clearly at the center of Gadda's concerns. In fact, in the years immediately framing the composition of *Meditazione*, Gadda had dedicated two essays to the topic: the 1927 "I viaggi, la morte" and the 1929 "Le belle lettere e i contributi espressivi delle tecniche.[22] In "I viaggi, la morte" Gadda returns to the issue of the relationship between writing and the representation of life intended, as in the pages of *Meditazione*, as a succession of time and space. The targets of Gadda's critique, however, are not the philosophers of idealism, but fantastic authors and symbolist poets. While the former are said to transcend reality through the production of phantasmagoric narratives, the latter do so by way of a practice based upon symbols of infinity and closure. And since, as Gadda puts it in *Meditazione*, a chapter of aesthetics is also a chapter of ethics, he cannot but condemn these writers for having abstracted themselves from the reality of experience: "La poesia . . . Quando voglia prescindere 'in absoluto' da un qualunque motivo della realtà complessa, rinnegarne un qualunque vincolo, si trasforma in arzigogolato ricamo, in 'immaginosa finzione,' nel senso più dilettantesco della parola" (580) [When poetry seeks to transcend, "in absoluto," any one aspect of the complex reality, when it seeks to deny reality's ties, it transforms itself into ornate embroidery, into an "imaginary fiction," in the most dilettante-ish sense of the word].

A viable alternative to this type of writing is proposed by Gadda in his second essay, "Le belle lettere e i contributi espressivi delle tecniche." Here he describes a language capable of actualizing the Vichian process introduced in *Meditazione* through a poetic word open to the ambiguity and temporality contained in the heteroglossia—that is, in the patrimony of lived and living speech-styles:

elaboratori del materiale estetico . . . sono un po' tutti . . . : agricoltori, avvocati, operai, preti, ingegneri, ladri, puttane, maestri, nottambuli, monache, bancarottieri, marinai, madri, ex-amanti, marchese, politicanti, vecchi danarosi, fattucchiere, malati, notai, soldati. Tutti, tutti. (479)

[Everybody . . . elaborates aesthetic material . . . : farmers, lawyers, workers, priests, engineers, thieves, whores, teachers, nightwalkers, nuns, bankrupt fellows, sailors, mothers, former lovers, marquises, politicians, rich old folks, witches, sick people, public notaries, soldiers. Everybody, everybody.]

As this quotation suggests, one of the most immediate correlatives to Gadda's conception of artistic language is that creation is no longer the domain of the demiurge, of the "*homo faber*," but becomes a nonauratic, collective endeavor. Hence, in this same article, Gadda not only proposes to conceive of the writer as a mason, building a wall with the bricks made by others, but extends an explicit invitation to abandon idealist views of authorship: "lo schilleriano gioco, ov'egli assume quella stessa parte che nell'universo il Creatore" (484) [the Schillerian game, where he plays the part of the Creator of the universe].[23] Nonetheless, Gadda does allow for some measure of creativity but relocates it in a reworking of the formed material, in a manipulation of the already said. This manipulation ranges from neutral citation and replay to negation by way of strategies of parodic reversal and uncrowning.[24] A longer quotation from the text finalizes well Gadda's rhetorical project:

Lo scrittore ha davanti a sé delle realtà storiche, esterne, come il cavatore ha dei cubi di granito da rimuovere. E' impossibile dimenticare una così povera e spesso dimenticata verità. Lo scrittore a sua posta rimove e coordina queste realtà date (storiche, esterne), o le ricrea, o, meglio, conferisce ad esse quel supersignificato che è il suo modo d'espedirsi. (476)

[External realities stand in front of the writer like those chunks of granite that a miner has to remove. It is impossible to forget such a simple and often forgotten truth. For his own part, the writer removes and coordinates these given realities (historical, external), or he recreates them, or better yet, confers upon them that added meaning which is his own way of proceeding.]

Gadda and the Avant-gardes

It is worth mentioning at this juncture, that Gadda's alternative poetics, much like that of Céline, appears to have benefited greatly from importing the aesthetic tenets of Italian avant-gardist movements. These include the turn-of-the-century *scapigliati* and their twentieth-century heirs: the futurists. Gadda himself suggests this genealogy. In "La scapigliatura Milanese," he writes: "'scapigliatura' . . . 'Una piccola rivoluzione sentimentale ed estetica che fiammeggiò in Milano, a un dipresso dal '60 al '77' come disse il Linati. Ma in una visuale più ampia . . . fino al 1910, fino al '14: fino al futurismo, a *Lacerba*, alla polemica antidannunziana" ["*scapigliatura*" . . . A small sentimental and aesthetic revolution that happened in Milan, from 1860 to 1877, as Linati said. But, in a larger perspective . . . up to 1910, 1914: up to futurism, to *Lacerba*, to the anti-Dannunzian polemic].[25]

Gadda's affiliation with the *scapigliatura* has been the focus of some attention.[26] However, despite an ever-growing interest in Gadda's work, most North American critics never address the rather intriguing possibility of an affinity between Gadda's poetics of pluralinguism and the "*paroliberismo*" of the futurist avant-garde.[27] Surprisingly, as this silence is in view of the chronological and even geographical proximity of the cultural activity of Gadda and that of the futurists, it can nonetheless be explained by the philological bent of much of Gaddian criticism, which has tended to contextualize the author's endeavor within more traditional forms.

Moreover, it is also quite possible that the overt endorsement of fascist ideology on the part of futurism might have played a part in the political unconscious of critics, bringing them to separate the author of the famous anti-fascist pamphlet *Eros e Priapo* (1968) and of the poignant, anti-Mussolinian satire of *Quer pasticciaccio brutto de via Merulana* (1957) from the work of Filippo Tommaso Marinetti and that of his followers. Last but not least, Gadda seems to legitimize critical assessments that emphasize the distance of his work from that of the futurist avant-garde. On several occasions, he expresses ironic, if not disparaging, comments toward Marinetti and his followers.[28]

In Italy, scholars of Gadda have generally been more attentive to the author's relationships with his own contemporaries. For example, Gianfranco Contini, one of the earlier and arguably still the finest among critics of Gadda, situated the author's work within the "post-romantic avant-garde." Contini also commented upon what he called Gadda's "futurist-like synthesis" and "unanimism."[29] Most recently Antonio Turolo has underlined the fact that Gadda's ironic comments should not prevent scholars from exploring possible connections.[30] Likewise, Micaela Lipparini has warned that the distance between Gadda and the futurist avant-garde is not as great as was previously assumed.[31]

By the turn of the century, the *scapigliati* had given new impetus to the Italian "*questione della lingua.*"[32] The group's daring contamination of normative Italian with the idioms of the country's enormously rich patrimony of dialects, did not go unnoticed. At the beginning of the new century, Marinetti seconded the stylistic transgression of the *scapigliati* in his "*barocco tecnificato*"[33]—that is to say, in the theory of *paroliberismo*.

Broadly outlined, the theory of *paroliberismo*, which was systematized theoretically between 1912 and 1914,[34] redefines traditional, established categories of representation. From the premise that the world of physical and perceived images of modernity is contingent and open-ended, Marinetti extends an invitation to engage in unstable symbolic practices. Thus, he not only voices the need to free words from the traditional ordering of the Latin sentence, but calls for a destruction of syntax in the abolition of all those elements of expressions that create finality and closure. These include grammatical units whose function is to encode stasis, such as adjectives, adverbs, punctuation marks, and finite verbs. What remains are words in freedom, "*parole in libertà*"[35] — that is to say, nouns and their doubles. Selected from the enormously rich patrimony of linguistic heteroglossia, these are no longer combined according to causality and linearity, but are juxtaposed paradigmatically, following an ever-expanding and dynamic net of analogies. In the words of "Manifesto tecnico della letteratura futurista": "L'analogia non é altro che l'amore profondo che collega cose distanti, apparentemente diverse e ostili. Solo per mezzo di analogie vastissime uno stile orchestrale, ad un tempo policromo, polifonico, e polimorfo può abbracciare la vita della materia" (43) [Analogy is nothing but the profound love that binds together things that are distant, and apparently different and incompatible. An orchestral style — a style that is polyphonic, polychromatic, and polymorphous — can embrace the life of matter only by means of the most vast net of analogies].

The implication of this model are of course far-reaching for the theory and practice of traditional representation. The departure of *paroliberismo* from the normative propositions of traditional syntax gives a theoretical justification to the unfinished, the tentative, the potential as the "proper" figuration to translate the metamorphic becoming of the modern experience.[36] The radical openness to a variety of speech styles, including those of prose, narrative exposition, poetry, and drama, as well as those of everyday languages and noises reproduced through phonetic spelling and onomatopoeia, has the effect of breaking up the integrity of literary language and its mediums. This inclusion by collage is, of course, crucial. The reproduction of the many cultural codes of modernity, of the texts of our daily, quotidian experience, ends up by questioning the traditional dichotomy between "art" and "life." In other words, when an object from the real world is imported into an artifact, the object's presence not only undermines the ontological status of the artifice as such, but also the status of the world itself, which now can become part of the art work. Last but not least, *paroliberismo* deeply affects the position of the subject of the enunciation. Because a self-identical subjectivity depends upon the possibility of persisting in time and space, the polyphony of expressions has, as its corollary, the pluralization of the subject in a multiplicity of positions. Hence, Marinetti's famous call, in the "Manifesto tecnico," to destroy the unary, symbolist Subject — "Distruggere nella letteratura 'l'io'" (44) [Destroy the literary "I"] — and his more enduring, and ultimately more fundamental practice of a group aesthetics replacing the demiurgic "I" with a collective "we."

It is well known that futurism fell short of actualizing in verbal practices the innovations called for in the manifestos. In fact, the best results of the group are not to be found in Marinetti's *Zang Tumb Tuuum* (1914), and in other mediocre creations, but in works by Boccioni, Carrà, and Severini, which translate the concept of collage in the more spatially conducive medium of painting. However, it is also undeniable that the impact of futurism was extremely far-reaching, not only for other avant-gardist practices, but also for a writer like Gadda, who was lacking a strong literary model.

We might recall how Pirandello had addressed "*la questione*" theoretically and had identified in the expressionistic practices of Folengo, Porta, Bersezio, and the *scapigliati*, the primary manifestations of "*umorismo*." Yet, as I pointed out earlier, Pirandello's *Il fu Mattia Pascal* and *Uno, nessuno e centomila* remained within the confines of a traditional model of representation. It was only in some of the short tales collected in *Novelle per un anno* that Pirandello departed from the security of monoglossia. He did so not so much by experimenting with forms of linguistic pastiche, but by fusing the voices of narrators and characters in the mode of free indirect discourse. Mirroring the outcome of Pirandello's novels, Italo Svevo's *La coscienza di Zeno* voiced the transgressive, destabilizing potential of Eastern Italian dialects while remaining firmly grounded in the security of monoglossia. Perhaps this explains why, in his copious essays, Gadda never addresses these writers' novels but does criticize the practices of Dante and Manzoni[37] for having included—and yet neutralized—the transgressive potential of plurilinguism. Conversely, he often endorses various types of avant-gardist expressionism in the rhetorical and in the visual arts, such as painting and cinema. For example, in the 1945 "L'arte del Belli," Gadda argues that Belli, like Manzoni, is sensitive to the problem of expression, but surpasses Manzoni by resisting all forms of linguistic neutralization.[38] In the already mentioned "La scapigliatura milanese" of 1949, he praises the *scapigliati* Arrighi, Dossi, Faldella, Praga, Rovani, Lucini, and Linati for having engendered, through their writing, a renewed sense of truth. As regards the visual arts, in the 1950 essay "Una mostra di Ensor," Gadda not only situates the nineteenth-

century painter Ensor in the pantheon of Bosch and Goya but com-
mends him for his willingness to experiment with a plurality of styles:

Egli non vuole installare le sue visioni multiformi nell'unità immobile
di uno 'stile' raggiunto ed unicamente sfruttato . . . . C'è nel suo lavoro
. . . un va e vieni continuo, un intercambio tematico, un fluire e un
rifluire di modi che imita lo 'ebb and flow' . . . .[39]

[He does not want to fix his multiform vision in the motionless unity of
one achieved style. . . . There is in his work a coming and going, a thematic interchange, a circulating and a recirculating of manners that
imitates the "ebb and flow."]

This praise for Ensor's style also explains Gadda's admiration for another
avant-gardist painter, the surrealist Giorgio de Chirico.[40]

Even more telling than these future displays of admiration for various
types of avant-gardism, however, is a letter to Carocci dated November 2,
1926. Gadda confesses his desire to be "moderno e diciamo cosí futurista
. . . una continuazione di mie idee sull'arte in rapporto alle espressioni
moderne della vita" [modern and futurist, so to speak . . . a continuation
of my idea of art in relation to the modern expressions of life].[41] In another letter to Carocci from the same volume, this one dated January 15,
1928, (61), Gadda again rejoins Marinetti, now in the fields of cinematic
art. As the latter had done in "La cinematografia futurista" of 1916,[42]
Gadda praises avant-gardist cinema, for which he intended to write an
essay entitled "Letterati and cinema" for a special 1927 issue of the journal Solaria. Although Gadda never completed the piece,[43] he nonetheless saw the cinematic medium as naturally conducive to that dynamic
expressionism theorized by the soviet futurist filmmakers Sergei Eisenstein and Dziga Vertov. The similarity of Racconto's conceptualization of
a novel proceeding by "La Norma . . . l'Abnorme . . . La Comprensione"
(415) with Sergei Eisenstein's theory of "dialectical montage" and Dziga
Vertov's "kino-eye" are so striking to merit further attention. As David
Cook has written, Eisenstein's theory, exemplified in the famous synthetic image of the lion at the end of Battleship Potemkin (1925), looks at
history and experience "as a perpetual conflict in which a force (thesis)
collides with a counterforce (antithesis) to produce from their collision a
wholly new phenomenon (synthesis) which is not the sum of two forces

but something greater and different from them both."[44] Further, the synthesis does not function as a step to a greater totality, but, much like Gadda's notion of comprehension, is "the thesis for a new dialectic, which will in turn generate a new synthesis and so on until the end of historical time" (180). As for Dziga Vertov, in movies such as *The Eleventh Year* (1928), *The Man with a Movie Camera* (1929), and *Enthusiasm, or Symphony of the Donbas* (1930), he was creating those conflicting and simultaneous images of the "kino-eye," a cinematic vision representing life's processes in all their spatial and temporal integrity. In the words of Vertov's most famous address, "The Council of Three" (1923), "[A] kino-eye [is] more perfect than the human eye, for the exploration of the chaos of visual phenomena that fills space. The kino-eye lives and moves in time and space; it gathers and records impressions in a manner wholly different from that of the human eye."[45]

At this juncture in my discussion, then, it is more than legitimate to ask why, despite these exhibits, there exist passages in the Gaddian corpus that contain disparaging comments toward futurism. I would like to venture the hypothesis that Gadda's comments have much to do with the desire to mark a distance between his work and the less enduring manifestations of futurism. In other words, Gadda might have intuited, very early on, that the importance of futurism was located in the destabilization of traditional models of representation and the premises upon which these rested, as opposed to futurism's more flamboyant, but ultimately more superficial expressions. To tell it with Giovanni Lista, Gadda understood the problematics of futurism: "the precedent of project to work, of metalanguage to creation."[46] Finally, Gadda's desire to repress the memory of fascist ideology—which he, like the futurists, at one point endorsed[47]—might have played a role in dispersing the possibility of an affinity between his project and the *barocco tecnificato* of the futurists. Nonetheless, this affinity manifests itself in his correspondence, in his essays, and, more significantly, in the space of his own rhetorical practices.

Gadda's Parodies: "La Madonna dei filosofi" (1931)

Turning now to Gadda's fictions, we cannot fail to realize that the literary space has departed successfully from the ideality of the modernist episteme. It has become the site of a displacement of the Platonic vision, of a parodic uncrowning of the already-said, coupled with a discursive practice willing to represent that heterogeneity irreducible to ideals of identity and closure.

The deterritorializing strategies employed by Gadda range from parodic, discrediting dethronings to more serious and even tragic probings of the impossible horizons of idealism. "La Madonna dei filosofi," a short story from 1931 now collected in *La Madonna dei filosofi* (69–107) typifies Gadda's carnivalesque, Rabelaisian mode, or what he had called in *Racconto* his "humoristic-ironic" manner (396). The text begins with a description of the Ripamontis. Once aristocrats, they are now well-off commoners because one of their ancestors dissipated the family's fortunes in an attempt to resolve the economic contradictions of society at large. The pitfalls of idealism, however, continue to haunt the family. The Ripamontis' last heir, Maria, is destined for a life of solitude. Her fiancé has volunteered to fight in World War I and is now missing in action. In a parallel narrative line, the story moves to the characterization of another Platonist: "L'Ingegnere Baronfo" (84). Baronfo, a successful businessman and occasional lover of Emma Renzi, represses all the materialistic components of life. He refuses to recognize Gigetto, the fruit of his relationship with Emma Renzi, as his son, and numbs his healthy body with large quantities of drugs. As the story progresses, Baronfo decides that, since only spirit matters, he will dedicate the rest of his days to the study of philosophical ideals. Thus, at the age of thirty-four, he sells his business and begins his lonely path in the company of Descartes and an old book about the English philosopher Ismaele Digbens. Digbens was a thinker who had distinguished himself by countering Lockeanism with absolute proofs of the existence of God. His fame, however, rests in the study of physics. Contrary to the arguments of Democritus, Epicurus, and Gassendi, he had sought to demonstrate(!) the absence of movement and matter in being. Fascinated by the philosophy of Digbens and hoping to acquire additional works of speculative idealism, Baronfo answers an advertisement for the sale of some of the contents of the Ripamontis' library. The sale, however, does not provide him with the reading material he seeks. It has been promoted to purge the collection of books allegedly too far removed "dallo spirito e dagli ideali della vera scienza" (93) [from the spirit and the ideals of true science], notably volumes by Darwin, Mill, Spencer, and Haeckel, as well as several studies on historical evolutionism. Yet, while Baronfo's wish for additional texts of philosophical idealism remains unfulfilled, in a parodic return of that repressed materiality and dynamism irreducible to totalizing systems, "La Madonna dei filosofi" sets the stage for a melodramatic turn of events. Baronfo begins cruising the countryside in Maria's car—a machine as dynamic as Boccioni's paintings—and, not immune to the owner's physical appearance—"splendide gambe (molto migliori di quelle del cavalicre Digbens)" (101) [wonderful legs (much better than those of monsieur Digbens)]—he goes from being an occasional visitor of the Ripamontis to becoming a faithful member of their circle. The story closes with Baronfo's marriage to Maria, the savior and, as the title suggests, merciful "Madonna" of philosophical idealists.

"La Casa" (1935–36) and "San Giorgio in casa Brocchi" (1931)

The seduction of Platonism is by no means confined to what *Meditazione* had called "certe menti anche elette" (640) [certain elevated minds], such as the Ripamontis and Baronfo. On the contrary, it appears to be endemic to the social and cultural behavior of the petit bourgeois, as two of Gadda's best-known short fictions, "La casa" and "San Giorgio in casa Brocchi" suggest.[48]

Written between 1935 and 1936, "La casa" is a humorous, parodic description of a construction project for a house capable of fulfilling the myth of total order and harmony. Much like Courtial des Pereires' "Chateau Polyvalent," it is intended to insulate its dweller from all the contingencies of life. For this reason, the design calls for granite walls, impermeable cement, and a roof composed of three layers of shingles. Against the advice of modern architects, whom the owner considers noisy futurists (1118), the interior design also reflects the vision informing the outer structure: "nulla di storto, di sconnesso, di semiaperto, di fatto per modo di dire. Tutto, in casa mia, è fatto in senso duramente classico, è perfetto" (1122) [nothing crooked, disconnected, half-opened, only half-done, so to speak. Everything, in my house, is done in a classical manner, all is perfect]. In one last act of repression, the heterology of the body is also distanced as two doors and an antechamber are placed before the toilet. Despite these enclosures, however, the tale foregrounds the impossibility of keeping the external, contingent world at bay. Hordes of people selling shoe polish, soap, journals, perfumes, and more, continue to knock on the door, while relatives pester the owner with daily phone calls.

Whereas the walls erected in "La casa" have a literal consistency, those of "San Giorgio in casa Brocchi" are of a more emblematic but no less incisive nature. The story opens in 1928, a time of changes threatening the social purity and the cultural identity of the northern Italian bourgeois aristocracy. Jole, the voluptuous servant of Count Agamènnone, has been seen conversing with the young scion, Gigi Brocchi: "il cane di razza, il quale non è se non il prodotto tipico di una lunga e laboriosa selezione" (651) [the thoroughbred, the typical product of a long and elaborated selection]. The futurists also contribute to the menace facing social and class purity represented by Jole. At the famous and illustrious "Triennale Milanese," they are exhibiting the portrait of Marchesa Cavalli. As a symbol of a "caledoscopico Novecento" (658) [the kaleidoscopic twentieth century], the piece is an affront to classical aesthetics. Not only is it a hybrid compound of materials, but it has eyes that can be rotated in an infinite number of directions. In adjacent rooms hang the even more transgressive paintings of the amazons and the bohemian whore. Whereas the first upset the security of a single vision by way of a synthesis of five hundred alternative perspectives (659), the second is an insult to artistic talent, to the symbolist notion of creation as a quasi-divine endeavor. At the base of the art work's frame, someone has left Duchampian ready-mades: spoons of ice cream, red paper cones, two garter belts, and other familiar, common objects "transposed" from the real world. To make matters worse, the avant-gardists are now expanding beyond the showrooms of the "Triennale" and are penetrating the enclosures of the bourgeois world. Count Agamènnone, Gigi's uncle and the brother of Gigi's mother, has acquired a futurist painting and dines now with its artist, Penella (679).

In an attempt to keep the external "contagio" (662) [contagion] at bay and preserve the ideals of her class, the countess puts great faith in auratic works: her own embroidered tablecloth for the altàr of San Giorgio and a book, Cicero's De Officiis. Since the latter was written at a time when the contradictions of Roman civilization were surfacing (671), and with the intent of "sistemare la vita, sia quella privata che quella pubblica" (676) [fix life, both private and public], the countess trusts that it will be a valuable guide to Gigi. However, in a caricature of all ideals of identity and sameness before the immanency of existence, the story describes the final, and ironic breach of the Brocchi's wall: one of Penella's paintings becomes a great success. The work, titled *L'uomo e l'angelo* [Man and the angel] represents a man conquered by the elements of nature and an angel whose total deprivation of sacral distance is symbolized by a very human sexual endowment. As the narrator comments, this endowment is necessary to the "propagazione della specie angelica" (683) [the spreading of the angelic species]. The cultural breach initiated by the new art finds its correlative in the social sphere when Jole is sent by Count Agamènnone to deliver additional readings to Gigi. Newly representing the futility of attempts to stop change and heterogeneity, in front of the voluptuous Jole (648), Gigi realizes that nothing can end "il rotolare del mondo " (694) [the world's rolling]. Thus, he closes Cicero's *De Officiis* and decides to walk with Jole into the bedroom. Approving of his character's decision, a self-reflexive narrator comments that in 1928 it is due time to retire reactionary models of thought in favor of more contemporary, modern epistemologies: "E poi, insomma, il Novecento ha o non ha i suoi diritti? Ceda l'Ottocento al Novecento" (683) [And then, after all, does or doesn't the twentieth century have its rights? Nineteenth century! Surrender to the twentieth].

La meccanica (1928) and *La cognizione del dolore* (1938–41)

If "La madonna dei filosofi," "San Giorgio in casa Brocchi," and "La casa" undo, by parodic laughter, the metaphysical ideals of the aristocracy and the bourgeoisie, it would be wrong to assume that other social groups are immune to the lure of Platonism. In other words, without denying Gadda's propensity to dethrone the epistemology of the ruling class, it would be incorrect to read Gadda as a champion of the leftist critique, as illustrious neo-Marxist scholars have done.[49] Like Céline, Gadda does not replace the myths of bourgeois idealism with those of the proletariat, but relentlessly probes the Platonic epistemologies informing all social groups.

Anticipating the discrediting representations of peasants, workers, and emigrants of *La cognizione*, *La meccanica* (1928)[50] opens with a pungent portrait of Gildo Pessina. A thief and a factory worker, Pessina is attempting to convince Zoraide, his cousin and the wife of a soldier at the front, to intercede on his behalf so he can avoid the draft. The novel itself is quite significant in bearing witness to Gadda's resistance to leftist ideals of resolving social contradictions. Set around 1915, it probes the frailty of absolutes in relation to the Italian socialist movement. It explores the historical climate of Milan surrounding Italy's intervention into World War I and dwells extensively on the institutionalization and demise of "*la Società Umanitaria*" (496). Founded by Prospero Moisè Loria, a man of "idee fatte, ferree, immutabili" (497) ["accomplished, ironlike, immutable ideas], *la Società Umanitaria* was to be the coalescence of Loria's many truths into one: the necessity of human redemption (497). For this purpose, Loria had delegated considerable sums of money to build a shelter for the care and instruction of the poor (497). After nine years, thanks to some Jewish money, or what an ironic narrator defines as the philanthropic kiss of a benefactor, the "*Casa di Lavoro*" was finally born. However, shortly after its official legitimation as a charitable institution, the *Casa di Lavoro* began exclusionary practices. Its director, Alessandrina Ravizza, expelled a nymphomaniac because "il suo spirito malato aveva interpretato l'Umanitaria non già come la soccorrevole casa del ravvedimento (*oh! ideale*) ma come un pullulante vivaio di possibilità scandalosamente ebbre" (501–2; my emphasis) [her sick spirit had interpreted the Umanitaria not as a charitable house for redemption (oh! ideal) but as a hatchery swarming with scandalous possibilities]. From then on, the managers of the *Casa* pursued Ravizza's efforts at redemption, convinced of the absolute truth of their beliefs and methods (506). When workers who had emigrated to Germany returned to Italy, however, the *Casa* failed, as the poor, the sick, and the maimed were left in the open fields. The institution itself proved to be superfluous and was soon dissolved.

The tone in which *La meccanica* closes foregrounds another of Gadda's many "*maniere*" to probe Platonism: A pathos-filled mode that is at work not just in the epilog of the above-mentioned text, but informs the middle sections of *La cognizione del dolore*,[51] which describe Gonzalo Pirobutirro and his mother, Elisabetta François. Amalgams of many of the myths dethroned by Gadda's earlier fictions, these are tragic figures of idealism. As Gadda commented in an interview, they are emblems of the pain caused by attempts to frame the meandering of being: "il dolore dell'essere oltre che dell'esistere" [the pain of being, in addition to that of existing].[52]

At the threshold of death, after an entire existence spent in the objectification of ideals—"Idea Matrice" (303–4) [Matrix idea]—the elderly Elisabetta begins to realize that she may have bartered the authenticity of life for illusory symbols of stability. During a storm, while seeking refuge from nature's forces in the enclosure of the cellar, she understands that any attempt at permanency and closure are but curtains fluttering in the wind: "Oh!, lungo il cammino delle generazioni, la luce! . . . che recede, recede . . . opaca . . . dell'immutato divenire. . . . Ogni prassi è un'immagine . . . zendado, impresa, nel vento bandiera" (97–8) [Oh!, along the road of generations, the light! . . . which recedes, recedes . . . opaque . . . of the unchanged becoming. . . . Every praxis is an image . . . sendal, device, flag in the wind]. Thus, she courageously emerges from her enclave and opens her house and persona to the light of the day and the entire population of Lukones: "Si sentì ripresa nell'evento, nel flusso antico della possibilità, della continuazione: come tutti, vicina a tutti . . . donandosi aveva superato la tenebra" (285) [She felt caught up in the event, in the ancient flux of possibility, of continuation: like all, close to all . . . giving herself she had overcome the darkness]. She tutors children at no cost and buys whatever produce the peasants offer her. However, in the course of the narrative, Elisabetta's newfound openness is the cause of pathos-filled tensions between herself and her son Gonzalo.

Afflicted by the same will for permanency and order that had shaped Elisabetta's life before the episode of the cellar, Gonzalo is allegedly prey to a "male oscuro" (310–11) [obscure sickness]. In a later review of Giuseppe Berto's novel *Il male oscuro* (1964),[53] Gadda will describe this sickness as the pain felt by some before the *"cinematismo"* (1201) of life, the cinematic quality of experience. In the words of the novel:

E c'era per lui il problema del male: la favola della malattia, la strana favola propalata dai conquistadores. . . . E' il "male invisibile" di cui narra Saverio López nel capitolo estremo de' suoi *Mirabilia Maragdagali*. . . . L'ultimo suo capitolo, in sul sopravvenir della morte, argomenta la è una discongiuntura o spegnimento d'ogni accozzo di possibilità compatite: tantoché la ti vien tacita, e come la ti camminassi dietro le stiene. (108–110)

[And there was, for him, the problem of ill: the fable of disease, the strange fable spread by the conquistadores. . . . It is the "invisible ill" of which Saverio López tells in the last chapter of his *Mirabilia Maragdagali*. . . . His last chapter, written on the approach of death, asserts that it is a separation or extinction of every combination of indulged possibilities: so that it comes quietly, as if it were walking behind your back.]

Identified as the last one in a long line of metaphysical questers,[54] Gonzalo always has manifested an impaired sense of the "real." As a child, he abhorred the town's carnival because of the plurality of bodies of the festive crowds (433). He was also horrified by the carnival's cotton candy, which appeared to him as a skein prey to continuous metamorphosis and stretching. By 1934, the main chronological frame of the novel, Gonzalo's metaphysical "fobie" (433) [phobias] have increased even further and are tragically revealed in his relationships to objects, people, and language. To cite Gian Paolo Biasin, "Gonzalo is at the center of a peculiar existential and narrative tension between the materiality of the world and the abstraction of the idea, between the body and the spirit, between noise and silence."[55] Precisely because experience appears to him as a series of dynamic and conflicting cinematic shots—"gli parve impossibile che la sua vita fosse venuta filmandosi" (429) [it seemed to him impossible that his life had become covered with the film of such nonsense]—Gonzalo engages in pathetic attempts to negate all the reminders of life's temporality. In the words of the narrator, he resists "la cara normalità della contingenza" (157) [the dear normality of contingency]. Not only does he refuse to own a watch, but he has recently broken one in an excess of rage. The sight of the bourgeois' wrists angers him and the daily tolling of church bells cause scatological outbursts and obscene comparisons with mythical Bacchanals: "dalla matrice di quelle mènadi scaravoltate a pancia all'aria . . . col batacchio per aria . . . il batacchio . . . a romperci i timpani per quarant'anni!" (178–9) [from the matrix of those maenads hurled belly first into the air . . . with clapper hanging out . . . the clapper . . . to break our eardrums for forty years]. The country's produce, a symbol of the earthly, seasonable cornucopia—"il bagaglio del mondo, del fenomènico mondo. L'evolversi di una consecuzione che si sdipana ricca, dal tempo" (156) [the baggage of the world, of the world of phe-

nomena. The evolution of a sequence that unravels, richly, from time] —
infuriates him. The heterogeneity of ethnic groups and races making up
the population of his city has become, to his diseased perception, an
ocean of mutability and lack of differentiation. It is a "Pomata
mercuriale" (324) [a mercurial ointment], "un olio" (327) [an oil], and a
"Tempestoso mare . . . delle genti sperse, slavate, con sargassi di cinesi o di
bracci di negri . . . armeni, russi, bianchi e rossi, arabi . . . levantini . . . "
(320) [Tempestuous sea . . . of lost, laved people, with sargassos of Chinese or of Negroes' arms . . . Armenians, Russians white or red, Arabs . . .
Levantines]. Yet, what enrages Gonzalo even more is the Wittgensteinian
discovery that language has lost the ability to order the world. The immi-
grants' dialect, based on a limited number of phonemes, or "sostantivi-
omnibus" (427) [omnibus-substantives], which are combined to express a
variety of thoughts, creates a measure of equivocality that he cannot tolerate. For example, the onomastics of the townsfolk, based on small variations on the names of Joseph and Mary, frustrates his will to discriminate
between the names' bearers. In a vertiginous confusion, Gonzalo cannot
separate "le Giovanne con le Giuseppine, e anche con le Teresine: ma
più che tutto, a terrorizzarlo, era l'insalata delle Marie e Marie pro-
clitiche, cioè le Mary, le May, le Marie Pie, le Anne Marie, le Marise, le
Luise Marie e le Marie Terese" (149) [the Juanas with the Pepitas, and
also with the Teresitas: but more than anything, to terrorize him, there
was the salad of Marias and proclitic Marias, that is the Marys, the Mays,
the Maria Pias, the Anne Maries, the Marisas, the Luisa Marias, and the
Maria Teresas].

Finally, not only the idiom of the townspeople comes to impede Gonzalo's "metafisica" (185) [metaphysics], but also the universal structure of
Western models of symbolization: the pronominal system. One of the
novel's most memorable passages is an invective against language's I: "il
più lurido di tutti i pronomi" (175) [the filthiest of all pronouns]. In an
anticipation of Samuel Beckett's The Unnamable, Gonzalo comes to the
painful truth that as a deictic, or a grammatical shifter, the pronoun "I"
can be appropriated by all. Hence, it prevents him from establishing in
language the ontological identity of his own, Cartesian "ergo sum": "I
think; già; but I'm ill of thinking . . . 'mormorò il figlio'. . . . I pronomi!
Sono i pidocchi del pensiero" (176) [Je pense; right; but J'en ai marre de
penser . . . 'murmured the son'. . . . Pronouns! they are the lice of

thought]. Just a few passages later, during a conversation with Doctor Figueroa, Gonzalo additionally comments on his hate for deictics. He now observes that their presence is a constant reminder of the inadequate, elusive elements of symbolization: "io, tu . . . certifica della nostra impotenza a predicar nulla di nulla . . . dacché ignoriamo . . . il soggetto di ogni proposizione possibile" (178) [I, you . . . guarantees our impotency in preaching anything at all . . . since we ignore . . . the subject of every possible proposition]. The realization that order in language has receded also brings him to abjure writing and seek a space beyond words. A would-be novelist, he has stopped working on his *"romanzo"* (417), and dreams now of being enveloped only in silence (186).

In addition to the failure of instrumental language, another tragic aspect of the novel is the exploration of the repercussions that negation has on Gonzalo's personal life. Because, most of the time, to deny means to deny oneself, to tear away all possibilities, Gonzalo has begun to repress the life of his physical body and its generative potential. Fearing, as Beckett's Belacqua will, the multiplication and temporality of progeny, he has given away his wedding suit and taken a vow of chastity. The town gossips that he is now "Celibe . . . come Beethoven, e anche più se fosse stato possibile immaginarlo" (73) [a bachelor . . . like Beethoven, and even more so, if that were imaginable]. As the narrative progresses, and despite a prophetic dream[56] that discloses the "thanatos" of metaphysics, Gonzalo is brought to the verge of madness and murder. Prey to the tendentious reasoning of "delirio interpretativo" (211) [interpretative delirium], like the engineer from "La casa" and the countess from "San Giorgio in casa Brocchi," Gonzalo begins to erect figural and literal walls—"imaginary" barriers of finality and self-coincidence—between himself and all life-forms surrounding the ancestral villa. At first, he considers writing an appendix to Plato's *Timaeus* but chooses instead to remain locked in his room while reading Kant's *Grundlegung zur Metaphysik der Sitten*, Plato's *Laws*, *Parmenides*, and *Symposium*. Then, he becomes obsessed with the idea of reinforcing the property's points of entry, despite daily reminders of the life surrounding it. For example, as Gonzalo projects additional enclosures, the wind continues to blow through doors and windows. Grasses and trees are growing at the base of the walls, while insects and lizards keep crossing them (190). Ultimately, Gonzalo becomes so frustrated with the life he cannot control, that one day, before what he considers to be "la pluralità sconcia" (417) [the filthy plurality] of his mother's visitors, he explodes with a death threat: "Se ti trovo ancora una volta nel braco dei maiali, scannerò te e loro" (436–7) [If I find you again in that pack of pigs, I will cut your throat and theirs]. A few days after this outburst, Gonzalo leaves town. That same evening, Elisabetta is victim of a brutal attack. The event remains a mystery, since the name of her perpetrator is never disclosed.

Reading Gadda's Narrative Discourse

The futility of absolutes suggested by Gadda's parodic and even tragic probing of idealism in the works considered thus far is by no means confined to the narrative structures of the text but doubles in a discourse of irreducible ambiguity and endless dynamism. As readers familiar with the author's work will recall, the fabulae of Gadda's novels are notorious for being additive and open-ended, "emboîtements senza fine" [endlessly nesting], as a sentence from *La meccanica* aptly puts it (587). Allowed to grow by paratactical accretion, they develop in a multiplicity of directions occasioned by the narrative context, without ever achieving that state of "purity" and completion that many of their characters seek. Two of Gadda's longer works, *La meccanica* and *La cognizione del dolore*, furnish numerous examples of this type of transgressive fabulation. They illustrate what Guido Guglielmi's *La prosa italiana del novecento* calls a retarded "structure" coupled with a mobile "texture" (15).

 La meccanica, a novel composed of eight chapters — five of which are "complete," while the remaining three are at the draft-stage — opens with Gildo's knock on Zoraide's door. However, before any speech is reported, the narrative frustrates the hierarchy of significance by focusing on a two-page-long description of Zoraide's physiognomy. When Gildo is finally allowed into the house, only fragments of conversation are reported and the narrative moves to relate Gildo's background. Since he is a rogue, a muddled crime story is included. A theft of bicycles and a gambling story unfold, and only at the end of the chapter does the reason for Gildo's visit become clear. An analogous fabulation informs chapter two. Zoraide's memories of her husband, the socialist Luigi Pessina, and of her lover Franco Velaschi are coordinated with the episode of "*La Società Umanitaria*," while the chapter as a whole expands by the inclusion of lengthy content-notes drawn from the most disparate extratextual sources. Chapter three opens with a description of Luigi Pessina's life, to which are added digressions on the year's political and military events as well as a romance between an admiral's daughter and *"l'ingegnere Ulivi."* Only at the end of chapter three does the narrative return to Luigi, to report his resigned response to the news that he has been drafted. The news itself is followed by a long depiction of the medical visit, complete with detailed medical reports. Chapter four begins with the description of the machinations of Velaschi's parents as they try to secure their son a job so that he can avoid enrollment in the conflict. Chapter five describes the outcome of their efforts, but to the plight of Velaschi's father is added a story about a landowner's suicide, a portrait of Dirce Raspagnotti's son, and further, unrelated narrative material.

If the fabula of *La meccanica* illustrates what the narrator calls the "laberinto delle selve ariostesche" (569) [the labyrinth of Ariostesque forests] in its resistance to containing multiple and open-ended matter, in an even more radical manner, *La cognizione del dolore* flattens narrative selection in favor of open-ended inclusion. Consisting of two parts comprising various sections and several "appendixes," it is a novel on the border of narration. Like *La meccanica*, it remains unfinished by "heuristic" intent, by the constitutive desire not to conclude.[57] Thus, from a panoramic opening on a country between 1925 and 1933, the novel expands through a number of macroscopic narratives to report a scandal in Lukones following the hiring of the veteran Pedro Mahagones; a story about lightning; the rise and death of the poet Carlo Caçoncelles; an involvement in the scandal of the local doctors Di Pascuale and Figueroa; a number of episodes about Gonzalo Pirobutirro's life told by José, La Battistina, La Peppa, and others; Gonzalo's and Elisabetta's pathos and the mysterious attack on the latter; the poem "Autunno"; and more. Because these digressions often have, as in the case of *La meccanica*, the self-sufficiency of independent, nonintegrated stories—*"Disjecta membra"* as Beckett might call them—Gadda transposes a number of them into other fictions. In *Accoppiamenti Giudiziosi* for example, "Una visita medica" and "La mamma" are taken from *La cognizione*, while the short stories "Cugino barbiere," "Le novissime armi," and "Papà e mamma," from the same collection, are parts of *La meccanica*.[58] Like Céline and certainly Beckett, this transposition extends well beyond the utilization of already available narrative material and creates what Dante Isella, in an interesting intertextual echo to André Breton's surrealist novel *Les vases communicants* (1932), has called a work akin to "a complex system of communicating vessels."[59]

It is in the novels' style, however, that Gadda's highly experimental narrative discourse finds its most macroscopic unfolding. Since his practice, like that of Céline, equates the singularity of voice with an absolutizing worldview, it pluralizes itself into a discourse of irreducible ambiguity and endless dynamism. The schizophrenic refraction of speeches of *La meccanica* is an early, yet important example of this synthesis. It illustrates what Contini's *Quarant'anni d'amicizia* quite suggestively called Gadda's "*resa unanimista*" (64), perhaps implicitly recognizing how this French avant-garde had been a major shaping influence on future avant-gardist projects, including that of Marinetti.[60]

Set during the period of Italy's entry into World War I, *La meccanica* does not allow the representation of the conflict to rest in any descriptive, apodictical stability. Through the antithetical words of contrasting ideologies, the conflict becomes a cluster of heroic feats and criminal acts. In the narrator's words, "intervento: i suoi patroni interventisti o, nel linguaggio degli avversarî, guerrafondaî, avventurieri della violenza" (517) [intervention: its patrons interventionists or, in the language of the adversaries, warmongers, seekers of violence]. The ambiguity generated by the juxtaposition of conflicting ideologies is increased by the addition of existential idioms in nonprivative oppositions. The war is to be accepted with stoic resignation by the honest socialist but becomes the source of rage for those who seek to avoid the draft, of pathos for the concerned mother, and even of relief for unfaithful wives like Zoraide. Since she has been having an affair while her husband is at the front, she symbolizes the conflict by "Questa guerra!"(488) [Oh! The war!], an exclamation disclosing the satisfaction of safely fulfilling illegitimate desires.

The absence of synonymic substitution, of a "true," predicative language in the representation of the conflict, is shared by a number of other elements of the novel. The muddled-crime story about the theft of bicycles specifies the name neither of the thief nor of the merchandise stolen. Since Gildo might be implicated in the crime along with two other people, the identity of the criminal is never established. The theft itself is presumably of four bicycles, yet anonymous voices speak of five. The investigators indicate the presence of other stolen wares, ranging from ties and underwear to cosmetics and gramophones. Even more figural is the discourse on characters, particularly in relation to Zoraide. Like Laurence Sterne's *Tristram Shandy*,[61] representation exists here in a zone of entanglement and forces the reader into an open-ended itinerary across discursive, rhizomatous maps. Suggestively introduced in the narrative while looking at herself in a mirror (the latter being, of course, an icon of specular refraction), Zoraide is characterized according to the language of desire of the literary archive. Thus, she is at first a *fin de siècle*, D'Annunzian figure of decadent sensuality, with limbs "fulgide per latte e per ambra" (471) [shining of milk and amber]. In the next paragraph, however, the mirror switches to a naturalistic representation modeled after Emile Zola: "funzionario della meticolosa analisi, fotografo de' lunghi cigli e delle lor ombre d'amore" (471–2) [the functionary of a meticulous analysis, the photographer of long lashes and of their shadows of love]. Additional discursive trajectories represent Zoraide according to Metastasian and preromantic topoi (486) as well as by way of the language of sensual mysticism. This is provided, among others, by Flaubert's *Madame Bovary*. When Zoraide goes to the Duomo, for example, like Emma Bovary, she replaces ascetic thoughts with languid sighs of "'l'amante': un misteriosa e torbida felicità, un peccato atroce e meraviglioso, l'amante, l'amante" (491–92) ["the lover": a mysterious and troubled happiness, an atrocious and marvelous sin, the lover, the lover]. A quotation from the novel provides a *"mise en abîme"* of this type of figural and amplified discourse. The narrator suggests that if the mirror were to represent the portrait of Zoraide by a "novecentista" [a twentieth-century artist] it would quite likely produce an image "catastroficamente sintetica," (472) [catastrophically synthetic]—that is to say, overdetermined and certainly a foil to *La meccanica* and Gadda's other endeavor, *La cognizione del dolore*.

As a mature actualization of Gadda's metamorphic word, of that Protean, ever-pliant "heuristic" language, this novel is, along with *Quer pasticciaccio*, the recognized stylistic masterpiece of twentieth-century Italian literature. Possibly inspired[62] by the daring experimentalism of Céline's *Voyage* (1932) and *Mort à crédit* (1936)—novels read and greatly admired by Gadda in the thirties[63]—*La cognizione* strikes the reader by its radical rejection of a normative, single register. In a macroscopic phenomenon of paradigmatic opening, or what Pasolini called "the hyper-taxis,"[64] it juxtaposes the national idiom spoken by native dialect speakers to normative expressions drawn from the Italian jargons of medicine, botany, and astronomy. Literary quotations are abundant and often linked to the idioms of architecture, advertisement, and jurisprudence, as well as Lombard, Neapolitan, and Tuscan sayings. In a relentless *Wortvermischung*, the French tongue comes to occupy the same space as the interjectional and scatological expressions of the Other, or what one is tempted to call Célinian examples of *"rendu émotif."*[65] Passages constructed according to poetic logic[66] are linked to Latin and Latinate passages but do not shy away from the inclusion of snatches of English and Spanish. The endless productivity of this discourse permeates the entire novel, clearly unsettling the stability of chronotope, characterization, and events.

At the threshold of the narrative, the title already resonates with ambiguity and regress: "la cognizione del dolore" meaning both "acquainted *of* and *through* grief" and echoing lines from Machiavelli's *Proemio* to *Discorsi*, Leopardi's "Detti Memorabili di Filippo Ottonieri" in *Operette*, and even a syntagma employed by Nietzsche in *Also Sprach Zarathustra*: "an der eignen Qual mehrt es sich das eigne Wissen" [through suffering, one increases one's knowledge].[67] The ambiguity of the title is continued in the first pages of the novel. These locate the city of Lukones in a temporal continuum between 1925 and 1933 and in a shifting space between fictional and historical reality. Allusions to the economic profile of the Brianza region, coupled with reference to a war with a neighboring country and frequent mention of a coercive regime (6) render it a foil to postwar Italy under the rise of fascism.[68] Yet, by way of a citational use of language, the city is also a mosaic of quotations from the literary intertext and the Other's wit. Surrounded by a chain of mountains called *"Il Serruchón"* (18), and subject to the divine scourge of draughts and hail, Lukones emerges as a hybrid of the Manzonian *"Resegone"* (20) and the mythical cities of the Old Testament. Further, it is also Yonville-l'Abbaye, from Flaubert's *Madame Bovary*, with which it shares the *"albergo del Leon d'oro"* (17), country doctors, bourgeois merchants, and maimed peasants. In one more fold, Lukones appears as the product of the Other's wit, with word-plays and puns across languages. Situated in the zigzagging space of the province of "Zigo-Zago" (15), it is connected by train to the neighboring town of "Novokomi" (17), or "Idon'tgo."

Objects, characters, and events partake of the ambiguity of the setting. The main agricultural product of the province is described by an amalgam of the specialized language of trade commodity, mythological idioms, and Carlo Cattaneo's scientific treatise on agrarian diseases. The name of the cereal itself, the *"banzavóis"* (6), is a coinage based on *"mais"* and the dialect *"panz vöj,"* an expression meaning "empty stomachs." The description of the villas of Lukones undergo a similar process of rhetorical amplification. Through the demotic pronunciation of the partitive *"di"* and the sibilant "s" in place of the correct "z," their initial presentation suggests the admiring words of the people; "Di ville, di ville!; di villette otto locali doppi servissi" (40) [Villas, villas! Villettas eight rooms, double baths]. Yet, because this paragraph is followed by a list of buildings' features, "Con palestra per i ragazzi . . . Con tetto a terrazzo . . . Con le vetrate a ghigliottina" (48) [with a gym for the children . . . with terraced rooftop . . . with guillotine glass walls], the villas are displaced from the realm of oral speech to that of printed advertisements. As the passage evolves, they become further defined through intertextual reminiscences of literary passages penned by Giosué Carducci and Ada Negri: They are idyllic refuges "che 'occhieggiavano di tra il verzicare dei colli'" (43) [that "flowered among the green cauls of the hills"], and enclosures "protette d'olmi o d'antique ombre dei faggi" (41) [guarded either by elms or by the antique shadows of the beeches]. They are also the haunted houses of northern gothic literature, inhabited by "misteriose luminescenze, larve, o lèmuri, notturne ali, spettrali parvenze" (61) [mysterious luminosities, of ghastly, or ghostly nocturnal wings, of spectral apparitions]. To no surprise, in the jargon of architecture, the villas emerge as stylistic clusters. Like Ulrich's house in Robert Musil's *Der Mann ohne Eigenschaften,* they include the neoclassical and neo-neoclassical, art nouveau, Liberty, Corinthian, Pompeian, Angevin, Sommaruga's Egyptian, and Alessio Coppedés (45–46). Even further at odds is the description of the Villa Pirobutirro. Its location not only is blurred by a pastiche of Spanish, Italian, and Tuscan idioms but is given geographical coordinates according to the hemispherical position of the observers:

Sicché, davanti al lato della casa e nel versante del colle que los toscanos llaman *a bacío,* es decir en el declive de la colina hacia el Norte (en España), o hacia el Sur antártico (en Maradagàl), un piccolo

spiazzo triangolare, con guijarrillos, dava a ogni intruso facoltà di per-
venire direttamente sul terrazzo. (378–9)

[So, before the side of the house that los Toscanos llaman a bacío, es
decir en el declive de la colina hacia el Norte (en España), o hacia el
Sur antártico (en Maradagàl), a little triangular open space, con guijarrillos, gave every intruder the opportunity of coming directly on the
terrace.]

To add to the destabilizing effect of this babelization of tongues, the discourse also makes extensive use of footnotes. Confirming, as Derrida has
suggested,[69] the uneasy relation that all marginalia entertain with the text
from which they are springing, La cognizione often includes an uniden-
tifiable voice commenting on the errors of the main body of the text. For
example, after the allusion to Manzoni's hymn "La Pentecoste," we read
that the citation is absolutely wrong and improper (338). Likewise, an
etymological variant on a proper name is said to be a mark of insufficient
philological research on the author's part (405). More subtly, the voice
shakes all illusion of textual omnicompetence by inviting the reader to
consult extratextual sources of reference, such as Virgil's Georgics (319),
Leibnitz's Nouveaux Essais (319), and so forth.

In addition to the town and its buildings, a host of other objects are
analogously subjected to the unsettling forces of this unstructured idiomatic opening. The medicines consumed by Gonzalo are not specifically
named but follow a course of close synonymy: "caolino a polvere, o
magistero di bismuto (sottonitrato di bismuto)" (95) [powdered Kaolin, or
discipline of bismuth (subnitrate of bismuth)]. A passage recounting one
of Gonzalo's meals never identifies the name of the food and allows its
definition to waver among paradigmatic entries for the genus of crusta-
ceans:

[S]i era detto . . . che egli fosse stato per morire . . . in seguito alla in-
gestione di un riccio, altri sostenevano un granchio, una specie di scor-
pione marino . . . qualcuno favoleggiava addirittura di un pesce-spada o
pesce-spilla . . . . Le persone colte . . . una aragosta del Fuerte del Rey.
(86)

[People had said . . . that he had been on the point of death . . . after
having swallowed a sea urchin, others said it was a crab, a kind of sea

scorpion . . . some mythologized also about a swordfish or a brooch-fish
. . . Cultivated people . . . a lobster of Fuerte del Rey.]

Like the above graft of urchin-crab-scorpion-swordfish-lobster, the ani-
mal of the region, or *"guarniko"* (67), wavers between zoological species,
being both a calf and a dromedary (67). A portrait hanging in Gonzalo's
room is both a daguerreotype of Generale Pastrufacio and a painting of
Mantegna or Giovanbellino (141). In this metamorphosis of forms, the
general might not even be Pastrufacio after all, since he is said to have the
blond hair, the poncho with two tips, and the South-American kerchief of
Garibaldi, the hero of the Italian Risorgimento. This figurality is so extensive that it infiltrates even the micro-level of the word. In what brings to
mind Marinetti's dictum that "every word needs to have its double. . . .
For example: man-torpedo, woman-gulf, crowd-surf, square-funnel,[70]
Gadda's discourse textualizes a wealth of hyphenated compounds. Thus,
bicycles become "[b]icicletta-mulo" (381) [bycicle-mule], ties "colletto-
cravatta" (333) [collar-tie], jewelry "collane-pavese" (335) [necklace-
shield], and flowers "fiori-briciole" (411) [flower-crumbs]. Words are also
pluralized by declension according to the close and rare synonymies to be
found across the registers of Italian or in the national patrimony of dialects. In one passage of the novel, for example, the word "tripe" is given in
the Italian version of *"trippa,"* but also by way of the dialect *"büsekka,*
plurale tripp, büsekk" (466). Likewise, clogs are both the Tuscan *"zoccoli"*
and the Lombard *"zòkur"* (465).

     Characterization does not escape Gadda's figural discourse and dra-
matically foregrounds the impropriety of "proper" nouns. As in the case
of Zoraide from *La meccanica*, a figural mirror is placed before the referent to foster the supplementary and displacing circulation of meaning.
Thus, if medical portraits and descriptions of malnutrition establish the
people as early-century emigrants from the Italian lower classes, allusions
to the population's trees of "nespola" (363) [medlar] and will to amass
"roba o robba" (365) ["stuff"], transport them into the intertext of literary
"verismo," notably the pages of Verga's *I Malavoglia*. The impeded
univocality of synonymic substitution at work in this panoramic, scenic
representation is extended to specific characters. Peppa is a "donna-
uomo" (29) [female-man], female drivers are "Argonauti-donne" (335)
[female-Argonauts], waiters "fracs-ossibuchi" (342) [ossobuchi-tailcoats],

and the peasants "pitecantropi-granoturco" (319) [maize-pithecanthropoid]. In this pervasive absence of finality, the identity of the population is further clouded by an abysmal paronomasia. The washer-woman, Peppino's sister, is also known as Peppa. The seller of fish is Beppina, and the wife of the mortician is Pina, also known as Pinina del Goêpp, officially registered as Giuseppina (32). In a vertiginous labyrinth of signs, the guardian of Gonzalo's villa is "José" (72), and the maid is "Battistina," cousin of "Batta" (75). Mahagones is also "Manganones o Pedro," "Gaetano Palumbo," and "Pietruccio," who later becomes "Pedro" (21).

Ambiguity, however, is by no means confined to the representation of lower classes. While bourgeois men are variously defined as an orphic-pithagoric community and a mathematic-geomantic elite (335), one of Gonzalo's ancestors, Gonzalo Pirobutirro d'Eltino, who died on April 14, 1695, emerges as a curious amalgam of history and fiction. He is said to have been one of the executors of decrees for the Crown of Castille. Yet, his cruelty and desire to hang Filarenzo Calzamaglia (103) locate him in the realm of Manzoni's *Promessi sposi* and in the legendary cruelty of the Borgias (104). The official poet of Maradagàl, Carlos Caçoncelles, is also poised in the shifting space between fiction and historical reality. Like Gadda and the *scapigliato* Carlo Dossi, he bears the Christian name "Carlo(s)" and practices an art of intertextual collage. We are told, for example, that Caçoncelles' epic compares the freedom-fighter Juan Muceno Pastrufacio to George Washington, Marlowe's Tamburlaine the Great, Giuseppe Garibaldi, and even Byron's Mazeppa. However, unlike the *scapigliato* Carlo Dossi and C. E. Gadda, Caçoncelles is a writer tending toward the horizon of absolute words. He shares the bombastic style and the prophetic rhetoric of Foscolo, Carducci, and D'Annunzio. In one more nomadic *"ligne de fuite,"* Caçoncelles is also a figure of northern gothic literature. Rumors speak of him as a ghost, a monstrous figure, a spectral apparition (61). Like Caçoncelles, Elisabetta François is an ontological cyborg, a serial being of historical reference and literary words. In one of her forms, she is a French tutor who has lost a son (256), and therefore an autobiographical reminiscence of Gadda's mother, the language teacher Adele Lehr, whose younger son Enrico perished on April 23, 1918. However, in a literary *"itinérance,"* Elisabetta is Shakespeare's *"Re Lear"* (295), Livius's Veturia, Carducci's *nonna Lucia* from "Davanti san Guido," and Virgil's Creusa from the *Aeneid* (170). As the discourse progresses, additional phrases increase the complexity of this already elusive characterization. For the population of Lukones, she is "*la Signora*" (118), the maternal and prodigal benefactress. However, in her son's speeches, she surfaces as the victimizer who has chosen the objectification of an ideal, "la villa" (305) [the villa], over the well-being of her family. Endlessly moving from one form to the next, on the night of her attack Elisabetta is a character from the naturalist era, covered, however, by a checkered blanket, as in the "tempo di Dickens" (466) [Dickens's times]: "Un orribile coagulo di sangue si era aggrumato, ancor vivo, sui capelli grigi, dissolti, due fili di sangue le colavano dalle narici. . . . Gli occhi erano dischiusi, la guancia destra tumefatta, la pelle lacerata" (467) [A horrible clot of blood had coagulated, still vivid, on the gray hair, loose, two threads of blood ran from her nostrils. . . . Her eyes were open, the right cheek swollen, the skin torn].

Likewise, Gonzalo is the product of a mercurial pen, the spiritual offspring of Hermes the alchemist. The surviving son of Elisabetta, Gonzalo is a novelist-engineer, like Gadda, and therefore a partially autobiographical figure. However, he is also a paper being, a tessellation of epic, novels, and drama. In what Eco would call a descriptive process by unlimited semiosis,[71] he is described, like the Homeric Odysseus and the modernist *Ulysses*, as he attempts to free his Penelope from the suitors Antínoös and Hugh "Blazes" Boylan. The narrative also represents him as a character-cluster of the cruel Smerdiakov from Dostoevski's *Brothers Karamazov*, the idealist Quixano from Cervantes' *Don Quixote*, Shakespeare's Hamlet, and a comic hero from the French classical theater of Molière (289). Additional speeches further unsettle Gonzalo's already tenuous consistency. Like Orestes from Euripides' *Oresteia*, he is said to harbor murderous impulses toward his mother. In another connection to classical tragedy, and specifically to Sophocles' *Oedipus*, Gonzalo suffers from an Oedipal complex and longs to be alone with Elisabetta: "Dentro, io, nella mia casa, con mia madre" (186) ["Inside, in my house, with my mother"]. Other, more prosaic passages, partake of this relativizing effect. For doctor Figueroa, Gonzalo is a madman, affected by what psychiatrists like Sérieux and Capgras call "'delirio interpretativo'" (210–11) [interpretative delirium] and is capable of actualizing the violence of his impulses. However, in a progression by paradox, the private, paternal voice of the doctor also represents him as a potential husband for his unmarried daughter, and therefore as a generally suitable son-in-law (73). When Gonzalo's speeches are reported, aporias continue to remain unresolved, since the space of writing undergoes further enrichment. Within a few pages, Gonzalo's language can render the rationality of a reader of Plato, the lamentation of a vengeful, almost bestial Other, and the cries of a child for the absent mother. Significantly, the narrator comments that Gonzalo's physiognomy remains irreducibly incoherent: "ora saturnino, ora dionisiaco, ora eleusino, ora coribàntico" (217) [now Saturnine, now Dyonisian, now Eleusinian, now Corybantian].

Such pervasive instability and lack of coincidence in novelistic settings, objects, and characters unfold throughout the events of *La cognizione*. Thereby, resolution is prevented by a paradigmatic opening outward, toward the endless, chiastic fabulation of the collectivity. The winner of the war, for example, remains unnamed. The mystery of the bolts of lightning that strike villas Enrichetta and Antonietta remains unresolved amid various hypotheses. Initial investigations suggest that the lightning rod of villa Maria Giuseppina has caused the damage, but this theory is weakened as others begin to surface. The mason of villa Enrichetta argues that the cause of the lightning resides in the plumbing, while the meteorologists present differential equations to prove the contrary. Meanwhile, in one more, Bakhtinian "loophole" phrase,[72] local folklore suggests the possibility of magic and explains the event by drawing upon the reservoir of such literature.

The dialogization of events is not restricted to the villas but also includes the attack on Elisabetta François. Impeding the hermeneutic code from bringing about the ultimate solution, Gadda's discourse finally joins the fictions of Nabokov and Borges in anticipating that reversal of the detective convention that has been used so often in postmodern narratives[73] by Robbe-Grillet, Sciascia, Calvino, Eco, and others.[74] The gossip of the population suggests that Gonzalo is the perpetrator and, as we recall, in one of his enraged speeches he did indeed threaten to murder his mother and her visitors (437). However, other voices point to Palumbo and the peasant Giuseppe as the guilty ones. Even the language of the victim's body participates in the ambiguity of the mystery. Keeping the reader in a state of sublime hesitation, the discourse twice tells (467, 469) how the kinetics of Elisabetta's arms produce a figural paradox: "parevano protese verso 'gli altri' come in una *difesa* o in una *implorazione* estrema" (467; emphasis added) [they appeared to be stretched out toward "the others" as if in *defense* or in an extreme *supplication*]. This synthesis by statement and counterstatement is maintained until the last episode of the text, where the narrator describes a group of visitors assembled in the Pirobutirro house. On Elisabetta's violated body they witness what we, as readers of *La cognizione*, have been experiencing all along—the constitutive impossibility of capturing the ephemerality and ambiguity of life in one eternal name and story: "Nella stanchezza senza soccorso in cui il povero volto si dovette raccogliere tumefatto . . . parve a tutti di leggere la parola terribile della morte e la sovrana coscienza dell'impossibilità di dire: Io" (472) [In the unassisted weariness where the poor countenance had to collect itself, swollen . . . it seemed to all to read the terrible word of death and the supreme awareness of the impossibility of saying: I].

Nonetheless, it is precisely through such supreme, and often tragic, awareness that a new practice can arise. To reprise Girard's title, it is a practice of "fictional truths," displacing "romantic lies" by novelistic, nonabsolute words and stories.[75] Like Céline's *Voyage au bout de la nuit*, which, as we might recall, ended "devant l'aurore" (635) [in front of dawn], *La cognizione* also finishes—without closing—at the dawn of a new day. It extends an invitation to stop trying to wrap being in the singularity of a proper name and start describing instead the being(s) of the *"gelsi."* These are the mulberry trees appearing on the horizon of a countryside yet to be peopled:

E alle stecche delle persiane già l'alba. Il gallo, improvvisamente, la suscitò dai monti lontani, perentorio ed ignaro, come ogni volta. La invitava ad accedere e ad elencare i gelsi, nella solitudine della campagna apparita. (472)

[And at the slats of the shutters already the dawn. The cock, suddenly, roused it from the distant mountains, peremptory and unaware, as always. He invited it to proceed and to number the mulberry trees, in the solitude of the countryside, disclosed.]

RITE OF PASSAGE
The Early Beckett between "Unwording" and "Linkwriting"

Ici tout bouge, nage, fuit, revient, se défait, se refait. Tout cesse,
sans cesse. On dirait l'insurrection des molécules, l'intérieur
d'une pierre un millième de seconde avant qu'elle ne se désa-
grège. C'est ça la littérature.
Samuel Beckett, "La peinture des van Velde ou le Monde et le Pantalon"[1]

[Here everything moves, floats, flees, returns, makes and un-
makes itself. Everything ends, without ending. It seems the insurrection of molecules, the inside of a stone a millionth of a second
before it disintegrates. This is what literature is.]

Much critical tradition has located Beckett's "postmodernist
turn" in the years following World War I, notably in works
such as *Molloy* (1951), *Malone meurt* (1951) and *L'Innomable*
(1953). By contrast, Beckett's "English period"—that is, the
time spanning from the early essays on Joyce and Proust to
Murphy (1938)— generally has been read as a corpus of writing consisting of derivative modernist work.[2] In this chapter,
I will argue that, on the contrary, Beckett's early works already illustrate a close affiliation with that revision of modernist assumptions about language, literary subjectivity and
narrative representation pursued during the same period by
Gadda[3] and Céline[4]. In order to argue this position, I will
begin by discussing a number of essays written by Beckett
during the 1930s, starting with the monograph *Proust*, and
then will proceed to a detailed reading of his fictional works:
Dream of Fair to Middling Women (1932), *More Pricks than
Kicks* (1934), and *Murphy* (1938).

Beckett's *Proust* (1931)

Written in 1931, as he was qualifying for a teaching post at Trinity College, Beckett's monograph on Proust[5] represents not so much the exegesis of one of our modernist giants by a young, promising scholar, but more properly should be interpreted as a work where Beckett is beginning to outline the coordinates of his future creative endeavor. The epigraph of the work, the verse "E fango è il mondo" [And mud is the world] is a crucial step in this direction and merits further reflection. As readers familiar with Italian literature will recognize, the epigraph is a citation from "A se stesso." Penned by the nineteenth-century poet Giacomo Leopardi, to this day "A se stesso" continues to be recognized as one of the most antisymbolist compositions ever written. In fact, through a series of discursive and stylistic negations, Leopardi voices the historical crisis of Enlightenment rationality, while making manifest the powerlessness of human endeavor when confronting the amorphous viscosity of life. Moreover, and perhaps more significantly to our purpose, the "canto" itself comes to admit of art only as the articulation of the chaotic, paradoxical nature of experience. This articulation will of course be realized by Leopardi himself through a radical allegorical poetics or, in his words, by way of wandering, bold metaphors.[6]

The significance of the epigraph is amply confirmed in the text that follows. Despite a foreword that promises a comprehensive reading of *A la recherche*—that is to say, a reading capable of accounting for both the allegorical and symbolic elements of the Proustian discourse[7]—Beckett clearly situates his discussion in the space where Proust no longer "assumes omniscience and omnipotence" (62) as the classical artist who "raises himself artificially out of Time in order to give relief to his chronology and causality to his development" (62). As Nicholas Zurbrugg has argued recently,[8] in an almost de Manian fashion Beckett focuses on the passages of *A la recherche* that precede the movement of appropriative sublimation. These are pages that inscribe the heterogeneous, open-ended text of materiality before the "blockage" in vertical significance. In short, Beckett's interest lies in the incommensurability and infinite interpretability of the "event," in the equivocal and paradoxical sublime brought forth in the postmodern Proustian phase. As we might recall, this is the same phase that, as Lyotard has cogently written, "in the modern, puts forward the unpresentable in presentation itself."[9] Considering Beckett's intent, then, it comes as no surprise that after a cursory exposition of the ways in which the Proustian forces of "Habit" and "Memory" stabilize the open-ended, contradictory events of experience through the imposition of "concepts" (60), the essay fastens upon periods of transition. These are phases when "Habit" and "Memory" have not been able to impose "blockages" to multiplicity and change. They interest Beckett because it is here that the reality of being as perception of particular— "the Idea" (11) freed from "the haze of conception—preconception" (11)—is disclosed: Our first nature . . . is laid bare during these periods of abandonment. And its cruelties and enchantments are the cruelties and enchantments of reality . . . the object is perceived as particular and unique . . . independent of any general notion . . . isolated and inexplicable in the light of ignorance (11).

Two passages where a complex and changing referent escapes categorization by discourse are cited as examples. The first deals with Marcel's bewilderment at the proliferation of discordant sounds and colors in the hotel room of Balbec-Plage. The second is concerned with his bafflement in the presence of a grandmother so transformed by time as to be beyond recognition. Then, the study proceeds to deflate the Proustian eidetic intuition of essences manifested in the episodes of involuntary memories. It uses, however, a more egregious weapon than the parodic dethroning voiced during the same year in the poem "Casket of Pralinen for a Daughter of a Dissipated Mandarin." Whereas in the latter the epiphanies are erased as "my memory's involuntary vomit—violently projected, oh beauty!,"[10] in the former Beckett more cavalierly glosses over them. The revelation of the madeleine is given a very cursory exposition, while the others occupy the space of only one page (23). Then, and revealing once more Beckett's incredulity towards Proustian and modernist metanarratives, the study focuses on other moments before the incommensurability of being. An incident at Balbec exemplifying metamorphosis and contradiction as it relates to the narrator's mother, is followed by a lengthy discussion of Marcel's troubled perception of Albertine. As "the many-headed goddess" (34), "a frieze, or a frescoed cortège" (31) of images, she is a "plastic" and "pictorial multiplicity" (32); a Deleuzian "haecceity" escaping the order of metaphysical discourse. Her "*choseté*,"[11] as Beckett also calls heterogeneous compounds in an intertextual anticipation of Deleuze, cannot be "synthesised into one single astral obsession" (31) but exists as an irreducible, kaleidoscopic constellation. The repeated attempts by the narrator of *A la recherche* to contain her multiplicity by "concepts" or, in more Proustian terms, to enclose her seriality in the univocal "cocoon" (31) of *La prisonnière*, are futile. Albertine remains the elusive being of *La fugitive*—an opaque, viscous "nebulae" (44), to be sure, yet also an embodiment of Corneille's "*obscure clarté*": "more" visible in her darkness because truer to the reality of life, to "All that is active, all that is enveloped in time and space" (41).[12]

The focus and the points raised by Beckett in *Proust* offer important insights into the author's understanding of the eventual nature of being, but the value of this work also lies in the introduction of a changing conception of literary subjectivity and narrative representation before referential exteriority.

Rejecting, like Gadda and Céline, logical methods of capturing reality in favor of an aesthetic attitude of "*pietas,*" or what Beckett calls the Schopenhauerian "contemplation of the world independently of the principle of reason" (66), the last sections of *Proust* critique absolutizing uses of language while extolling weaker, "will-less" (70) subjects and symbolizations. In short, the essay polarizes two distinct signifying practices and, without wholly abandoning a desire for representation,[13] it moves to an alternative and nonmetaphysical formulation of the visible. On one hand stands a model of symbolist, Baudelairian derivation. Informed by linguistic ideality, it neutralizes the sublime encounter, the event of the "Idea," through the categories of the "concept." On the other hand, Beckett introduces a symbolic activity that shrinks "from the nullity of extracircumferential phenomena" (48), and does not fear the contemplation of the sedimented "depth(s)" (47): It therefore "pursues the Idea, the concrete" (60). The following quotation summarizes both models. Because the Proustian narrative allows the kaleidoscopic, open-ended being of Albertine to be textualized in the pages of *A la recherche*, representation is "a multiplicity in depth, a turmoil of objective and immanent contradictions over which the subject has no control" (32). It is with this insight that Beckett's study on Proust ends. Observing how the Proustian sentence both originates and recedes from symbolist discourse, and even proposing the neologic epithet of "autosymbolism" (60) to define it, Beckett concludes with words of praise. In Proust's moments of impres-

sionism—"his non-logical statement of phenomena in the order and ex-
actitude of their perception before they have been distorted into intelligi-
bility" (66)—the young Beckett locates the presence of a writing closer to
the articulation of the processes of existence. Unlike the metaphysical
Word, this is a sign that no longer neutralizes equivocality and paradox,
but continues to register images of excess and ambiguity by overdetermined and regressive tropes. As Beckett writes, "The rhetorical equivalent of the Proustian real is the chain-figure of the metaphor. It is a tiring
style, but it does not tire the mind. The clarity of the phrase is cumulative
and explosive. . . . One is exhausted . . . submerged, dominated by the
crest and break of metaphor after metaphor" (68). This important conclusion of *Proust* returns, albeit greatly expanded, in other works from the
same, thirties decade, most of which have been collected in *Disjecta*.

Beckett's Disjecta Membra: *Disjecta* and Other Fragments from the Thirties

Disjecta, which bears Beckett's own title for a miscellany of writings unpublished or published obscurely, did not become available until 1984.
Thanks to the plea of James Acheson, Beckett gave Ruby Cohn permis-
sion to edit the volume, which she rightly considered an invaluable document harboring the seeds of the author's mature aesthetics. Cohn's assessment finds confirmation as early as the letter to Axel Kaun, now known as
the "German Letter of 1937," and printed in the first section of the volume (51–54). Beckett laments the idealism informing literature and argues that while other arts have progressed to newer symbolic modalities,[14]
narrative and poetry continue practicing a "paralyzingly holy . . . word"
(172). Official English is said to contain referential exteriority by "a veil . . .
A mask" (171). Rigid as "a Victorian bathing suit" and imperturbable as "a
true gentleman" (171), it imposes the analytic, determining representations of a scientific knowledge to that which is entangled and horizontal.
Analogously, in a second piece, entitled "Les Deux Besoins," Beckett
describes—and even iconically represents—a symbolization that pursues
the rigid frames of an "idealistic geometry."[15] Allegedly bearing the "signature de Pythagore" (56), it is a practice faithful to the mathematician's
dictum that we can understand and order being within confining, binary
taxonomies: "Dodécahèdre régulier, suivant les dimensions duquel l'in-

fortuné Tout-puissant, se serait proposé d'arranger les quatres éléments"
(56) [Regular dodecahedron, following the dimension of which, the unfortunate All-powerful intends to arrange the four elements]. The images
of the mask, the veil, and Pythagoras' geometric figures, are translated in
a predicative practice in the essay "An Imaginative Work!." "Miss—*absit
nomen!*," an anonymous artist and one of "The chartered recountants"
(89), is said to produce an art of "horology" (89) and to contain the
Ariostesque "indifference" and "mobility" (90) of existence in the symbolic grids of discursive predication. Thus, the need for words capable of
undoing metaphysical structures by a carnivalizing, dethroning textuality
is regarded as imperative by Beckett.[16] In "Les Deux Besoins," Beckett
maintains that the role—indeed the artist's "grand besoin" (55) [great
need]—is to make visible "la monotone centralité" (55) [the monotonous
centrality] in which, despite its Galilean motion, experience has been
enclosed. It is for this reason that, within the mathematical context of this
essay, Beckett resurrects the spirit of Hippasos. Not only did Hippasos
unveil the fiction of mathematical "truths" by demonstrating the incommensurability of the side and diagonal of the square, but his teachings
might have undermined the confining dodecahedron of Pythagoras as
well. As critics have indicated,[17] since Beckett represents this geometric
figure by six triangles surrounding a hexagon, he is suggesting how centripetal, mathematical impulses are now being tested by centrifugal ones.
Mirroring the dehiscing program of "Les Deux Besoins," in the letter to
Axel Kaun, Beckett also issues an invitation to slash the apodictic veil and
perforate its rigid mask through a practice of "unwording" and "linkwriting":

To bore one hole after another in it, until what lurks behind it—be it
something or nothing—begins to seep through; I cannot imagine a
higher goal for a writer today. . . . Is there any reason why that terrible
materiality of the word surface should not be capable of being dissolved,
like for example, the sound surface, torn by enormous pauses . . . so that
through whole pages we can perceive nothing but a path of sounds sus-
pended in giddy heights, linking unfathomable abysses of silence? An
answer is requested. (172)

In the remaining sentences, the above quotation is expanded to outline
the possible paths to be taken, and, under the term of "Nominalist irony"

(173), Beckett promotes a new parodic textuality. Yet, this textuality is but a preliminary step since "it is not enough for the game to lose some of its sacred seriousness. It should stop. Let us therefore act like the mad (?) mathematician who used a different principle of measurement at each step of the calculation" (173). The image of the gaming madman producing inconclusive tropes not only establishes Beckett's practice within a figural model of discourse, much like the "autosymbolism" (60) of the unsublimated pages of *A la recherche* discussed in *Proust*, but the reduction of the enunciative, humanistic subject to a nonachieving, clownish figure deflates the importance of *all* symbolization. Since such deflation might very well be at the origin of the much discussed Beckettian *Sprachkrise*[18] and corresponding aesthetics of failure and mess,[19] it certainly deserves further reflection.

As outlined in the essay on Proust, in Beckett's signifying economy being evolves in time and space. Thus, its symbolic apprehension can never achieve the fullness of presence but, as in the case of Gadda and Céline, tends instead to a form that admits and even reinforces the inconsequence and ephemerality of life. In the words of Beckett's "Three Dialogues," Beckett's best-known essay on painting, from *Disjecta* (138–45), it is a writing obliged to express and, within a metaphysical perspective, doomed to fail because it articulates the fleeting, contradictory occurrences of life. Such profession of failure is nonetheless the occasion of an important break with the traditional representational system and ultimately an indication of success. Precisely because this aesthetics resists a stable, denotative *"paysage"* and proposes instead a *"passage"*[20] of nomadic, Kafkaesque linguistic structures, it is, as Thomas Trezise[21] has pointed out, diametrically opposed to the structuralist and phenomenological epistemes informing modernity, to the logocentric use of language as metaphysical "techne." As such, it comes to be situated outside early and late modernism. To be more specific, since the Beckettian literary space is kept in a state of constant overdetermination and regress, it clearly marks a departure from the stability of metaphysical symbolization informing the epiphanic moments of modernist novels such as Joyce's *A Portrait* and Woolf's *To the Lighthouse*. Further, since Beckett's figuration is also historical, it displaces premises of artistic endeavor as atemporal monuments in favor of a poetic language that does not stand apart from the ephemerality of life but comes into existence and passes away in death.[22] This is of course a crucial development that helps situate Beckett's points of divergence from the ideology informing the practices of late modernists such as Gertrude Stein and the later James Joyce.

It is well known that Beckett's first published essay, the 1929 "Dante . . . Bruno . Vico . . Joyce," now in *Disjecta*, praised the style of *Finnegans Wake*.[23] The piece traces the relationship of "Work in Progress" to Vico's theory of "hieroglyphics" (25)—that is to say, to that conception of poetry as a productive extension of metaphors and metonymies crucial to the work of Gadda also. Yet, whereas Gadda had spoken of a "heuristic" use of the word, Beckett follows Vico more closely. He calls these tropes the "Type-names" (25) located in those passages of the Joycean novel where the sentence not only describes Earwigger's traits of dynamism and contradiction but mimetically reproduces them by a language of paratactical accretion and paradox. Yet it is important to point out that the *Wake*'s figurality reflects only one side of the younger writer's program. Precisely because Joyce's tropes are still close to that romantic, Coleridgian aesthetics of "multeity-in-unity," they tend to be all masterful, overinclusive containers of the universal "riverrunning." Hence, they are directed less toward a representation of being as organic growth and decay and more toward being's enclosure in the immobility of the eternal artifact. This impulse is reflected in that circular, all-encompassing structure of the first and last sentence of the novel and is often explicitly voiced. If "What has gone" we "Begin to forget," writes Joyce in the *Wake*, art functions as the purveyor of the eternal: "It will remember itself from every side, with all gestures, in each our words. Today's truth, tomorrow's trend. Forget, remember!."[24] Thus, it comes as no surprise that after having praised the novel in the 1929 essay, Beckett will differentiate his own approach from that of the *Wake*. As Breon Mitchell has suggested,[25] in the letter to Kaun of 1937 Beckett does plot a course away from Joyce. "With such a program," Beckett writes, "the latest work of Joyce has nothing whatever to do. There it seems rather to be a matter of an apotheosis of the word . . . we want to confine ourselves to the mere intention" (172). In the same document, Beckett locates an analogous practice in Gertrude Stein's "logographs" but again points out that they do not belong to a self-conscious practice. "The unfortunate lady," Beckett comments, "is doubtless still in love with her vehicle" (172) and makes use of tropes "alas, quite by chance" (172).

It is for these reasons that Beckett's endeavors, despite the formal similarity with the results of late modernists, represent more properly a departure. As in the case of Gadda and Céline, Beckett's work is situated within that new "ontological-epochal opening" detected by Gianni Vattimo[26] in the weaker avant-gardist aesthetics of the recollection of being as contradictory and transitory "Ereignis."

Avant-gardizing Beckett

Beckett's avant-gardist affiliation is amply confirmed in his numerous contacts with the unanimists, the surrealists, and the verticalists.[27] Knowlson's biography, *Damned to Fame*, recalls that, while at Trinity, Beckett was doing research on the unanimists Jouve and Romains, whose work was then in the process of being anthologized by Beckett's teacher Rudmose-Brown. Deirdre Bair also maintains that Beckett had met Romains personally at a party in honor of Joyce in 1929 (85). Romains' name also occurs frequently in *Disjecta* (77–78; 84–88), and it is usually cited with approval.

Beckett's involvement with the avant-garde, however, was by no means confined to unanimism. By 1928 he had moved to Paris to teach at the Ecole Normale. Throughout the city, avant-gardist manifestations of futurism, dadaism, and surrealism were highly visible. As Lois Gordon recalls in her *The World of Samuel Beckett*, André Breton had recently published *Surrealism and Painting* and *Nadja* (35) and was firmly established as the leading voice of surrealism. Roger Vitrac and Antonin Artaud were carrying out a project of avant-gardist drama at the Théâtre Alfred Jarry, which they had cofounded in 1927. Other art forms also contributed to the vitality of the movements. The galleries Georges Bernheim and Galérie Surréaliste were showing the work of Arp, Mirò, Mondrian, Dalì, Giacometti, Duchamp, and Magritte, while the most important artistic event of the year, the 1928 art show "Au Sacré Printemps," was exhibiting the paintings of De Chirico, one of Gadda's beloved artists. In the movie theaters of the Parisian boulevards, Ray's *L'Etoile de Mer*, Duchamp's *Anaemic Cinema*, and the films of Eisenstein were being shown. Meanwhile, Louis Buñuel and Salvador Dalì were making *Un Chien Andalou*.

It could be argued that Beckett's response to the avant-garde was nothing more than mere passive observation, but this is not the case. Thanks
to Pelorson, whom Beckett had met that same year, Beckett began translating the work of the dadaist Tzara and the surrealists Breton, Eluard,
and Crevel for the September 1936 issue of *This Quarter*, edited by Ed-
ward Titus and reprinted in Julian Levy's *Surrealism* (1936). Moreover,
during this time he had repeated contacts with Eugene Jolas and the
verticalists. Eugene Jolas, a former reporter for the *Chicago Tribune*, had
founded the journal *Transition* in 1926. The publication was intended as
an outlet for the work of the expatriates. It included selections of Joyce's
Finnegans Wake as well as early prose and poems by Beckett.[28] More im-
portantly, it sought to introduce to an English audience the work of the
European avant-gardes. A cursory reading of the table of contents of
Transition's numbers,[29] reveals that Jolas was printing works by the surrealists Desnos, Soupault, Eluard, Artaud, and the dadaists Tristan Tzara
and Hugo Ball. Even the works of Marinetti and Jules Romains made an
appearance. One of Romains' pieces was printed in the journal's thir-
teenth issue. Marinetti's work, already well-known to the French after the
publication of the manifesto of 1909 in the Parisian *Figaro* and in
Apollinaire's "L'Anti-tradition Futuriste" of 1913, was made available
again in the fourth issue of the journal. Further, the journal was receptive
to avant-gardist works in areas other than literature and included reproductions of paintings by Giorgio De Chirico, as well as articles on the
sculpture of Boccioni, Brancusi, Duchamp, and Giacometti. Worthy of
mention is also the inclusion in *Transition* of two ground-breaking pieces
on film: Erwin Panofsky's "Style and Medium in the Moving Picture"
and Sergei's Eisenstein's "The Cinematographic Principle." While Panofsky argued that cinema was questioning the traditional notion of space
and time and was subjecting language to the principle of "coexpressibility," Eisenstein was attempting to define his alternative theory of montage, or what at this stage he still called the "intellectual cinema." Drawing upon the Japanese system of hieroglyphs as a combination "to be
regarded not as their sum, but as their product, i.e., as a value of another
dimension, another degree,"[30] Eisenstein's piece promoted an image
based on the serial juxtaposition of contradictory shots. In his words, "By
what, then, is montage characterized and consequently, its cell—the

shot? By collision. By the conflict of two pieces in opposition to each other. By conflict. By collision" (37).

The receptivity of *Transition* to avant-gardism eventually crystallized in the verticalist manifesto of 1932, which Beckett signed, along with eight other writers. These included Jolas, Pelorson, and Carl Einstein. The last had been associated with the German expressionist avant-garde gathered by Herwarth Walden to form *Der Sturm* and became the cofounder, with Georges Bataille, of *Documents*.[31] The manifesto, entitled "Poetry Is Vertical" and now reprinted in McMillan's volume (66), calls for an alternative and weaker "nexus between the 'I' and the 'You'" (66): It rejects "the classical ideal," its "factitious sense of harmony," and champions synthetic and alogical, dreamlike representations. As such, it does share some of the tenets of surrealism. However, its last sections take the surrealist ideology one step further by wishing for a radical destructuring of expression. Proposition number eight outlines a "mantic language"; one, we are told, that "does not hesitate to adopt a revolutionary attitude toward word and syntax, going even so far as to invent a hermetic language, if necessary" (66).

Beckett's affiliation with avant-gardism is additionally cemented in other documents from the same period. Some of his thirties' pieces from *Disjecta* for example, are comic pages of praise for a fictional avant-gardist, Jean du Chas (35–42). The collection also includes numerous reviews that champion the new generation of Irish poets, painters, and playwrights, who exhibit distrust of and irony toward the metaphysical Word—notably McGreevy, Devlin, Coffey, Yeats, and Sean O'Casey. Yeats is associated with "the great of our time, Kandinsky and Klee, Ballmer and Bram van Velde, Rouault and Braque" (97). O'Casey is admired for practicing a theater of dissociation and consummation, "the principle of disintegration in even the most complacent solidities" (82); for allowing his material to escape and his "set (to) come to pieces" (83). The poets McGreevy, Devlin, and Coffey, who represent the Irish "voice of the avant-garde railing against the establishment,"[32] are writers who, like Joyce and Stein, practice a sign of connection and plurality. Unlike the latter, however, they have learned the avant-gardist lesson of submission to material[33] and are bearing in mind the protosurrealist messages of Rimbaud's letter to Georges Izambard, Laforgue's *Complaints* (1885), and Corbière's *Yellow Loves* (1873) concerning the mortality of *all* words. Beckett's correspondence from the same decade is also worthy of note, particularly as it relates to the subject of Eisenstein and his theory of montage.[34] In the letters, Beckett not only asks Sergei Eisenstein for an invitation to work for him for a year, but praises the innovative possibilities of the young art form. Like Gadda, the technique of montage appears to him as a medium naturally conducive to the linkage of conflicting shots and to the representation of coexistence and simultaneity that Beckett himself realized in *Film*, a work produced in 1964 but significantly set in 1929.[35]

It is in this context of the avant-gardist critique of modernist representational assumptions that one must place the fictions of Beckett's "English period": *Dream of Fair to Middling Women* (1932), the collection of short stories *More Pricks than Kicks* (1934), and *Murphy* (1938).

Rereading Beckett's *Dream* (1932)

Written in 1932, or perhaps even a year earlier, as Knowlson's *Damned to Fame* suggests, this novel was, for its time, so transgressive in style and subject that Beckett could not find a publisher for it.[36] Consequently, he used sections in later works, while the manuscript was laid to rest in the Dartmouth archives. Available to the general public since 1992 in an American and an English edition, *Dream* is the Ur-text behind the practice of "unwording" and "linkwriting" actualized in *More Pricks than Kicks* and *Murphy*. Perhaps this explains why Beckett compared it to a container: "the chest into which I threw my wild thoughts."[37]

Dream is both a theory and a praxis for an alternative novel rather than a derivative of modernist works, and, within the Beckettian corpus, "a practice-pad" for later novels.[38] Like Gadda's *Racconto*, it is composed of narrative sections and theoretical notes. Together, these probe both the impossibility of metaphysics and the end of the viability of the "book." In the process, they inaugurate yet another thirties' emergence of the "text."

The first note, from the chapter "Two," mounts a corrosive, "unwording" critique of the presumed authority and omnipotence of enunciative subjects and their language. It does so through a genealogy, much as Céline had done by retelling the archetypal fable of *Genesis* in a context of compromising power structures. By way of a Chinese parable, quite likely of Beckett's own invention, the note demolishes the natural premise of absolutizing representation and shows it to be the product of a chance occurrence and of the human, Apollonian will to mastery.

Lîng-Liûn, a minister and a man "without passion" (10), Beckett writes, went one day to Bamboo Valley, where, after having cut a bamboo shoot, he realized that if he blew into it, he could hear his own, mono-tonal voice. Meanwhile in the forest, a male and a female phoenix were singing and had "the kindness" (10) to emit six notes apiece. Projecting the experience of his own voice onto that of the birds, the minister be-came convinced that six notes each were all the birds were capable of, and that they could be adequately captured in the sounds of a musical instrument. Thus, he proceeded to cut eleven more stems, for a total of twelve "liu-liu" (10), and brought them to his master. Each of the twelve sounds, or symbols, corresponded to a character: "the Yellow Bell . . . the Great Liu, the Great Steepleiron, the Stifled Bell, the Ancient Purifica-tion, the Young Liu, the Beneficent Fecundity, the Bell of the Woods, the Equable Rule, the Southern Liu, the Imperfect, the Echo Bell" (10). The premise of symbolic enclosure of referential exteriority was born. With it came the assumptions that subjects could provide absolute, totalizing representation of life in the space of narrative. As the narrator puts it, the logocentric mythos emerged, the idea of "a book that would be purely melodic . . . linear, a lovely Pythagorean chain-chant solo of cause and effect, a one-figured teleo-phony that would be a pleasure to hear" (10).

The credo of the Chinese minister was long-lived. In a subsequent note, the narrator argues that it informs the practices of nineteenth-cen-tury authors, such as "the divine Jane and many others" (119). Like Lîng-Liûn, they still believe that referential exteriority can be "artificially im-mobilized in a backwash of composure" (119), and that with one, single note the assurance of substance and finality can be won. Subsequently, the scholarly note focuses at length on the novels of Balzac and observes that they are far removed from the contemplation of being that their titles imply. In yet another geometric metaphor, Balzac's novels are said to be scientific exercises cast in the language of the French Academy: ". . . why call a distillation of Euclid and Perrault 'Scenes from Life'? Why 'Human Comedy'? Why anything? Why bother about it?" (120). Another quotation analogously demolishes the guiding premises and representational values of Balzac's fiction and states how formal order implies a radical falsity:

To read Balzac is to receive the impression of a chloroformed world. He is absolute master of his material, he can do what he likes with it, he can foresee and calculate its least vicissitude, he can write the end of the book before he has finished the first paragraph, because he has turned all his creatures into clockwork cabbages and can rely on their staying put wherever needed or staying going at whatever speed in whatever direction he chooses. (119–120)

This passage deserves further attention, since it extends well beyond the nineteenth-century novel to point to more contemporary practices addressed in other documents from the Beckettian intertext. Balzac's characterization by "clockwork" closely mirrors the art of "horology" (89) of the anonymous "Miss—*absit nomen!*," the "chartered recountant" (89) described by Beckett in "An Imaginative Work!." More significantly, the observations on the organization of the Balzacian novel not only bring to mind the circular structure of *Ulysses* and the *Wake,* but the sentence on artistic omnipotence is a verbatim anticipation of some statements made by Beckett on Joyce in the course of Shenker's interview of May 5, 1956.[39]

Beckett's revisionary aesthetics, however, is by no means confined to these examples of "unwording." Newly mirroring the coeval field of enunciation, the critique of absolutizing premises about language and literary subjectivity gives way to an alternative rhetorical economy. This economy is concretized in the practice of a "linkwriting." Since life is made of molecules that "will not suffer . . . to be absorbed in the cluster of a greater system, and then, and chiefly, because they themselves tend to disappear as systems" (119), the narrative voice now starts to advocate a use of language that closely follows that of Gadda and Céline. Like Gadda who, as early as the 1924 *Racconto,* not only had resisted the metaphysical will to reduce the continuum of the "real" in a narrative of thematic and stylistic coherency, but had proposed a novel of plurality, a symphony of signifieds and signifiers, the narrator of *Dream* also wishes for a "symphonic, not a melodic unity" (11). This is a type of narrative that implies a weaker enunciative figuration, one incapable as well as unwilling to bring the complexity and immanency of the "real" within an explanatory range. In short, this is a literary subjectivity "diametrically opposed to the one Joyce expresses through Stephen Daedalus."[40] No longer an Apollonian image of artistic omnipotence and Benjaminian "aura," it emerges as a foil to the impotent and abject "Bard(a)mu"; the embodiment of a "scrivener who has no very near or dear or clear ideas" (168). "Neither Deus nor ex machina enough" (117), it can only traffic with the "muck" (187) and the "bog" (239) of the world. Clearly departing from the Proustian narrator as well, it has lost the key to the mystical epiphanic revelation: "Behold, Mr. Beckett . . . a dud mystic . . . mystique raté" (186). More like Gadda's manifold, "omnipotential" narrator, it is often referred to as a one that is many. It is a "we, extenuate consensus of me" (112), an I as *Company* (1980), whose talent does not lie in the "*narratio recta*" (169), in the strong "architectonics" (179), but in the "Gehenna of links" (211). Therefore, it will state the meandering of the world, the Gaddian "*Est quod est*," the Célinian "Voyage," by "wander(ing) about vaguely," (118), allowing the pen to "r(u)n away" (73) with "no plans, but none at all" (178). Hence, the literary subject proposes to relinquish authoritarian premises of enclosing being in the Being of predication—the "landscape of a dream of integration" (13)—and promises to write by a radically temporal figuration. The latter certainly emerges less as a sign of nihilist despair and more as a practice respectful of the particularity and uniqueness of its referent. As such, it is akin to that ethical encounter with the irreducibly other described by Levinas as the epiphany of the "face."[41]

Introduced by an epigraph that casts doubts on the categories we use to frame experience—"A thousand sythes have I herd men telle, That the is joye in heven, and peyne in helle; But"—the "Type-names" shape the very beginning of the novel, where a group of characters emerges from the Irish drizzle. As molecules not only affected by chronotopicity, but allowed to be so, they are constituent refractory to any form of binding. If not yet narratable by the cinematic montage practiced by Beckett in his later production for television, they are nonetheless recordable by tracing the itinerary of the "linkwriting," or the "this and that and then this" that Mrs. Ramsay from Woolf's *To the Lighthouse* (239) had sought to overcome in her letters. In the narrator's words, "We can state them as a succession of terms, but we can't sum them and we can't define them. They tail off vaguely at both ends and the intervals of their series are demented" (124).

One of the female characters,[42] Smeraldina-Rima, the daughter of the Mandarin and Mammy, is a symphony, or "concert of effects" (12). A convulsive beauty like Breton's Nadja, from the homonymous novel, she has a grotesque body, a composite of beauty and ugliness, firmness and flabbiness: "Botticelli thighs, knock-knees, ankles all fat nodules, wobbly, mammose, slobbery-blubbery. . . . Then, perched aloft on top of this porpoise prism, the loveliest little pale firm cameo of a birdface" (15). Her eyes, which recall the futurist sculpture described by Gadda in "San Giorgio in casa Brocchi," mirror the rest of her physique, since they are "darting this way and that" (30). The heterogeneity of Smeraldina in space is increased by horizontal differentiation and by the infinite interpretability of her being. In her journey from Dublin to Vienna, and at different periods during her stay in Austria, she embodies a series of female characters. These range from virginal girl to departing lover to incontinent female to abandoned lover, and more, "four of her and many another" (115). Syra-Cusa similarly straddles the bar of difference and identity. A woman presented as "very uterine" (50), and a hybrid of the unappeasable women of history and literary tradition—Clytemnestra, Semiramide, and Lucrezia—coupled, however, with equine features, she remains totally indifferent to Belacqua's gift of an edition of Dante's *Commedia*. In fact, she leaves the gift in a café. However, she is also interested in spiritual uplifting and busies herself with "Abstract drawing! Can you beat that one?" (116). Another female character, Alba, or "Alba and Co." (179), is she who has "practically no occasion to be herselves" (115), lives according to the "non-simpl(e)" and is constantly propelled to make a Gaddian tangle, or, in Beckett's words, "a mess and a knot" (164) of all human relations, including amorous encounters and friendly conversations. The Frica, or perhaps "Lilly, Jane or Caleken Frica? Or just plain Mary? " (180) is "both mare and filly" (195), as well as a "throttled gazelle" (215).

The male characters analogously probe the readerly frames of semic and symbolic denotation and emerge as intersections of images. Lucien not only converses on Leibnitz, but conducts his life as if it were a passage from the *Monadology*: "He was a crucible of volatilisation . . . his contours in perpetual erosion . . . his whole person a stew of disruption and flux" (116–17). Liebert is "l'inénarrable . . . engagé profondément dans le marais . . . " (20) [the non-narratable . . . profoundly engaged in the

marshes]. Even Nemo, who remains for many pages the immobile, self-
identical image carved on the parapet of O'Connell Bridge, does not
escape the forces of the Spinozian "affect." Towards the end of the narrative, an article in the *Twilight Herald* informs the reader that he has fallen
in the waters.

Among these characters, however, it is Belacqua, otherwise called "the
principal boy" (11), who comes to embody the temporal and spatial displacement of the "syllepsis." A tumult of contradictory impulses—"A
trine man! Centripetal, centrifugal and . . . not" (120)—Belacqua stands
at the center of a tension between Cartesianism and non-Cartesianism,
matter and spirit, phenomenon and noumenon. As such, he mirrors the
"omnipotentiality" of Gadda and the Célinian impossibility of being
"Jean, Pierre, and Gaston," in a body of centrifugal molecules. In his
afferent version, he is seduced, like Gonzalo from *La cognizione* and the
Marchesa from "San Giorgio in casa Brocchi," by a modernist, metaphysical desire. His will to order is evident not only in his feet, "mon-
strously symmetrical" (133), but it is foregrounded in an impossible desire
to enclose the manifold complexity and horizontality of life. For example, from that compound of beauty and ugliness that Smeraldina con-
stitutes, Belacqua selects only her face, and reduces her being to the fixity
of a painting: "the living spit of Madonna Lucrezia del Fede" (15). By an
analogous phantasmagoria, or as the narrator puts it, admitting her "according to his God" (25) only, he cannot accept her passivity and liveliness at once. Therefore, he freezes her into that "stillness" (23) in which
he had seen her the first time: "So he would always have her be, rapt, like
a spirit of a troubadour, casting no shade, herself shade" (23). An explanation for this reduction is offered by Belacqua himself, who comments that
"the true Shekinah . . . is Woman." As Kroll has observed acutely,[43] since
the Shekinah is a revelation of holiness in the profane, the allusion emphasizes Bel's desire to absorb the transitoriness of the Flesh into the
absolute of the Symbol. Two other passages, both dealing with Belacqua's
mental efforts to establish difference between and within woman, articulate with even greater clarity his Cartesian, paranoid striving for wholeness. In the first, Belacqua has met Syra-Cusa, a brunette like Smeraldina, and tries to categorize the former in opposition to the latter:
"Somewhere is the magic point where skirted beauty forks" (35). His taxonomy, however, is at an impasse: "I cannot establish on a base Aa . . . a

triangle with the desired apex, because . . . I am unable to imagine the base Aa" (35). The second passage describes a discussion between Belacqua and Smeraldina's father, the Mandarin, on the issue of that pre-Oedipal, "choric" coexistence of spirituality and sexuality in woman. For Belacqua, this is again the source of a horrible confusion: "There is no such thing . . . as a simultaneity of incoherence, there is no such thing as love in the thalamus . . . 'I am this and that'-altogether abominable. I admit Beatrice . . . and the brothel . . . but not Beatrice in the brothel" (102). Despite Belacqua's articulate speech, his interlocutor is not convinced, and argues that this is a sign of Belacqua's metaphysical vision. In a commentary that certainly voices the issues raised in Beckett's essays, the Mandarin replies to Belacqua: "You simplify . . . the whole thing with the literary mathematics . . . your type never accepts experience, nor the notion of experience. So I speak merely from a need . . . The need to live, to be authentically and seriously and totally involved" (101). Ultimately, the Mandarin dismisses him as one whose understanding of the "continuum" is preordained to failure because it is inherently "cock-eyed" (102). Confirming the Mandarin's suggestions, we are often told that a rat, which in *Dream* functions as an icon of dehiscing force, "an escape into being,"[44] much as the insects and the reptiles do in Gadda's fictions, lives with Belacqua. Here, it is "gnawing its way into a globe" (9), "galavanting and cataracting behind the sweating wall-paper . . . slashing the close invisible plane with ghastly muted slithers" (15).[45] Belacqua's mind often refuses to perform the "chamber-work of sublimation" (5), and despite his attempts to keep Smeraldina in the stillness of a portrait and in the absence of corporeality of troubadouric poetry, she is very much alive. In what appears to be a parodic reversal of many modernist assimilations of reality into art, the repressed "physis" returns. In the course of Belacqua's visit to Vienna, it obliterates the Shekinah, and Smeraldina rapes him.

Because of failed attempts to assign identity and sameness to the "inchoate liminal presentations" (33) of life, Belacqua, who has a "fetid head" (17) and for this reason is often the object of the narrator's scorn, begins to seek the total indifference of Limbo. This is a physical and mental state oblivious to referential exteriority and separated from that heterogeneity and contradiction that women embody. At first Limbo is achieved by the palliative of sleep. As Belacqua grows older, however, he further refines this strategy. In another analogy to the walls erected by many characters of Gadda's and Céline's fictions, Belacqua engages for long periods of time in "wombtombing" (148), shutting himself up in dark, protective enclosures: "the cup, the umbra, the tunnel" (46). Here, so he believes, two goals will be achieved. On one hand, it will be possible to escape the ebb and the flow of a temporal, complex macrocosm, "sheltered from the winds and sheltered from the waters" (44). On the other hand, his mind will find rest from all attempts at enclosing heterogeneous entities: "disinterested, indifferent, its miserable erethisms and discriminations and futile sallies suppressed" (44).

Such emancipation from life, however, remains a quixotic remedy. As a symptom of the pathetic desire to "troglodyse" (128) oneself, it is but "the salve on the prurigo of living" (181). In what Zurbrugg has identified as an intertextual allusion and revision of Proust's imagery of tunnels and light in *Le Temps retrouvé*,[46] not only do the forces of externality assail Belacqua's house and wall of fiction, forcing him out into the open "the way a crab would be that was hauled out of its dim pool" (46), but he himself is part of that materiality he seeks to suppress.

Heterologically unbounded, as another writer of the 1930s, the surrealist Georges Bataille, would say, Belacqua is the "acephalic" man; the one who embodies the rupture of physical and social homogeneity of Platonism. Like Céline's Ferdinand, he is somewhat of a "*clochard*," often prey to excessive physical discharge by onanism and vomit and to unrestrained intake of drinks. In this efferent version, he also occupies different positions in time and space. If he is a child in "One," an adolescent in "Two," and a young man in "Und" and in "Three," as an adult he emerges as the pursuer as well as the pursued. From Dublin to Vienna and Vienna to Paris, he becomes infinitely interpretable, being both "Phoebus, chasing Daphne, Narcissus flying from Echo and . . . neither" (120). More significantly, his will to reduce life to sameness and identity is contradicted by his literary tastes and ambitions. An emerging "homo rhetoricus"—he is studying to become a professor (48) and occasionally composes poetry—he clearly privileges the literary heterogeneous. He dislikes "The uniform, horizontal writing, flowing without accidence, of the man with a style" (48), and prefers syntagmas where clichés and commonplaces disrupt the even tone. From his acquaintances we learn that "Il ne sait jamais résister à l'extase du décollage" (20) [He can never resist the ecstasy of unsticking] and is discovered quoting sentences by aposiopesis. Like Célinian phrases, these sentences lack predicative closures: "'Mais elle viendra . . .' 'Du bist so . . .' 'La belle, la . . .'" (148) ["'But she will come . . .' 'You are so . . .' 'The beautiful, the . . .'"]. Belacqua's rhetorical penchant also explains his profound hate for Chas. The latter is said to be affected by the "Anal complex" (148), or a will to apply "closure" (148) to whatever is expressed, be it a conversational sentence or a poetic verse. Moreover, Belacqua also has dreams, albeit never realized, of composing a book. Since he intends this to be a novel that abdicates all thematic and stylistic cohesion—a "dynamic décousu," full of "flowers that cannot coexist" (138)—it is a foil to Beckett's own, a *mise en abîme* of the author's practices. Hence, it has led critics to read *Dream* as a thinly veiled autobiography.[47] The narrative voice, however, warns us against such symbolic equations and introduces what will become a constant preoccupation of much Beckettian fiction: a will to probe the hermeneutic frames by which not only authors provide tuning forks, but, as Iser has suggested,[48] we, as readers, do as well, assigning identity by excluding the excess and privileging structure to the detriment of conflict in order to consolidate significance into meaning. In anticipation of an analogous practice in *Murphy* and later novels, a Sternian aside admonishes the audience against choosing the centripetal forces at the expense of centrifugal ones. It calls for halting the "wretched" (53) practice of "squar(ing) up to the book . . . hiss(ing) up his mind and peck(ing) and pick(ing) wherever he smells a chink" (53). Additionally, the aside extends an invitation to a more contemplative, less masterful reception of being: "let yourself go to the book, and it do the work and dephlogisticate you like a current of just the right frequency" (53). In another passage, we are told to stop suppressing the facts we cannot account for and be ready to follow the indefinite disarray instead: "if . . . we could only learn to see all things great and small . . . all the articles of bric-à-brac through which we move, as so many tunics of so many onions, if we could only learn to school ourselves to nurture that . . . curiosity struck from the desire to bind forever in imperishable relation the object to its representation . . . there is no knowing on what sublime platform . . . we may find ourselves . . . through reefless airs for a magic land" (160–1).

It is toward such a place that the fabula of *Dream* tends, to that apex of epiphenomenal heterogeneity introduced at the Frica's party. Here, a great theatrical happening unfolds, a "soirée Dada" of coming and going, cries and laughter, sexual attraction and physical repulsion. *Dream*'s lius, "all, one and sundry" (206), meet the bibliomaniacs, the paleographers, the violinists, the professors of Bullscrit and Comparative Ovoidology, the cicisbeos, the whores, the communist decorators, and "the nondescripts" (217). At the party, we see Belacqua again, one last time, before he disappears into that Irish rain that produces a "mitigation of contours" (240), that color gray where, as Marie Claire Pasquier has written, "all differences are drowned,"[49] as he listens to a voice enjoining him "to move on" (241), on that path of being that no longer knows closure.

More of Belacqua: Beckett's *More Pricks than Kicks* (1934)

The counterideology of *Dream* invades Samuel Beckett's two other early narrative works, *More Pricks than Kicks* and *Murphy*. Of the two texts, the first owes more to the "chest," since here we find not only entire sections lifted from *Dream*, but an older version of Belacqua in Belacqua Shuah. This state of "work in progress" is certainly justifiable as a utilization of a rejected text but ought more properly be interpreted as the manifestation of a constitutive avoidance of completion, one comparable to that of Gadda and Céline and corroborated by the overall compositional tendencies of the Beckettian oeuvre. Further, it is an anticipation of the practice of "exile writing," an additional divestment of words' power to name and circumscribe that will ultimately inform Beckett's decision to write in French, a non-native, deterritorialized language.

Like the earlier Belacqua, the Belacqua from *More Pricks* embodies the will to withdraw from participation in the heterogeneity and openendedness of life. This trait is already inscribed in his name. "Belacqua" is the name of the indolent lute-maker in canto IV of Dante's *Purgatorio*, doomed to wait at the foot of the mountain as he had waited on earth before repenting. "Shuah" recalls the grandfather of Onan, punished in *Genesis* 38:8–10 for having prevented life by engaging in coitus interruptus.[50]

The indolence and withdrawal of "Belacqua Shuah" unfold in his scholarly, domestic, and social behavior. In the narrative section entitled "Dante and the Lobster," Belacqua is struggling with a verse from Dante's *Paradiso*: "stuck in the first of the canti of the moon . . . so bogged that he could move neither backward nor forward."[51] The "tiller of the field" (12), the common man, has made peace with the notion that the spots on the moon stand for the wandering condition of Cain and for the contradictory truth of God's vengeful pity. Belacqua, however, cannot accept it: "he pored over the enigma, he would not concede himself conquered, he would understand at least the meanings of the words, the order in which they were spoken and the nature of the satisfaction that they conferred on the misinformed poet" (9). Yet, the clock strikes twelve, and since Belacqua, in his attempt to reduce open-endedness to a minimum, has segmented the rest of his day linearly according to the teleology "one, lunch; two, the lobster; three, the Italian lesson" (10), he needs to attend to his meal and postpone the explanation of Dante to a later time. Thus, in order to achieve the first of the day's goals, he locks his door—"he must be left in absolute tranquillity . . . He must be left strictly alone" (10)—and sets out to prepare a cheese sandwich. In what brings to mind yet another scene from Gadda's La cognizione, specifically the episode of Gonzalo and the cotton-candy, Belacqua abhors the "pith and dough" (11) of the bread. As a substance amorphous and elastic, it is an objective correlative of life's condition: "He laid his cheek against the soft of the bread, it was spongy and warm, alive. But he would very soon take that plush feel off it, by God but he would very quickly take that fat white look off its face" (11). So, Belacqua proceeds to toast the slices according to ritualistic specifications—"precisely" and "properly" (11)—before covering them with Savora and spices: "No butter, God forbid. . . . Butter was a blunder, it made the toast soggy" (12).

Belacqua's desire to repress life's condition and the material reminders of it—or, as the narrator puts it, his admitting of "life, we dare almost say, in the abstract" (114)—is by no means limited to his scholarly and domestic activities but is manifested at the level of his personal and social existence. Mirroring his younger version from Dream, Belacqua of More Pricks shuns the carnal aspect of woman. For example, in "Fingal" Belacqua is at the Hill of the Wolves with Winnie Coates, "pretty, hot and witty, in that order" (23). She welcomes the prospect of some intimacy with her companion, but Belacqua is more interested in the landscape. This is why he uses a chance encounter with Dr. Sholto and a bicycle to run away from Winnie and hide in a public house. In "Love and Lethe," we are told that another woman, Ruby Tough, tolerates Belacqua's idiosyncrasies "in the hope that sooner or later, in a fit of ebriety or of common or garden incontinence, he would so far forget himself as to take her in his arms" (87). In "Walking Out" a reversal appears to have occurred, since Belacqua is betrothed to Lucy. Nonetheless, and confirming his earlier patterns, on the eve of the wedding he attempts to convince his bride to take a "cicisbeo" (103) and suggests a Platonic arrangement: "her living with him like a music while being the wife in body of another" (109). Belacqua only settles happily into marriage when an accident renders the body of Lucy permanently crippled. The couple will also move in to a house where all chronometers, reminders of temporality, are banned. Belacqua's next two weddings follow a similar pattern. The second is to Thelma bboggs, a woman said to have "a most chercharming personality, together with intense appeal, as he repudiated with no less insistence, from the strictly sexual standpoint" (117). The third is to Smeraldina-Rima, and follows the spiritual dynamics already foregrounded in the narrative of *Dream*.

Contrary to one of the most enduring myths in Beckett's criticism,[52] one finds that it is within the social fabric that Belacqua's nonparticipation in and indifference to life is most clearly foregrounded. In "Dante and the Lobster," for example, Belacqua is shown to have very little compassion for living beings, such as the lobster that is destined to a pot of boiling water: "Well, thought Belacqua, it's a quick death, God help us all" (22), to which the narrator replies by commenting "It is not" (22). In another episode, titled "Ding-Dong," Belacqua shows no emotion when witnessing an accident on Pearse Street, where a little girl is run down by a bus while carrying some milk and bread to her tenement house. In Fleet Street, a blind paralytic appears to catch Belacqua's most superficial attention only. In "What a Misfortune" the death of Lucy leaves him unaffected, since Belacqua "could produce no tears" (114). During the preparations for the wedding to Thelma, he is "so quiescent" (129) and "overtaken by this inertia" (128), that he leaves all the arrangements to his best man, Capper Quin. Not surprisingly, and anticipating the penchants of Murphy, Belacqua is greatly attracted to the lunatics of the Portrane Asylum. The lunatics' existential apathy embody the fulfillment of his desire "to be back in the caul, on my back in the dark for ever" (29).

Like *Dream*, however, the narrative of *More Pricks* also emphasizes that ambiguity and temporality of being of which Belacqua, despite his nonparticipation, is still a part. If Belacqua abhors contradiction, nonetheless he is prone to an incongruous juxtaposition of words and actions. Not only does he occasionally utter paradoxes (162–3), but he easily juxtaposes gorgonzola cheese with theology, and pubs with philosophy. On the whole, as the narrator comments, he is a "compound of ephebe and old woman" (176), a hybrid whose "guarantee of identity" might only be "the baby anthrax that he wore just above the collar" (70). The narrative also textualizes the return of the irreducible, contingent elements of life. In the first episode, for example, and despite Belacqua's teleological planning, the "end" is inserted in the "one, two, three." The toast does not turn out to be what Belacqua expected, and his locked door appears to be insufficient to block the events of the macrocosm. A photograph of McCabe, a man destined to be hanged for arson and murder despite a petition, lays on the table and, ratlike, crosses Belacqua's thoughts throughout the day. The lobster that Belacqua picks up for his aunt is almost devoured by a cat, and the lesson with the Ottolenghi does not provide the explanation of the theological "quodlibet" (10) that he had hoped for.

The collection also focuses extensively on the temporality that Belacqua seeks to control, and does so by representing him in time and by sprinkling each story with examples of *memento mori*. These range from meticulous recollections of the time of the day and the season of the year, to more subtle reflections on chronotopicity. In "Dante and the Lobster," for example, the passage from Dante that the Ottolenghi refuses to translate—"qui vive la pietà quando è ben morta" (19) [here lives pity, when pity is dead] is not only emblematic of contradictoriness, being a play on the words "piety" and "pity," but is also an ironic commentary on Belacqua's desires by way of the literary archive. As a verse from canto XX of *Inferno*, it belongs to the context of the fourth bolgia. Here are punished characters much like Belacqua—souls, that is, who have not accepted life's linear opacity and have chosen to engage in various practices of divination of the future. In "Ding-Dong" another event probes the impossibility of Belacqua's will "to consecrate his life to stasis" (42), to live "a Beethoven pause" (38). In a public house in Lombard Street, a "woman of the people" (44) and a foil to the previously mentioned "tiller of the field" (12) is selling "Seats in heaven" (45). Yet, when Belacqua approaches her, she comments that even the celestial sphere participates in motion: "'Heaven goes round' she said, whirling her arm, 'and round and round and round and round and round'" (45). In "What a Misfortune," Thelma lifts Belacqua's ban on chronometers. As the future Mrs. Shuah, she presents to him, "for whom . . . even the sun's shadow a torment" (129), "The grand-father and mother . . . of a period clock" (129). Other episodes analogously emphasize the failure of Belacqua who, like his ear lier version in *Dream,* will develop the curious strategy of the "moving pause" (38) to avoid movement. This is a deambulation by boomerang, whereby to each step forward corresponds a movement backward, or a return to its point of departure. As such, it is a visual icon of the circular structure of Joyce's narratives.

Because of the counterideology informing the novel—an ideology voiced by the intradiegetic commentary of "Ding-Dong"[53]—it comes as no surprise that the last two stories of the collection, "Yellow" and "Draff," describe the demise of Belacqua in a triumph of contradiction and open-endedness. Here we learn that Belacqua has been hospitalized and awaits surgery, scheduled for noon. The description of the different nursing and housekeeping activities occurring as the morning progresses are set against his fears: "He dashed out his cigarette and put on the lamp . . . in order to postpone daybreak . . . Daybreak, with its suggestion of a nasty birth, he could not bear" (159). Nonetheless, and in what Zurbrugg iden-tifies as a reversal of the positive role attributed by the Proustian *Recher-che* to Vermeer's yellow wall,[54] the sun's rays creep through the windows and flood the room with color: "But on the grand yaller wall . . . a pillar of higher tone, representing the sun, was spinning out its placid deisal. This dribble of time, thought Belacqua, like sanies into a bucket, the world wants a new washer. He would draw the blind, both blinds" (167). Time however, cannot be concealed. When the clock strikes twelve, Belacqua is taken to the operating room, where he dies, the victim of a chance event: "By Christ! he did die! They had clean forgotten to auscultate him!" (174). In the final piece in the collection, "Draff," life reaffirms itself in all its open-endedness and contradictions. In an analogy to the law of Dantesque divine retribution for sins—an analogy prompted by the mortician's and the driver's names of Malacoda and Scarmiglione, respectively, from *Inferno* XX—Belacqua's body is unaffected by rigor mortis. As such, it is akin to the soft and pliant pith he had attempted to correct in his ritualized lunches. Further, Belacqua's widow, Smerry, and his best man, Capper, seem to have benefited greatly from this sudden death: The "commerce with the things of time" (180) has rendered Capper more self-confident. Smeraldina can now afford to live also that carnal existence that Belacqua had denied her. On the way back from the cemetery, in one more irony to all protective enclosures erected by metaphysical questers, the two find Belacqua's house in flame and decide to leave together. The last scene describes a groundskeeper, or a third "tiller of the field" (12), comfortably straddled between contradictory moods, "Calm and wistful" (191), and immersed in a landscape that is "classico-romantic" (191); affected by heterogeneity and temporality, because — ultimately — "So it goes in the world" (191).[55]

Overturning Metaphysics: *Murphy* (1938)

Samuel Beckett's last narrative work of the thirties, the novel *Murphy*, is an even more radical probing of the impossibility of a determining, scientific representation of being. This achievement was acknowledged even by James Joyce who, in a letter to Adrienne Monnier in 1940, recommended *Murphy* along with Flannery O'Brien's *At Swim-Two-Birds* as "new theories of composition."[56]

The alternative episteme informing the novel is revealed quite early in the narrative by way of a geometrical analogy. Mr. Kelly's kite, a hexagon and therefore an icon of analytic, totalizing narration, is loosing its strength. Much like the "Zélé" of Céline's Courtial des Pereires, its sails are said to be worn by much exposure and its "tassels have come adrift."[57] Confirming the impossibility of governing anchors and perimeters, *Murphy* explodes the identity of characters and their actions by a discourse of radical heterogeneity and becoming.

Murphy, the first "liu" to be presented in the novel, bursts the singularity of form, that oneness of being that characters and readers are often prone to seek. Born under the sign of Mercury/Hermes, the god that "has no fixed color" (31–32), he has occupied, like Leibnitz before him, a garret in Hanover[58] and leads a life narratable only by a chain of paradoxes and oxymorons: "My life-warrant . . . My little bull of incommunication" (31). A reader and a nonreader, willing "to engage in some pursuit, yet not" (32), inclined to "Purity" (32) and the life of the mind, but also ruled by the senses and the body, Murphy embodies a state of pre-Oedipal indifference. His use of language reflects the predicament of his existence. As his girlfriend Celia describes it, Murphy's symbolization is one that upsets dichotomies and stasis: "She felt, as she felt so often with Murphy, spattered with words that went dead as soon as they sounded; each word obliterated before it had time to make sense, by the word that came next; so that in the end she did not know what had been said" (40). Elsewhere, we learn that Murphy's way of classifying experience is conducted under the aegis of figurality; the ambiguity of metaphor and the infinity of metonymy: "In the beginning was the pun. And so on" (65).[59] In one more analogy to Beckett's theoretical pieces, Murphy's vision is not that of the "*voyeur*" (90), dependent "on light, object, view point, etc." (90), but of the "*voyant*," or that "vision that all those things embarrass" (90).

Manifold complexity, however, is by no means confined to Murphy, but is a condition shared by other characters. To reprise again the figure of the kite, all the hexagon's sides are "worn and wan" (114). Murphy's girlfriend, Celia, for example, is initially identified structurally, and therefore in her antonymous, privative difference from Murphy. Whereas Murphy hates the sun, the street noises, and has "cold and unwavering" (2) eyes, she is said to have opposite features. She walks the road daily, has a roving eye, and enjoys the noises. As the story progresses, however, and in another analogy to the coeval field, the narrative discourse subjects Celia to the logic of the simulacrum. Almost by contagion of morphogenic fields, she takes on a number of Murphy's traits. As such, she becomes the double, the copy that, unlike the "bare" model of repetition, no longer establishes the original but has an unsettling, differential effect.[60] An analogous dynamic is at work in the representation of other characters, such as Mr. Kelly, Wylie, and Neary. It is well illustrated in a comment by Wylie that suggests that "Our medians . . . or whatever the hell they are, meet in Murphy" (213). Wylie is said to have come "a little closer to Murphy" (90), as have Mr. Kelly and Neary. While Mr. Kelly had been characterized in the beginning of the narrative as the punctual, calculating man of scientific knowledge, he slowly begins to be described by sentences used for Murphy. Neary also comes to know Murphy's predicament of being and loses his ability to mediate.

However, it is not only Murphy who is the go-between (32), leaving his traces on other characters, and further confusing both his and their borders. Anticipating the descriptive logic of permutations and interchange-ability of the *nouveau roman,* all names lose fixity and become events, ephemeral and transitional moments in the passage of being. Tickle-penny is said to have "certain points . . . in common with Neary" (89), notably a "fear of going mad" (89) and "the inability to look on" (89). Neary comes to repeat the same sentences uttered by Wylie. Even more macroscopic is the case of Rosie Dew. Like many of Beckett's later char-acters who become contiguous with the objects they use, Rosie has incor-porated her disease and her dog. She now looks like a cyborg of "a duck, or a stunted penguin" (102), and a dachshund.

Loss of distinction, however, also occurs in the novel without synec-dochic contagion. Ticklepenny is the poet and nonpoet, the rapist and the raped, the homosexual and the heterosexual. The behavior of Miss Counihan is described in its patterns of oscillatory alternation: "cruel, kind, cruel and kind" (55). Celia is a whore, but one who is also, as her name suggests, a celestial madonna. Miss Carridge, Celia's and Murphy's new landlady, is well known for her aversion to bathing, yet this trait does not prevent her from appearing one day "thoroughly scoured and anointed in every nook and corner, rashly glowing with the sense of being what she called 'pristine'" (132). The "old-boy," the upstairs tenant in Miss Carridge's house, is described as ceaselessly mobile, but toward the end of the novel achieves complete stasis by committing suicide. Cooper, whose face is an icon of the surrealist overimage—"irresolution, revul-sion, doglike devotion, catlike discretion, fatigue, hunger, thirst and re-serves of strength" (205)—never sits down or takes off his hat, but in the novel's last scene does both. Even state officials and service employees are subject to crisscrossing. In a London street of the 1930s is an unlikely "policewoman" (86), while the work force of the mental hospital is com-posed of several "male sister(s)" (158), including Bom, "younger twin and dead spit of Bim" (165). Here also works a physician, Dr. Fist, a curious hybrid of specialties and "more philosophical than medical" (88).

Yet the world at large, Murphy included, has little tolerance for this state of being and desperately seeks an alethic, scientific knowledge. Mr. Kelly urges Celia to end her relationship with Murphy, who, Godot-like, cannot be categorized in the who and the what, but exists as an irreduc-ible particular: "Murphy was Murphy" (17). Murphy himself is attempting to escape contradictions. In the first pages of the novel, we learn that he has been studying in Cork to learn what his teacher Neary, who was at that time a Koffkian gestaltist[61] and a Pythagorean, calls "Apmonia" (3). This is a mediation of opposites, also known as "isonomy" or "attunement" (4). It consists of stopping the ebb and the flow of the heart. Neary's teachings, however, are to no avail. Murphy has "an irrational heart" (3), prone to seize one moment and burst the next. Even Neary's second strategy of appeasement—the "tetrakyt," the "short circuit" of "love requited" (5)—whereby the beloved functions as "the single, brilliant, organized, compact blotch in the tumult of heterogeneous stimulation" (6)—proves to be as unsuccessful as the first. So, to find respite from the discriminations of "Zion's antipodes" (78), Murphy has developed a palliative of his own. Since he is convinced that such landscape might reside in his mind, in that "Amor intellectualis quo Murphy se ipso amat" (107), he minimizes the contacts with the physical world by confining himself to a dark room and quieting his body by strapping it to a chair. A more detailed description of this process occurs in chapter six. To be sure, it might initially appear that Murphy has reached a state of nonmetaphysical bliss, since in the third area of the mind there are no distinctions: "The third, the dark, was a flux of forms, a perpetual coming together and falling asunder of forms . . . neither elements nor states, nothing but forms becoming and crumbling into the fragments of a new becoming. Here there was nothing but commotion and the pure forms of commotion. Here he was not free, but a mote in the dark of absolute freedom. He did not move, he was a point in the ceaseless unconditioned generation and passing away of line. Matrix of surds." (112)

Such existence, however, clearly depends on a Cartesian gesture of reduction, and, not surprisingly, this novel has earned precisely this epithet,[62] although *Murphy* is more a critique[63] of Cartesianism than a rehearsal of it. In other words, if Murphy's retreat is motivated by a desire to reach a zone where neither "good and bad" (108) nor "right forms and wrong forms" (108) exist, it is achieved by a suppression of the physical aspect of being and thereby ends by reproducing metaphysical structures. This explains why the narrator observes that if Murphy was not "involve(d) in the idealistic tar," (108) his mind activity was nonetheless a "little dungeon in Spain" (180), a "Belacqua fantasy" (78), and an ultimate failure: "How should he tolerate, let alone cultivate the occasion of fiasco, having once beheld the beatific idols of his cave? In the beautiful Belgo-Latin of Arnold Guelincx: *Ubi nihil vales, ibi nihil velis*" (178), where the allusion refers to the well-known occasionalist and follower of Descartes.[64]

The metaphysical fantasy of Murphy unfolds throughout the rest of the novel as he becomes the object of the remaining characters' quest for a singularity of form: "The eternal tautology" (41) of privative oppositions, the either or, yes or no. Murphy's girlfriend, Celia, seeks to reduce him to a bourgeois episteme. She has abandoned her profession as whore and now pushes him to earn a living. To use the words uttered by her grandfather, Mr. Kelly, Celia is attempting to contain Murphy in the alethic frame of "who, what, where, by what means, why, in what way and when" (17). To avoid losing her, Murphy has agreed to settle into a new life and, following the horoscope prepared by Suk, is now in London. Dressed in a suit made of a material that does not allow his vapors to escape, he walks the street, apparently in search of a job. In addition to Celia, three more characters engage in a communal quest for Murphy: Miss Counihan, Wylie, and Neary, who also has hired Cooper as the official detective. Miss Counihan thinks that Murphy is already economically well established and pursues him for the large fortune he supposedly is amassing. Neary and Wylie, both in love with Miss Counihan, see in Murphy their rival.

Singularity of form, however, is revealed to be a fantasy. The metamorphic plot sequence of the novel explodes the identity of the objects and subjects involved in the chase and, in the terminology of Derrida's *La vérité en peinture*, probes the rigidity of frames by "parergonality."[65] For example, while Neary and Wylie seek the same rival, they nonetheless describe the object of their chase differently. Neary sees Murphy's fidelity and economic success as the factors that give the latter an advantage, while Wylie feels it rests in Murphy's sexual prowess. Even the denotative finality of this trait, however, is undermined by the voice of the narrator. Weakening Wylie's statement on Murphy's "surgical quality" (62), he comments that "surgical" is "not quite the right word" (62). As the narrative progresses, the identity of the object of the quest becomes increasingly elusive. Neary stops regarding Murphy as a rival and begins instead to look for him as a lost friend. Further, Neary himself slowly changes from being the subject of a quest to its object: "His problem was not only how to find Murphy, but how to find him without being found himself by Ariadne née Cox" (116). Shortly thereafter, Needle Wylie no longer appears to need to outdo Murphy as his rival, since he is now sharing his famed "oyster kiss" (117) with Miss Counihan. Celia, who has become more and more like Murphy, is steadily losing her desire to mold her companion into a bourgeois form. In the midst of exploding frames, the pattern of the alliances between the questers and the location of the quest itself becomes subjected to additional shifts. In his latest *"voltefesse"* (200), Neary double-crosses Wylie and Miss Counihan. Wylie betrays Neary, and Miss Counihan asks Cooper—who initially had been hired by Neary—to follow her directions only. Moreover, since Cooper has discovered where Celia lives, the quest shifts from the search for Murphy in London to that of Celia in Brewery Road. In one last commentary by "parergonality," the quest pattern changes configuration again. Neary is now in love with Celia and regards Murphy as a rival. In short, as Leslie Hill has argued cogently in *Beckett's Fiction in Different Words*, "Whichever way one looks, the same logic of paradox, inversion, chiasmus and oxymoron undermines the foundations of meaning, stripping them of stability and coherence. Oppositions are set up to be subverted, convergences established only to diverge again" (18).

Meanwhile, Murphy has found employment at the hospital M.M.M. The hospital's building is located outside the contradiction of life at large, "on the boundary of the countries" (156), and it is full of padded, insulated cells. The job itself has brought Murphy close to beings who have "that self-immersed indifference to the contingencies of the contingent world" (169) that he seeks, and more particularly to Mr. Endon. True to his name (Greek for the preposition "within"), Mr. Endon is immersed in a complete state of self-enclosure. Murphy is very pleased with his new condition; he begins to lose connection with being and ultimately surrenders to metaphysical desire. The turning point, as critics have argued,[66] is the episode of the game of chess (243–44), an activity traditionally associated with symmetry, foundations, logic, and, within Beckett's signifying economy, removed from life. Murphy, who plays white, loses to Endon's black at the forty-third move. Shortly thereafter, the images of the macrocosm abandon his thoughts: "Then this also faded and Murphy began to see nothing . . . the absence (to abuse a nice distinction) not of *percipere* but of *percipi*" (246).

Beckett's world, however, does not admit of reduction and proceeds to dismantle Murphy's endeavor by a powerful narrative return of the repressed, a return of that primeval irreducibility of being that Murphy wished to escape. Murphy has chosen a garret as living quarters. This is a space ideally separated from the rest of the compound, with just a small skylight and a bed conducive to the immobility he seeks. Unaware of a gas leak (the word "gas," the narrator reminds us, derives from "chaos"—"gas would be chaos, and chaos gas" [175]), Murphy explodes. The explosion not only represents the Abderite's guffaws at the follies of Murphy,[67] but serves as the gateway to other laughters. Indeed, the body that Murphy had sought to transcend becomes instrumental in the identification of his cadaver. Since the coroner can establish the "how" of death but not the "who" (261), he summons the entire group of questers, and Celia recognizes Murphy by a birthmark on his charred buttocks. The fate of the ashes themselves further confirm one of the novel's "truths," specifically that "The syndrome known as life is too diffuse to admit of palliation. For every symptom that is eased, another is made worst" (200). In a British pub, Cooper becomes prey to a fit of anger and throws the packet of Murphy's ashes to a stranger. By the end of the day, they are scattered with the rest of the pub's refuse and rejoin, as does the brain of Céline's Courtial des Pereires from *Mort*, the heterotopic mess of the world: "the sand, the beer, the butts, the glass, the matches, the spits, the vomit" (275). The novel closes with Celia who has returned to her profession and is now wheeling Mr. Kelly to a park, where he intends to fly a kite. The string, however, snaps, and the kite disappears into the sky while the rangers urge everybody to depart: "All out. All out "(281). Celia begins toiling up the hill on a narrow path, conscious now that there are no shortcuts before being, that life cannot be controlled and enclosed into the singularity of one, self-identical form: "There was no shorter way home" (282).

Beckett's Tropes

In addition to lifting the structuralist bar by way of subtle metaphoric and metonymic signifying processes, Beckett's "English works" also do so by a

language of defiant paradigmatic declinations and paratactic cumula-
tions. Gilles Deleuze has quite aptly defined it as the *"langue I"* — that is,
a linguistic expression that is "atomized, disjunctive, broken, choppy,
where enumeration replaces propositions, where combination replaces
syntax: in short, a language of names."[68] Pervasive throughout Beckett's
"English period," *"langue I"* engenders the most daring forms of verbal
experimentation. At the threshold of the texts, the titles emerge already as
propagations from other works. The title of *Dream* is a composite of
Tennyson's *Dream of Fair Women*, Henry Williamson's *The Dream of Fair
Women* (1922) and even, as its epigraph illustrates, of Geoffrey Chaucer's
Legend of Good Women. *More Pricks than Kicks* is a variation on a sentence heard by Saint Paul in Acts IX of the Bible: "It is hard for thee to
kick against the pricks." Even the title of *Murphy* cannot escape the graft-
ing logic since it refers to the "Eumaeus" chapter of *Ulysses*, Ovid's *Metamorphosis*, Plato's *Republic*, and even suggests more mundane references
to the chess player Paul Morphy and the inventor of the fold-up bed,
William L. Murphy.[69] The texts themselves emerge as an additional multiplication of tissues. Because *Dream* alternates theoretical notes on the
novel with representations of Belacqua over time and across the social
and amorous milieus of Dublin, Vienna, and Paris, it is a cyborg of theory
and fiction. Thus, it includes the larger frames of romance, the *Bildungsroman*, and the novel of manners. This macroscopic cumulation of heterogeneous narrative speech is doubled in the chapters and is manifested
at the level of syntax and even single word units. Here it creates an almost
complete absence of tonal and stylistic consistency; one comparable, as
Richard Coe has argued, to Raymond Queneau's *Exercices de style*.[70]

There are five chapters of *Dream*. Their lengths vary widely, from one-
paragraph to half of the novel, and bear the sequential, open-ended titles
of "One," "Two," "Und," "Three," "And." The sections themselves are a
montage of literary models, a pastiche of nomination resulting in a cultural entropy more akin to that of the late Flaubert than to the mastery of
Joyce.[71] The hawthorn imagery of "One," for example, recalls Proust,
even if the outcome of the story in excremental matter is far removed
from all lyricism. "Two" begins with a description, cast in a third narrative
voice, of Belacqua's nostalgia for Smeraldina-Rima but moves to a
memory of childhood prayers akin to the stream of consciousness of
Stephen Daedalus from Joyce's *A Portrait*: "God bless dear Daddy . . .

Mummy Johnny Bibby . . . and all that I love and make me a good boy for
Jesus Christ sake Amen" (8). The section also includes a theoretical note,
a Chinese fable counterpointed by reflections in the first person, and a
description of Smeraldina. This description develops as a parody of the
theory of "ananké," voiced by Taine in his 1853 *Essais sur les fables de la
Fontaine*: "Milieu, race, family, structure, temperament, past and present
and consequent and antecedent back to the first combination" (12–13). In
an increased movement of definitional expenditure, more memories of
childhood in the early Joycean style are linked to a French sonnet written
by Lucien, a line of troubadour poetry (23), and a famous *"terzina"* from
Dante's second canto of *Inferno* III, where Virgil admonishes Charon for
not wanting to ferry the Pilgrim across the River Acheron: "Vuolsi così
colà dove si puote ciò che si vuole, e più non dimandare" (37) [Thus it is
willed where everything may be, simply if it is willed. Therefore, oblige,
and ask no more]. Similar examples multiply throughout the section. In
a further itinerary across speeches, characters from Laclos' 1782 epistolary
novel *Les liaisons dangereuses* stand side by side with verses from Jean de
Meun's thirteeenth-century continuation of Guillaume de Lorris's *Roman de la rose*, which are said to be cited, however, by the imaginary
avant-gardist writer Jean du Chas: "toutes êtes, serez ou fûtes, De fait ou
de volonté, putes, Et qui bien vous chercheroit, Toutes putes vous
trouveroit . . . " (52) [In body or spirit, you are, you will be, or you were
whores, and whomever will know you well, will find you to be all
whores]. More third-person narration follows and is juxtaposed with another Joycean passage of stream of consciousness, albeit in the later, vi-
sionary mode of the "Circe" section of *Ulysses* (77 ff.). "Und" is just as
protean, including as it does theoretical notes, sections of reported
speech and "paraphrased abrégé" (117) [paraphrased summary], allusions
to Balzac and Jane Austen, Greek mythology, references to the setting of
Manzoni's *Promessi sposi*, Dante's *Inferno* V, and so on. "Three" juxtaposes a conversation between the Polar Bear and Alba on the subject of
Belacqua written as a dramatic scene, allusions to Louise Labé, Homeric
descriptions of the dusk, Ronsard's numerous sixteenth-century poems
on the rose, and two dream narrations. The sustained form of literary
Latin is also a constant element and makes its presence felt in expressions
such as "credo quia absurdum, ut intelligam" (39), "Pinus puella quon-
dam fuit" (23), or in precepts from the Decalogue: "signo crucis se

munire . . . Virginem . . . angelum custodem" (52). *More Pricks than Kicks*
derives, of course, from *Dream* and therefore proposes the stylistic
defiance of the latter. However, it appears to be fraught with even more
allusions to Dante and Joyce. Numerous passages suggests the *"flânerie"*
of Bloom in Dublin, and in "What a misfortune" there is a reference to
Mina Purefoy's triplets from *Ulysses*. *Murphy* alludes to the Old and New
Testaments; Balzac; Lord Chesterfield; Campanella; Higgins; Hugo;
Malraux; Milton; Rimbaud; Shelley; Wordsworth; Proust's, or rather,
Swann's cattleyas; and much more.

Besides this unstructured use of the literary intertext, these works,
much like the novels penned by Gadda and Céline, do not shy away from
linking a variety of other registers in a compendium of codes contained in
numerous European national languages and varieties of English. In this
sense, they offer ample confirmation of the self-reflexive commentary by
the narrator of *Dream* as one who can't "spigot the faucet and throttle the
cock, the cockwash, and cut the cackle" (168). Among the other codes of
Dream, for example, is a vast terminology drawn from scientific jargon, as
illustrated by terms such as "calisthenic" (13), "cerebro-hygienic (13), "he-
patic colics" (61). In addition to the elevated vocabulary of medicine,
Murphy also makes extensive use of the idioms of astrology, alludes to the
astronomers Adams and Herschel, and Gestalt psychology, as well as the
philosophies of Campanella, Democritus, Descartes, Leibnitz, Hegel,
and William of Champeaux. Both texts also abound in expressions
decodable only with a dictionary of art history. In *Murphy*, there are sustained allusions to the painters Avercamp, Bellini, Parmigiano, Tin-
toretto, Vermeer, and the sculptors Barlach, Phidias, Puget, Scopas, and
Watts. *Dream* often uses these artists' work to describe the bodies of its
female characters. Syra-Cusa's is said to be a compound of "Brancusi
bird," with "the Bilitis breasts" (33), and the "Primavera buttocks" (50).
Analogously, the Countess of Parabimbi honors the Frica using the jargon of classical Italian fine art. Hence, Frica is "Sistine" and "a positive
gem of ravished Quattrocento" (216). Among less elevated codes, often
comically linked to the higher ones, *Dream* contains personal letters in
French from queers; missives in broken English from heterosexual lovers;
French advertisements for apartments; obituaries in "horrid Latin"; English commercials for corsets; and oral and obscene jargon derived from
French, English, Italian, and Spanish sources. For example, "One,"

which deals with the fantasies of the younger Belacqua, begins by way of an archaic form, but ends with American-English colloquialisms: "Behold Belacqua, an overfed child pedalling . . . after Findlater's van . . . till he cruise alongside of the hoss. Whip him up, vanman, flickem, flapem, collop-wallop fat Sambo. Stiffly . . . the tail arches for a gush of mard. Ah . . . !" (1). Elsewhere, the oral code of English is suggested in the speakers' abbreviations, such as "Lav on the lef. Won't be a sec. Mind the bike. Mind the skis" (73), or in words and sentences that reproduce the sounds of speech at the cost of proper spelling, such as "pewer" (18), "wunnerful" (24), "Gawd" (161), and "Belacqua laffed and laffed" (37). French argot also makes its appearance, in expressions such as "Ça n'existe pas" (49) [It's unreal]. Emotive and obscene expressions in numerous languages also abound. The pages are often counterpointed by "Hah!" (62) and "Ooooaaah" (9), and other interjectional signs such as aposiopesis and exclamation points. They also include French and German dilation of syllables, as in "Amourr" (50), "je veux pââââlir" (72), and "Gnnnädiges Fräulein" (132); the Italian interjection "*Macché*" (129); and the swearwords "*chiappate*" (50) and "Be off, *puttanina*" (51), the Spanish "*cojonazos*" (209), and so forth. The jewel of such hybridization is to be found in "Two," where a letter from Smeraldina to Belacqua casts the Germanic, oral pronunciation of English phonemes in a written style. It is illustrated in sentences such as "I have read it ofer and ofer again" (55), and "I had allso a letter from a man who asked me . . . to dance . . . I sopose I will go, I know my beloved dosent mind" (57). In the description of Belacqua's visit to Smeraldina in Vienna that follows the above missive, the English text also becomes infected by Germanic syntactic inversion of the auxiliary verb in compound tenses: "here she comes advancing up the railway-platform like a Gozzi-Epstein, careful not to lose the platform ticket that yet ten Pfenige cost had . . . " (65). A residue of *Dream*'s broken German can also be found in *Murphy*, where Dr. Fist advises Ticklepenny to "Giff de pooze ub or go kaputt" (88). Mirroring the heteroglossia of the "chest," Beckett also links Gaelic and argotic expressions to horoscopes, telegrams, visiting cards, and even a schemata for the configuration of the chess pieces after Endon's "*Zwei-springerspott*" move.

This complex pastiche of codes is increased by the inclusion of visual effects of symbolization. *Dream* reproduces musical notations and abounds in heterogeneous typefaces. Not only are entire sentences italicized and words shortened, as in "P.B." for "the Polar Bear" (27), but they are randomly capitalized, as in "That I onely know ONE THING and that is that I LOVE YOU AND I AM ALLWAYS YOUR SMERRY and that is the thing that matters the most in our life YOU LOVE ME AND ARE ALLWAYS MY BEL" (58). In addition to a variable use of typefaces, spacing is also a favorite device to disturb visual homogeneity. Often *Dream* appears to the eye as a montage of documents, particularly when the page reproduces the borders and the divisions commonly employed in letter writing and postscripts, stage directions, and lyrical poetry. Yet, it can also give this appearance without respecting any of these motivating conventions, as the location of words is often defamiliarized by being set off from the rest of the text and centered in the middle of the page. It can also be written by periodizing and capitalization as in the case of "S.M.E.R.A.L.D.I.N.A.-R.I.M.A." (82), or by hyphenation, aposiopesis, and periodization, as in "Con . . . stan-ti-no.pel." (82). Analogously, *Murphy* also uses effects of capitalization, italicization, and abbreviations. The Magdalen Mental Mercyseat is often called "M.M.M.," the word "music" capitalized and even enlarged to occupy two lines of typespace (236). This high degree of experimentation infiltrates all the elements of the text and the "incontinence of . . . poliloquy" (195) shapes even the smaller units of words. *Murphy* is a rich plethora of word plays. These may include puns, as when Murphy asks Celia "Why did the barmaid champagne?" and replies "Because the stout porter bitter." (139), or refers to a dog in heat as a "hot dog" (102). Double-entendres are also common. The speeches of Neary and Wylie are often fraught with risqué sexual connotations, as in the case of "love requited . . . a ball that gave rise to a sparkling rally" (5). Other times, language is unsettled by redefinition and/or distortion of familiar expressions, as is the case of "God blast you" (7), "Romiet" and "Juleo" (86), the "divine flatus" (89). Such deformation almost always has comic overtones, as in the case of the "truant sphincters" (167) polluting the air of the M.M.M., and the milk referred to as "cowjuice" (83). *Dream* presents even more extreme forms of poliloquy. Its most commonly employed grammatical construction is the coordination, or what a self-reflexive commentary calls the "dumb-bell phrase" (27). Much like Gadda's spiraling periods, this is a sentence that unsettles the stability of meaning by spinning out chaotic, paradigmatic enumerations. At work throughout the text, it molds the construction of numerous passages, such as "He felt queasy from all the rubbing and pawning and petting and nuzzling" (107), or "And all day it was dancing and singing and music and douches and frictions and bending and stretching and classes" (13–14).[72] Single words do not escape the force of the expressive link, and *Dream* is a rich container of neologic formations by explicit or implicit hyphenation. Not only are proper nouns often the sum of two, as in the case of "Smeraldina-Rima," "Syra-Cusa," "Polar Bear," but adjectives and common nouns are equally subject to the compounding logic. The result is a wealth of neologic formation of the like of "slobbery-blubbery" (84), "Smeraldinalgia" (5), "reliefhilarity," (67) "vomitdribble" (67), and "thighjoy" (71). The apex of such linking is reached toward the end of the novel. Here, on a rainy Christmas in Dublin, a Leipzig prostitute condenses in one sentence the rite of passage of the early Beckett by thundering at Belacqua the following parody of the *Wake*'s omnipotent Word of God: "Himmisacrakrüzidirkenjesusmariaundjosefundblütigeskreuz" (239).

In summary, then, far from consisting merely of derivative modernist work, Samuel Beckett's thirties production represents an important theoretical and fictional departure from modernist discursive practices. The essay *Proust* clearly locates Beckett's interest on those passages of *A la recherche* where a complex and changing referent elicits a figural formulation. This formulation is identified in the essay "Dante . . . Bruno . Vico . . Joyce" as a writing based upon a productive extension of metaphors and metonymies, akin to Vico's conceptualization of poetry. In the essays collected in *Disjecta*, this writing is distinguished from late modernist endeavors and is aligned with the transitory and revisionary logic of the avant-garde, whose influence on Beckett is amply documented. Against this background, the fictions of the "English period" emerge as texts that, in both discourse and style, depart from modernist representational assumptions to move toward the horizon of postmodernity.

5

POSTPONING A CONCLUSION . . .

Through the exploration of works by Céline, Beckett, and
Gadda, I have suggested that the fiction of the 1930s is much
more than an example of belated or weakened modernism,
as the critical tradition unfortunately suggests. When discussed in the light of its real achievement, it anticipates the
plural, ambiguous rhetorical formations available to the second, postmodern half of the century.

To be sure, thirties fiction originates at the point where
modernism begins. This is a point where a figural rhetoric
articulates the wane of traditional certainties brought about
by the sociopolitical and cultural developments of modernization: the disestablishing of communal societies for urban
and isolated forms of life, the end of slower-paced economic
organizations for ever-accelerating modes of capitalist production, and the reinterpretation of nineteenth-century beliefs and practices by Heinseberg, Marx, Nietzsche, and
Freud.

Yet if we are to retain a sense of historicity, it is important
to recall that modernist art, despite its ambiguities and paradoxes, despite its chaos and fragmentation, also seeks an order above the spatial and temporal intricacies of experience.
To reprise McFarlane, "the defining thing in the Modernist
mode is not so much that things fall *apart* but that they fall
together (recalling appropriately the derivation of 'symbol'

from *symballein*, to throw together). In Modernism, the center is seen as exerting not a centrifugal but a centripetal force; and the consequence is not disintegration but (as it were) superintegration."[1] It is precisely this lack of a centripetal, integrative desire that is the force that propels the thirties' writings of Céline, Gadda, and Beckett to decenter the formal and thematic order sought by literary modernism. This is a decenterment that will deploy itself in a variety of strategies. Through the character of Ferdinand, Céline's *Voyage au bout de la nuit* (1932) and *Mort à crédit* (1936) inscribe an apprenticeship novel into the fallen state of language affecting most particularly the words of the father. Gadda's *La meccanica* (1928) and *La cognizione del dolore* (1938–41) opt for a parodic and, at times, even tragic reversal of modernist metaphysical quests to order the self and the self's relation to the world. The same could be said of Beckett's *Dream of Fair to Middling Women* (1932), *More Pricks than Kicks* (1934), and *Murphy* (1938). The subversive intent of these authors, however, is by no means limited to narrativized critiques, but doubles in discursive practices tolerant of the ambiguity and open-endedness of our twentieth-century experience of the world. To tell it with Krysinski, as in the case of the metatexts of Broch and Musil, the critique of language of thirties' fiction is always accompanied by an affirmative praxis: "The *ethos* of Viennese writing . . . presupposes an overcoming of negative categories and it is founded on the creative postulate of an artistic language that would be truthful, apophatic and dialectic beyond petrified negativities. *Sprachkritik* presupposes *Sprachpraxis*. The . . . metatext is a sort of therapeutic semiosis of language and novelistic discourse."[2] Because of this double gesture of *Sprachkritik* and *Sprackpraxis*, the thirties' endeavors of Céline, Gadda, and Beckett, configure a broader, transnational evolution and genealogy for European art: a transitional space between a fading modernist vision and an emerging postmodernist sensibility.

If the texts themselves remain, as they rightly should, the undisputed exhibits of a thirties' emergence, a final reference to their belated reception further witnesses the presence of an anticipatory, albeit often unacknowledged, potential.

In *La Force des choses*,[3] Simone de Beauvoir recounts how, just before the war, Nathalie Sarraute had sent *Tropismes* to Jean-Paul Sartre. Despite its merits, the book received no critical attention at the time of its appearance. Then, in 1957, the Minuit publishing house decided to re-print it in the context of the *nouveau roman*. This decision proved to be a timely one, and both Sarraute and *Tropismes* finally received their well-deserved recognition.

The fate of Sarraute's thirties' work was shared by Gadda, Céline, and, partially, Beckett. Despite the fact that, by 1946, Gadda had almost com-pleted his oeuvre, it was only in 1957 that he reached a wider audience with *Quer pasticciaccio brutto de via Merulana*. The interest generated by this novel prompted the publisher Einaudi to reprint *La cognizione del dolore* in 1963. In the course of that same year, the narrative of Gonzalo Pirobutirro won the prestigious *Prix international de littérature* held in the city of Corfú. As in the case of Sarraute's *Tropismes*, this was a novel written at a much earlier time. Yet it began to attract interest only in the fifties and sixties. The Italian cultural scene was, at that point, undergo-ing rapid changes. The widespread success of Tomasi di Lampedusa's *Il Gattopardo* (1958) made it apparent that the long parenthesis of "neo-realism" was closed. Lampedusa's novel no longer conveyed the beliefs that had been at the center of the neorealist endeavor—that is, the faith that the moral, political, and social problems of the Italian cultural com-munity could be resolved in and by narrative. Unlike Vittorini's *Uomini e no* (1945), or Pavese's *Compagno* (1947), for example, *Il Gattopardo* showed no faith in the progress of humanity and history. On the contrary, by representing the fall of an aristocratic Sicilian family against the back-ground of the events leading to the unification of Italy, it textualized a vision of life as irreducible decay and anarchy. Last but not least, *Il Gattopardo* also departed from the documentary types of writing that had been preeminent in the years of neorealism. The style of the novel was the product of a contamination of nineteenth-and twentieth-century lit-erary models. While the careful reconstruction of an epoch owed much to the codes of traditional historical fiction, the attention paid to the psy-chological analysis of characters and the nonlinear, noncausal develop-ment of the plot were indebted to modernist practices. This stylistic con-tamination explains the appeal of the novel for the neo-avant-gardes of the 1960s, particularly that of the *Gruppo 63*. Founded by a younger gen-eration of poets, narrators, and critics, including Umberto Eco, Giorgio Manganelli, Edoardo Sanguineti, and Luigi Malerba, *Gruppo 63* had mounted a poignant critique of neorealism on the basis of its uncritical adoption of the language of nineteenth-century bourgeois realism. As the work of Eco on the subject makes clear, for the neo-avant-garde, authentic ideological resistance and social protest could occur only in experimental writings: "we had to call into question the grand system [of bourgeois society] by means of a critique of the superstructural dimension that directly concerned us and could easily be administered by our group. Hence we decided to set up a debate about language. We became convinced . . . that to renew forms of communication and destroy established methods would be an effective and far-reaching platform for criticizing— that is, overturning—everything that those cultural forms expressed."[4]

In the context of a changing cultural climate, the neo-avant-gardists as well as other emerging artists began to look for models to legitimize their departure from neorealist premises. Among the favorite foreign authors were Jack Kerouac, Saul Bellow, Gunther Grass, Jorge Luis Borges, García Marquez and the French *nouveaux romanciers.* To the latter, Italo Calvino dedicated much attention by publishing several essays in which he discussed, at length, the vision informing novels by Butor, Robbe-Grillet, Sarraute, and others.[5] Also worthy of mention is *Il Verri*, a journal associated with the neo-avant-gardist *Gruppo 63*, which issued a special volume dedicated to the new novel in 1959.

The reorientation in taste that was occurring in Italy during the fifties and sixties also brought about the (re)discovery of Italian writers who had been neglected in the past. Gadda was a case in point. Not only did his radical practice of expressionism and pastiche fail to conform to the neorealist model, but, in a 1950 essay, Gadda had voiced one of the most poignant critiques of the cultural practices of neorealism. The piece, entitled "Un opinione sul neorealismo," argued that the crudely objectifying [*crudamente obbiettivante*] writings of neorealism remained incapable of articulating that which his oeuvre had always pursued: "le meravigliose ambiguità di ogni umana cognizione" [the marvelous ambiguities of every form of human knowledge].[6]

Hence, Gadda's works became important points of reference for a number of writers. During the sixties, these included newly emerging practitioners of expressionism such as Bianciardi, Mastronardi, and Pizzuto. Luciano Bianciardi's *La vita agra* (1962) as well as Lucio Mastronardi's *Il maestro di Vigevano* (1962) and *Il meridionale di Vigevano* (1963) revealed a pastiche of national idioms and dialects similar to that of

Gadda's *La cognizione* and *Quer pasticciaccio*. Gaetano Pizzuto, in his attempt to find a form to accommodate a view of reality as an on-going process of constant transformation and change, also drew upon the models developed by Gadda. This affiliation was revealed in the style of Pizzuto's *Ravenna* (1962) and *Paginette* (1964), in which a daring, almost "heuristic" use of grammatical and syntactical forms becomes an effective rhetorical device to suggest a lack of determination and closure.

However, the influence of Gadda has proven to be crucial even to those authors who have not engaged directly in expressionistic practices. These include Umberto Eco and Italo Calvino, arguably the nation's most eminent postmodern authors. Both Calvino and Eco have questioned the ability of novelistic discourse to order reality. While Eco has structured two of his three best-selling novels, *The Name of the Rose* and *Foucault's Pendulum*, in the genre of the anti-detective practiced by Gadda, Calvino's *Se una notte d'inverno un viaggiatore* (1979) and *Palomar* (1985) share Gadda's view of a world so complex as to exceed all representational models that would try to define it.

Today Gadda's name is frequently mentioned not only in relation to Eco and Calvino but also in connection with the contemporary generation of Italian novelists. This is a generation that has emerged in the recent cultural context of the 1980s and '90s and includes writers such as Gesualdo Bufalino, Vincenzo Consolo, Aldo Busi, Sebastiano Vassalli, Pier Vittorio Tondelli, and Stefano Benni.[7] Bufalino's *La diceria dell'untore* (1981), and Consolo's *Lunaria* (1985) and *Retablo* (1987) often have been described as baroque novels. Their pluralinguism and pastiche is the rhetorical outcome of an epistemological will to represent the multiple realities existing at the margins of history and its official discourse. Likewise, Busi, Tondelli, and Benni, provide a dissenting, polemical perspective on the world through a sophisticated manipulation of the Italian linguistic patrimony. Benni's *Comici spaventati guerrieri* (1986) seems to be particularly close to the Gaddian text. Compared by critics to Gadda's *Quer pasticciaccio*,[8] this is a novel that juxtaposes the specialized idioms of advertising, consumerism, and the elevated jargon of academia with a wealth of archaisms and neologisms. In short, like the writers associated with the neo-avant-garde of *Gruppo 63*, today's Italian novelists also confirm the crucial role Gadda played by having provided a historical model for alternative forms of conceiving literary discourse.

The case of Céline's reception has been somewhat different from that of Sarraute and Gadda, but has nonetheless seen the same end results. The publication of *Voyage au bout de la nuit* certainly did not go unnoticed, and the novel's thematic and stylistic transgressions generated a scandal in French literary circles in 1932. Yet, because Céline's pamphlets had branded him as an anti-Semite and therefore a politically compromised author, his work was, for many years, consigned to oblivion. From the fifties onwards, however, his name began to resurface. In 1953, in *Writing Degree Zero*, Roland Barthes mentioned Céline in connection with the poststructuralist polemic against the premises of formal and epistemological authority of normative French.[9] Barthes' work prompted Julia Kristeva to tread along analogous "Célinian" paths. Kristeva first mentioned Céline in a collection of essays from 1969 to 1977[10] and then dedicated a longer treatment to Céline's work in *Powers of Horror*.[11] Critics of the *nouveau roman*, such as Michel Jean-Bloch,[12] also began to indicate the possibility of connections between Céline's figural practices and those of Robbe-Grillet and other "new novelists." In 1972, with the publication of a special issue of *Cahier de l'Herne*, the importance of Céline was firmly established for the contemporary French novel. Moreover, the journal also included documents from Jack Kerouac and Henry Miller, thereby suggesting how Céline's influence extended far beyond France to encompass the larger group of American writers from the "beat generation."[13] The impact of Céline's work on American authors has been most recently reassessed by critics. Drawing upon Georges Brassaï's memoir *Henry Miller: grandeur nature*, Alice Kaplan has revisited the events surrounding the publication of Miller's *Tropic of Cancer*.[14] Miller, who was in Paris in 1932, had completed the manuscript of *Tropic* and was trying to find a publisher for it. However, reading Céline's *Voyage au bout de la nuit* made such a lasting impression that he rewrote *Tropic*, which he then published two years later, in 1934. Throughout the thirties and forties Miller remained an active supporter of Céline, trying to rescue the politically compromised writer from critical oblivion. However, mirroring the outcome of the French cultural scene, Miller's endorsement of Céline remained an isolated phenomenon. It was only in the fifties that Céline's reputation among the younger "beat" writers, including Burroughs, Ginsberg, and Kerouac, began to be established. Like Kerouac, Burroughs and Ginsberg publicly acknowledged the role of Céline in providing them with a model to counter the ossified structures of the American literary establishment.[15] In the sixties, Céline's reputation continued to grow and would crystallize in the 1965 anthology *Black Humor*.[16] Here excerpts from Céline's *Voyage* appeared next to today's best-known postmodern practitioners: Thomas Pynchon, John Barth, and Joseph Heller. Implicitly, then, the turn in the American reception of the fifties and sixties confirmed George Steiner's famous reminder[17] that moral standards are often independent of artistic greatness, that a politically compromised writer can have a fundamental role in shaping future literary endeavors. This is a reminder that is particularly pressing today, when in the 1990s context of ethnic and gender studies, the work of Céline again faces oblivion.[18] Yet, as I have previously argued, even though one cannot justify Céline's paranoid return, his pamphlets are an important, valuable warning against all facile celebration of postmodern plurality and ambiguity. Their presence reminds us of the imperative of negotiating "local," provisional truths in the absence of strong certainties and beliefs.

Samuel Beckett is, of course, a well-known, established author in all discussions of postmodern literature and, after Claude Mauriac's 1958 study—a study that placed Beckett in the context of the fiction of Robbe-Grillet, Sarraute, Leiris, and other *nouveaux romanciers*[19]—has become a staple figure for students of contemporary art. According to Breon Mitchell, Beckett's importance to the development of contemporary fiction "makes any discussion of Postmodernism which omits him seem pallid."[20] Nonetheless, despite the publication in 1992 of Samuel Beckett's ur-novel—the 1932 *Dream of Fair to Middling Women*— descriptive accounts of Samuel Beckett's postmodernism often tend to forget that later works such as *Molloy* (1951), *Malone meurt* (1952) and *L'innomable* (1953) hark back precisely to Beckett's *Dream*, and other lesser-known prewar fiction such as *More Pricks than Kicks* and *Murphy*. Much more than examples of belated modernism, these are works that decenter the narratives of Proust and Joyce from within while disclosing a new mode of conceiving of literary discourse analogous to that pursued by Gadda and Céline.

The fate of the reception of Beckett's work, like that of other thirties' writers, additionally points out the importance of learning how to read backwards—how to revisit the past from the vantage point of today—and, in a sense, realize through our critical endeavors, the understanding of art that these writers sought to suggest. If there is a fundamental message to be treasured from the work of Céline, Gadda, and Beckett, it is that narrative and its language no longer can claim the status of self-enclosed, atemporal objects, but emerge in an irreducible continuum of time and space.

I believe that this message can be extended to encompass the larger frame of literary history. After all, since no word is ever absolute and final, but always exists in a space of open-endedness and regress, we should continue to question our critical assumptions about the past and particularly the frames we employ to assign a meaning to it. If we are willing to do so, we might be able to engage our literature in a temporal and spatial dialogic relation with the words that have preceded it. Hopefully, we will be able to shed more light on our present linguistic and cultural consciousness and map not just one genealogy of postmodernity, such as the Céline, Gadda, and Beckett trio that I have proposed, but many of the "discursive events" that still stand unacknowledged behind the narrative possibilities that shaped the second half of the last century.

Notes

Introduction: An Archaeology of the 1930s

1. Foucault, *Archeology of Knowledge*, 26ff.

2. See, for example, the following representative titles: Gindin, *British Fiction in the Thirties*; Norman, *The Thirties*; Cunningham, *British Writers of the Thirties*; Randall Stevenson, *British Novel since the Thirties*; Green, *Fiction in the Historical Present*.

3. Sartre, *What Is Literature?*, 25.

4. Robbe-Grillet, *For a New Novel*, 15.

5. "Les textes qui composaient ce premier ouvrage étaient l'expression spontanée d'impressions très vives, et leur forme était aussi spontanée. . . . Ce sont des mouvements indéfinissables, qui glissent très rapidement aux limites de notre conscience. . . . Ils me paraissaient et me paraissent encore constituer la source secrète de notre existence" (Sarraute, *L'Ere du soupçon*, ii). Regrettably, the English version of this work, *The Age of Suspicion*, has omitted Sarraute's important statement.

6. Samuel Beckett, *The Unnamable*. In *Three Novels by Samuel Beckett*, 303.

7. It is well known that the explosion of the 1970s' and 1980s' debate on postmodernity often has tended toward the assimilation of the whole of twentieth-century art to its postmodernist half, with the concomitant result of flattening all distinctions between the writing practices of authors as diverse as Woolf and Borges, Proust and Nabokov, Svevo and Eco, to name just a few. For a sample of this reception, see Buccheri and Costa, eds., *Italo Svevo:*; Margaret Gray, *Postmodern Proust*; and Attridge and Ferrer, *Post-structuralist Joyce*.

8. From his early *Blindness and Insight* and *Allegories of Reading* to *Resistance to Theory*, Paul de Man has criticized interpretations focused on the authority vested in the symbol by romantic-symbolist aesthetics. Against Wasserman, M. H. Abrams, the New Critics, and present-day Gadamerian hermeneutics, de Man has valorized the allegorical element at the expense of the symbolic one—the latter also identified by him as metaphor, a term used with the connotation of conciliation and retotalization of antinomies and regress that are typical of the symbol. (For clarification on the issue of terminology, I recommend Culler, *Pursuit of Signs*, 194 ff.). Without denying the important insights that de Man's work has provided on the figural element traversing romantic and postromantic literature—an element that is often the source of much reconciliatory difficulty—I believe that this critic's excessive fastening on the problematic element has a flattening effect on literary history and ultimately cannot account for changes and developments in writing practices. For this reason, my approach is closer to the descriptive categories developed by Auerbach, Spitzer, and Lukács and followed most recently by Franco Moretti. In short, and like these critics, I will not deconstruct the modernist symbol for the figures but will observe the passage from the latter to the former.

1. Contextualizing Modernism

1. McFarlane, "Name and Nature of Modernism," 27. For additional discussion of the intersection between the process of socioeconomic development of modernization and cultural Modernism, compare also Callinicos, *Against Postmodernism*, 29ff.

2. Benjamin, "The Work of Art in the Age of Mechanical Reproduction," *Illuminations*, 222.

3. Panofsky, "Style and Medium," 96.

4. Compare also Bürger, *Decline of Modernism*, and *Theory of the Avant-garde*, 22, where the avant-garde's aim is defined as a "reintegrat[ion] of art into the praxis of life. Of interest is also the concept of the "*Verwindung*" of modernity proposed by Vattimo in the chapter "Art and Oscillation," from *The Transparent Society*, to describe the "new ontological-epochal opening" brought about by those weaker avant-gardist aesthetics of recollection of being as contradictory and transitory *Ereignis*. As in the case of Benjamin and Bürger, Vattimo locates the end of modernity within the orbit of the avant-gardist programs of eventuality and transitoriness. These programs are for Vattimo radically new since they represent a departure from the Aristotelian catharsis and the Hegelian congruity of inside and outside. Significantly, Vattimo builds his argument upon the concepts of aesthetic "*schock*" and "*Stoss*" developed in 1936 by Benjamin's "The Work of Art in the Age of Mechanical Reproduction" and Heidegger's "The Origin of the Work of Art." For a further treatment of these same issues, compare also Vattimo's "The End of (Hi)story, *Zeitgeist in Babel*, 132–41 and *The End of Modernity*.

5. Benjamin, "Surrealism," *Reflections*, 179.

6. Benjamin, "The Storyteller," *Illuminations*, 83–109. Compare also Panofsky,

who noted that with the invention of the cinematic sound-track, verbal practices became affected by a "principle of coexpressibility" ("Style and Medium in the Motion Pictures," 101).

7. Benjamin, *Origin of German Tragic Drama*. For additional discussion on the issue of the allegorical pluralization of meaning, compare also Benjamin's notion of linguistic hypernomination in "On Language as Such and on the Language of Man," *Reflections*, 314–32.

8. Benjamin, "Franz Kafka," *Illuminations*, 120.

9. Lyotard, *The Postmodern Condition: A Report on Knowledge*, 79.

10. Lyotard, "Rewriting Modernity," 25. I should observe, however, that Lyotard reformulates his previous understanding of the postmodern. Reflecting upon the recent introduction of technologies based upon laws of recognition, concept, and prediction, Lyotard comes to the conclusion that what we now call postmodernity is "the rewriting of some of the features claimed by modernity, and first of all modernity's claim to ground its legitimacy on the project of liberating humanity as a whole through science and technology" ("Rewriting Modernity," 34). Thereby, from the perspective of the present moment, postmodernity ought to be articulated as the repetition of the grounding, legitimizing metanarratives of modernity or, to reprise Lyotard's title, as a "rewriting (of) modernity." In addition to Lyotard, other critics have recently commented on the failures of postmodernism to bring about a qualitative break from the modernism of the first quarter of the twentieth century. Drawing upon the vast field of philosophy, aesthetics, and social theory, Callinicos, in *Against Postmodernism*, forcefully argues that postmodernism does not represent an epochal change in our social and cultural life. Moreover, Callinicos also suggests that the project of modernity has not been overcome but only sidelined.

11. Lyotard, *Lessons on the Analytic of the Sublime*, 12–25 and *Discours, figure*, 31; 202–8. Of course, Lyotard's description parallels the Freudian and, more recently, the Lacanian notion of the pre-Oedipal, presymbolic stage as a space of nondifferentiation.

12. Deleuze, *The Deleuze Reader*, 166.

13. See in particular the section "Minor Literature: Kafka," *The Deleuze Reader*, 152–164; a selection from Deleuze's *Kafka: Toward a Minor Literature*.

14. I am referring here to the issue of an excessive textualism imputed to Derrida, mostly by American and Anglo-Saxon critics, which derives from a too-literal interpretation of Derrida's statement that "Il n'y a pas d'hors-texte" [There is nothing outside the text], from *Of Grammatology*, 158. Without denying Derrida's focus on the linguistic construction of the referent, it should nonetheless be observed that his account of rhetoric often has intersected with that of heterogeneous materiality. On this issue, compare the following statement by Derrida: "It is totally false to suggest that deconstruction is a suspension of reference. . . . I never cease to be surprised by critics who see my work as a declaration that there is nothing beyond language, that we are imprisoned in language; it is, in fact, saying the exact opposite" (originally from an interview with Kearney, in Kearney, *Dialogues with Contemporary Conti-*

nental Thinkers, 123–24). For additional discussion, see also the exchange of letters between Houdebine and Derrida, now in Derrida, *Positions*, 91–6, Culler, *On Deconstruction*, and Gasché, *The Tain of the Mirror*. While in the section "Critical Consequences," 180–225, Culler connects nonframeable, heterogeneous objects with deconstruction's conceptualization of writing as differential, Gasché not only describes how Derrida has been misconstrued by critics, but observes that his work is philosophically involved with material, phenomenal categories of spatiality and temporality.

15. Compare also Derrida, "Différance," in Adams and Searle, *Critical Theory since 1965*, 120–36, and *Positions*, 3–14.

16. Joyce, *Ulysses*, 164. Compare also Marx's famous description of capitalism: "Constant revolutionizing of production, uninterrupted disturbances of all social conditions, everlasting uncertainty and agitation distinguish the bourgeois epoch from all earlier ones. All fixed, fast-frozen relations . . . are swept away, all new-formed ones become antiquated before they can ossify. All that is solid melts into air" (*Communist Manifesto*, 23).

17. Foucault, *The Order of Things*, xiii.

18. It is well known that Joyce was interested in film and in 1923, as he was planning his second novel, *Finnegans Wake*, wrote the following entry in his notebook: "cine-graphist/leitmotifs and décor idéal/Proust—max[imum] text-min[imum] action/Cine [-maximum action—minimum text] (quoted in Hayman, *The "Wake" in Transit*, 159).

19. In "La Enumeración caótica en la poesía moderna," 247–300, Spitzer develops the concept of "chaotic enumeration" to describe the supplementary and para-tactical assemblage of meaning in the modernist poetry of Rilke, Darío, Whitman, and Claudel.

20. Proust, *Du côté de chez Swann*, 9 (my translation).

21. Benjamin, "The Image of Proust," *Illuminations*, 214.

22. Woolf, *To the Lighthouse*, 47.

23. Woolf, *Mrs. Dalloway*, 231.

24. Svevo, *La coscienza di Zeno*, 82 (my translation).

25. Pirandello, *Il fu Mattia Pascal*, 3; 83; 219ff. (my translation).

26. Pirandello, *Uno, nessuno e centomila*, 22 (my translation).

27. Nietzsche, *The Birth of Tragedy and The Genealogy of Morals*, 1–146. For Nietzsche, tragedy originated in the crossing of boundaries. This crossing is exemplified in the transgression of human and divine space from Aeschylus' *Prometheus* and in the collapse of sexual barriers between blood relatives from Sophocles' *Oedipus*.

28. Proust, *Le Temps retrouvé*, 169.

29. Auerbach, *Mimesis*, 551.

30. Lukács, *Realism in Our Time*, 21.

31. Flaubert, *Letters*, 154. See also Baudelaire's much-cited essay "The Painter of Modern Life," where art is defined as the discovery of the eternal in "modernity . . . that which is ephemeral, fugitive, contingent upon the occasion," 37.

32. "*Sprachkrise*" refers to an ongoing skepticism about language traversing German culture, which antedates the German expressionist avant-gardism. It begins roughly from Nietzsche's announcement of the "death of God" and the collapse of all meaning and order in *Human, All Too Human* (1878). Just a year after Nietzsche's death, Mauthner gives a new impulse to the question. In his *Wörterbuch der Philosophie* (1901) and *Beiträge zu einer Kritik der Sprache* (1901–2), he argues that language is inherently metaphorical and allows meaning to emerge only in a state of flux. Throughout the modern period, in addition to the expressionist avant-gardes, numerous German works have voiced some of the concerns foregrounded by Mauthner and Nietzsche. These include von Hofmannsthal's "The Letter of Lord Chandos" (1902), Rilke's *Malte Laurids Brigge* (1910) and *Duisener Elegien* (1912), and, of course, Kafka's novels and short stories. According to Benjamin, Kafka's entire endeavor remains utterly figural. Like Klee's *Angelus Novus*, Kafka cannot give wholeness to the figures of his writing: "The angel would like to stay, awaken the dead, and make whole what has been smashed. But a storm is blowing from Paradise; it has got caught in his wings with such violence that the angel can no longer close them" ("Theses on the Philosophy of History," *Illuminations*, 257). In "Franz Kafka," Benjamin also notes that Kafka's sirens are "silent. Perhaps because for Kafka music and singing are an expression or at least a token of escape" (*Illuminations*, 118).

33. According to Benjamin, the fate of historical avant-gardism is either implosion, as was the case with dadaism, or a reactionary transformation akin to that of surrealism, but certainly applicable to Italian futurism also, whose more innovative impulses began to wane with the outbreak of World War I. In Benjamin's words, "There is always, in such movements a moment when the original tension of the secret society must either explode in a matter-of-fact . . . or decay . . . and be transformed. Surrealism is in this phase of transformation at present" ("Surrealism," *Illuminations*, 178). For additional discussion on the nihilist, often self-destructive element inhabiting the program of historical avant-gardism, compare also Calinescu, *Five Faces of Modernity*, particularly the chapter "The Idea of the Avant-Garde," 95–148.

34. Benjamin, "On Some Motifs in Baudelaire," *Illuminations*, 159. Compare also the following: "At that time, art reacted with the doctrine of *l'art pour l'art*, that is with a theology of art. This gave rise to what might be called a negative theology in the form of the idea of 'pure' art, which not only denied any social function of art but also any categorizing by subject matter" ("The Work of Art in the Age of Mechanical Reproduction," *Illuminations*, 224).

35. This is a concept developed by Neil Hertz through the categories of Freudian psychoanalysis to describe the Oedipal identification sought by the subject before the scary proliferation of textuality. See, in particular his "The Notion of Blockage in the Literature of the Sublime," *Psychoanalysis and the Question of the Text*, 62–85.

36. See Lyotard's *Discours, figure* and *Phenomenology*, Derrida's *Speech and Phenomena, and Other Essays on Husserl's Theory of Signs*.

37. Derrida, *Dissemination*, 184 ff.

38. In addition to the work of Derrida and Lyotard, for further discussion on the relations between Husserlian phenomenology and Saussurean linguistics, particularly as it relates to the notion of the Subject, compare also Kristeva, *Desire in Language*, 128 ff., Coward and Ellis, *Language and Materialism*, 129 ff., Eagleton, *Literary Theory*, 91–126, and Culler, "Phenomenology and Structuralism," 35–42. To some extent, even a later theorist, such as Hjelmslev, participates in this modernist tradition of thought, since in his *Prolegomena to a Theory of Language* he conceptualizes communication as the result of a reduction in the continuum of content and expression present in natural languages.

39. In *Théories du symbole*, Todorov connects structural linguistics to the "*Symphilosophie*" of Moritz, the Schlegels, Schelling, and particularly Novalis, for whom the symbol reunites plurality and asymmetry in absolute, self-sufficient, and harmonious "wholes."

40. De Saussure, *Course in General Linguistics*, 9.

41. Jakobson, "Linguistics and Poetics" and "Two Aspects of Language and Two Types of Aphasic Disturbances," 62–94; 95–114.

42. Joyce, *Portrait of the Artist*, 167.

43. Bakhtin, *Speech Genres and Other Late Essays*, 11. For additional discussion, compare also Bakhtin's *The Dialogic Imagination*, particularly the section "Forms of Time and of the Chronotope in the Novel," 84–258.

44. Deleuze distinguishes between "bared" as opposed to "disguised" models of repetition: "The first representation is representation of the Same, explained by the identity of the concept to representation; the second includes difference, and includes itself in the alterity of the Idea, in the heterogeneity of an 'a-presentation'" (*Difference and Repetition*, 23–24). Compare also Derrida, where repetition is described as one of the constitutive structures of metaphysical writing practices (*Writing and Difference*, 294–300).

45. James, "Preface" to *Portrait of a Lady*, 7.

46. I am referring to the authorial keys recorded in Budgen's *James Joyce and the Making of Ulysses* and in Gilbert's *James Joyce's Ulysses*.

47. For further discussion of Joyce's "mythic method," see "T. S. Eliot, "Ulysses, Order and Myth," 210ff.; quoted in Iser, *Implied Reader*, 179. A discussion of the Medieval spatial ordering is to be found in Eco, *Aesthetics of Chaosmos*.

48. Deleuze, *Deleuze Reader*, 155.

49. ". . . realizza l'emergere verticale del senso dal mondo orizzontale della prosa" (Moretti, *Opere Mondo*, 145 [my translation]).

50. Derrida, *Between the Blinds*, 588–89.

51. Spitzer, *Marcel Proust*, 234; quoted in Moretti, *Opere mondo*, 141.

52. See, for example, Guglielmi, *La prosa italiana del novecento*, DeBenedetti, *Il romanzo italiano del 900*, Mazzacurati, *Pirandello nel romanzo europeo*, Ghidetti, *Italo Svevo*.

53. Pirandello, "L'umorismo," *Saggi, poesie, scritti varii*, 110–11.

54. These practices are analyzed by Pirandello in another 1908 piece—the vol-

ume *Arte e scienza*. See, in particular, the sections "Soggettivismo e Oggettivismo," and "Per le ragioni estetiche della parola," *Saggi, poesie, scritti varii*, 183 ff.; 923 ff.

55. Terracini, *Analisi stilistica*, Luperini, "Pirandello e D'Annunzio novellieri," *L'allegoria del moderno*, 203–19.

56. Pirandello, "Rondone e Rondinella," "Lontano," "Nenia," *Novelle per un anno*, 1463–1468; 775–815; 509–12.

57. Pirandello, "Ciaùla scopre la luna," in *Novelle per un anno*, 1278–85.

58. Jameson, *The Political Unconscious*, 242. Jameson sees a great political significance in Modernist novels' promotion of the aesthetic realm—notably a "political unconscious"—whose absence in postmodernism is criticized as a conversion to the reality of capitalism. On this point, see in particular, the chapter "The Cultural Logic of Late Capitalism," in his *Postmodernism*, 1–54.

59. On this issue, see Lucente, "'Non conclude,'" 21–47, Dombrosky, *La totalità dell'artificio*, and the section dedicated to Svevo in *Properties of Writing*.

60. Biasin, *Literary Diseases*, 73–74.

61. Svevo, *Il vecchione*, 137.

62. Svevo, "Scritti su Joyce," *Il vecchione*, 741.

63. Joyce, *Finnegans Wake*, 602.

64. Mitchell, "Samuel Beckett and the Postmodernism Controversy," 113–14.

65. On this point, see Hassan, "Joyce, Beckett, and the Postmodern Imagination," 179–200, and Shaw Sailer, *On the Void To Be*. Eco's *The Aesthetics of Chaosmos* also reminds the reader of the influences of Romanticism and French Decadentism on the work of Joyce as a whole.

66. Quoted in Colum, *Our Friend James Joyce*, 123.

67. Derrida, "Two Words for Joyce," 158. Derrida arrives at this conclusion by analyzing the word(s) "HEWAR;" a compound of the Anglo-Saxon "war" and Germanic past tense of to be, or "war."

68. The figurality of language foregrounded in Wittgenstein's work was also being embodied in the work of Kafka, which became available from the mid-to late twenties only.

69. For a good discussion of the Parisian intellectual scene developing around Kojève in the 1930s, see Pefanis, *Heterology and the Postmodern*.

70. Bataille's theory is formulated in *Visions of Excess*.

71. Lacan, "The Mirror Stage," 734–38.

72. I shall note that there is also evidence that by the late twenties modernist writers themselves appear uncertain about the possibility of diegetically mastering the field of experience. Alan Wilde, for example, comments that, in the thirties, the modernist desire to stabilize experience is accompanied by a feeling of inability to succeed, in *Horizons of Assents*, 93 ff. Likewise, L. J. Swingle, in "Virginia Woolf and Romantic Prometheanism," argues that the pressing question in the thirties' essays by Virginia Woolf is to assess whether language can indeed retotalize experience. Woolf's doubt might very well have unfolded in her 1931 novel, *The Waves*, which often questions the authority of the artist and of his/her medium.

73. Heidegger, "The Origin of the Work of Art," 17–87.

74. Compare the following, from Lyotard, *The Postmodern Explained*, 79–80: "I do observe that the true process of avant- gardism was in reality a kind of work . . . a working through *(durcharbeiten)* performed by modernity on its own meaning." See also his *Postmodern Condition* and "The Sublime and the Avant- Garde," 244–256. Worthy of mention are also Huyssen, *After the Great Divide*, and Calinescu, *Five Faces of Modernity*. Calinescu emphasizes the antagonistic role played by the avant-garde in relation to the project of modernism and proposes to think of the avant-garde as "a deliberate and self-conscious parody of modernity itself" (141). I should observe, however, that the descriptive categories of Calinescu, as opposed to those employed by Vattimo, Lyotard, and Huyssen, have tended increasingly to sever the connections between historical avant-gardism and postmodern intellectual developments on the grounds that the former's program is based on a logic of "radical innovation" as opposed to the latter's "logic of renovation" and "reconstructive dialogue with the old and the past" (*Five Faces*, 276). If I agree with this broad distinction, I nonetheless will recall how postmodern authors and intellectuals have a particular bent toward revisiting precisely their avant-gardist past. Furthermore, the historical avant-garde itself—dada notwithstanding—is by no means monolithically oriented toward the destruction of tradition. Breton, for example, in *Manifeste du surréalisme*, draws upon a literary genealogy that includes, among others, Ducasse, Young, Swift, Sade, Chateaubriand, Rimbaud, Baudelaire, Dante, and Shakespeare. Marinetti himself allows for at least some precursors, including Zola, Whitman, Rosny aîné, Paul Adam, Gustave Kahn, and Verhaeren, "Guerra sola igiene del mondo" (*Teoria e invenzione*, 261).

2. Turning the "S" Into the "Z": Céline's *Voyage au bout de la nuit* and *Mort à crédit*

1. Céline, *Entretiens avec le Professeur Y*, 131. All translations of these and other passages are mine, but I have drawn freely from published versions, when available.

2. Because of ties of themes and genres between Céline's novels and those of modernist writers—ties that are often necessary for a parodic reversal—several critics have described the author's work as a modernist endeavor. See, for example, Vitoux, *Louis-Ferdinand Céline*; Thomas, *Louis-Ferdinand Céline*; Nettelbeck, "Notion and Function of Transposition," 186–95; Godard, "Un art poétique," 7–40; Thiher, "Le 'je' Célinien: ouverture, extase et clôture," 47–54. Among those who have avoided this temptation, and in whose orbit of discussion the argument of this chapter is situated, are Muray, *Céline*; Noble, *Language and Narration in Céline's Writings*; Hewitt, *The Golden Age of Louis-Ferdinand Céline*; Bellosta, *Céline ou l'art de la contradiction*.

3. "Autofiction" is a name coined by Serge Doubrovsky to define a genre that stands midway between novelistic representation and autobiography, or more precisely, "a false fiction which is the story of a true life" (*Autobiographies*, 70). This concept is particularly viable for scholars of Céline, an author who consciously

blurred his personal history and identity of Louis Ferdinand Auguste Destouches by naming all fictional voices "Ferdinand," "Ferdinand Céline," and "Dr. Destouches." On this issue of unresolved ontologies, see the excellent essay by Thomas Spear "Céline and 'Autofictional' First-Person Narration," and Godard's "Préface" to Louis-Ferdinand Céline, ix–liii.

4. Céline, *Mort à crédit*, 49.

5. LeBlanc, in "On Excrement, Time and Style," makes a number of suggestive observations on the character's "chronomania" and *"Ordentlichkeit,"* without, however, connecting these traits to a dethronement of modernist discursive practices.

6. ". . . nime les fantômes . . . transforme moméntanément les vaincus en vainqueurs" (Smith, *La Nuit de Louis-Ferdinand Céline*, 76).

7. Althusser, *Lenin and Philosophy*, 164–65.

8. On the polemic toward Hollywood cinema, compare also Céline's *Entretiens avec le Professeur Y*. Many passages of this work seem to anticipate the critique of classic Hollywood style voiced by the theoreticians of avant-gardist films and later by the writers associated with the journal *Screen*. To be more specific, these authors have pointed out how in America during the 1930s, and therefore in a time framed on one side by the economic depression initiated in the Wall Street crash of 1929 and on the other side by the political tensions culminating in the bombing of Pearl Harbor in 1941, Hollywood cinema evolved into a redemptive medium. By means of narrative progress and thematic resolution coupled with formal techniques of highlighting, reduced camera movement, and unambiguous focalization, screwball comedies, gangsters, and musicals, hid the contradiction and confusion of lived experience. Precisely because in classic Hollywood content interacted so deeply with form, films such as *Little Caesar* (1930), *The Public Enemy* (1931), and *A Farewell to Arms* (1932) became a very potent tool to appease the viewing public and to promote the ideals of the American dominant ideology. For additional discussion on classic Hollywood cinema, see also Ray, *A Certain Tendency of Hollywood Cinema*; Schatz, *Old Hollywood/New Hollywood*; and Burch, *Life to Those Shadows*.

9. See, for example, Adorno and Horkheimer, *Dialectics of Enlightenment*, 139ff. The authors argue that popular art forms lack all "import" against mediated totality and foster instead quiescence and consumption by redundancy and iteration. Of interest is also Marcuse's 1937 essay "The Affirmative Character of Culture," 88–133. For a broader discussion of the critique of the bourgeois project developed by the Frankfurt School in the early 1930s, see Buck-Morss, *Origin of Negative Dialectics*, 63–81.

10. The concept of "suture" has an illustrious history in twentieth-century Marxist literary theory. It harks back to Lacan's 1936 formulation of "The Mirror Phase," where the phenomenal subject is said to be constructed by the language and culture of the Other. The concept has been given a linguistic formulation by Benveniste's work on deictics, in *Problems in General Linguistics*, and a Marxist one by Althusser, who calls "interpellation" the hailing of ideology: "ideology . . . 'recruits' subjects among the individuals . . . or 'transforms' the individuals into subjects . . . by interpel-

lation or hailing" (*Lenin and Philosophy*, 174–75). One of Lacan's disciples, Jacques-Alain Miller, named this concept "suture," and Jean-Pierre Oudart subsequently transported it into film studies. For additional discussion, see Coward and Ellis, *Language and Materialism*, 93–121, as well as Silverman, *The Subject of Semiotics*, 194–236. I find the concept of "suture" particularly interesting not just for the chronological concomitance with Céline's work and Lacan's thirties' piece on "The Mirror Phase," but also in view of Céline's declared antipathy toward Hollywood cinema and its ideology.

11. Caroline, Ferdinand's grandmother, "parlait pas beaucoup et ça dejà c'est énorme"(*Mort*, 340) [didn't speak much and this is already very good] (*Mort*, 64). Uncle Edouard "faisait jamais des discours . . . Jamais . . . " [never spoke . . . never].

12. For additional discussion on the topic of silence, see Vitoux, *Louis-Ferdinand Céline*.

13. Spengler, *Decline of the West*, 29. I would like to recall that the concepts of *Zivilization* and *Kultur* were developed by Spengler between 1926 and 1928.

14. Raymond Queneau, "Préface" to Gustave Flaubert, *Bouvard et Pécuchet*, 11.

15. I have in mind Umberto Eco's *The Name of the Rose* and *Foucault's Pendulum*.

16. For additional discussion on this aspect of *Mort* from the perspective of Butor's "philosophie de l'ameublement" [the philosophy of furnishing] see Bellosta, "Le capharnaüm Célinien," 3–126.

17. Latin-Racelle, "*Voyage au bout de la nuit*," 69.

18. Céline, *Voyage au bout de la nuit*, 15.

19. Foucault, *Les Mots et les choses*, translated as *The Order of Things*.

20. There are other references to Proust, such as the following passage which satirizes the Proustian notion of the all-empowering memory: "Les souvenirs eux-mêmes ont leur jeunesse . . . Ils tournent dès qu'on les laisse moisir en dégoûtants fantômes tout suintants d'égoïsme, de vanités et de mensonges . . . Ils pourissent comme des pommes" (*Voyage*, 418) [Memories themselves are young at one time only . . . As soon as they are allowed to go a little mouldy, they turn into the most repulsive ghosts, oozing selfishness, vanity, and lies . . . They rot like apples].

21. Céline, *La Vie et l'oeuvre de Semmelweis*, 123.

22. Kristeva, *Powers of Horror*, has discussed the connection at length, particularly in the section "Those Females Who Wreck the Infinite," 157–73. Richard, *Microlectures*, makes some interesting comments also in the section "Mots de Passe," 221–37.

23. On this point, compare Kristeva, *Powers of Horror*; de la Quérière, "'Sacer Esto,'" 278–300; Knapp, *Céline: Man of Hate*; and Stanford, "Céline's Sources," 141–53. Stanford implicitly connects Céline to surrealism via Jarry and Lautréamont, both Surrealism's acknowledged precursors. Of interest is also Vitoux's *A Biography*, where it is recalled that in 1927 Céline set up a practice in Montmartre, the capital of the avant-garde, and by 1932 became acquainted with Denoël, Artaud's publisher. It is also well known that Aragon, along with Elsa Triolet, translated *Voyage* into

Russian and in 1933 solicited Céline for a contribution to an issue of *Commune*. I would like to point out, however, that both Céline and the surrealist avant-garde came to deny the connection between each other's work. In the biography, Vitoux states that Breton, in the 1950 issue of *Le libertaire*, claimed to have been disgusted by Céline's work very early on. For his own part, by 1937, with the publication of the pamphlet *Bagatelles pour un massacre*, Céline criticized the surrealist style as "pleasing" and also engaged in a polemic against surrealism's conversion to the doctrine of dialectical materialism exemplified by communist Russia. See, in particular, *Bagatelles*, 144–45; 309 ff.

24. The metaphor of writing as a journey into the undifferentiated and opaque space of life straddles the tenets of both the unanimist and surrealist avant-gardes. As we might recall, as early as *La Vie Unanime* (1908) and *Un être en marche* (1908–10), Jules Romains had championed a return to direct experience by calling for an antisymbolist practice of a decentered subject in the organic and shifting materiality of life. Opposing the realism of Zola and Verhaeren, Romains had wished for a practice of depth, or *"profondeur,"* whereby the poet was a being *"en errance,"* following the extension of the object in space and tracing its meandering path from one aggregate to the next in a series of dynamic events. Romains' credo had resulted in a writing of dynamism and contradictions, one that strongly influenced later avant-gardes. Romains' distrust for abstraction and his call for a weaker subject unfolds in the alogic and automatic writing of Breton's manifestos of 1924 and 1930, while his antithetical representations are clearly a main source of inspiration for the famous concept of the surreal paradoxical image. For a selection of Romains' work, see Figueras, *Poètes d'Aujourd'hui: Jules Romains*. For additional discussion on the metaphor of the journey as it relates to Céline's aesthetics, see Richard, *Microlectures*, particularly the section "Prendre le métro," 205–19; and Dherbey, "L'Esthétique de Louis-Ferdinand Céline," 53–67.

25. Quite tellingly, Céline often compares his artistic production to the work of a humble manual laborer and in the 1932 letter to Edmond Jaloux presents it as the product of a narrator "non comme auteur . . . mais d'ouvrier" ["not as an author . . . but as a worker"], "Première lettre à Edmond Jaloux," reprinted in Céline, *Romans I*, 1107 ("Appendices").

26. Regarding Bataille, see the essays collected in his *Visions of Excess*. Of particular interest are Bataille's thirties' essays: "The Use Value of D. A. F. de Sade" (1930) and "The Notion of Expenditure" (1933). Considering the affinities between Céline's narratives and Bataille's polemical "sovereignty" against the metaphysical tradition, it is perhaps not surprising that Bataille himself praised Céline in his review "Louis-Ferdinand Céline: *Voyage au bout de la nuit*," 47.

27. Artaud, *Selected Writings*, 59. Additional references to Artaud's work refer to writings collected in this volume and will be given parenthetically in the text.

28. *Céline ou l'art de la contradiction*, 80–110, has connected Céline's descriptions of the proletariat to two leftist movements occurring in France during the 1930s. The first, or "l'école populiste" [populist school], was developed around

André Thérive and Léon Lemonnier; the second, or "le courant prolétarien" [prole-
tarian current], around Poulaille and Dabit. Wolf, "Un mauvais français," 123–40,
has made analogous suggestions. It should be noticed, however, that Céline's interest in the lower classes neither is romanticized nor develops into a leftist ideology as
his anti-Soviet pamphlet of 1936, *Mea Culpa*, illustrates. Inspired by a visit to Russia
at the invitation of the Soviet government, *Mea Culpa* offers a devastating view of
communist society.

   29. Hewitt, "*Mort à crédit* et la crise de la petite bourgeoisie," 110–18. Compare
also Burns, *A Contextualized Reading*.

   30. As regards the absurdity of the war, see also Céline's unfinished 1949 work,
Casse-pipe, where he describes a group of soldiers who, unable to find the "mot de
passe" [password], cannot return to their quarters. The significance of this novel for
Céline's critique of language has been discussed by Richard, *Microlectures*. See the
sections "Mots de passe" and "Casque-Pipe," 221–37; 239–55.

   31. Beaujour, "Céline: Artist of the Repulsive," 52–63. See also the following
statement by Céline: "Je suis peut-être un artiste dans ce genre-là. Après tout,
pourquoi n'y aurait-il pas autant d'art possible dand la laideur que dans la beauté?
C'est un genre à cultiver, voilà tout" (*Voyage*, 104) [Perhaps I am an artist in that line.
After all, why should there not be as much artistry in ugliness as there is in beauty?
It's one line to take up, that's all].

   32. For a discussion focused on the dark side of modernization in America, see
Loselle, "Bardamu's American Dream," 225–42.

   33. The concept of "expenditure" was applied by Bataille to physical forms of
excess also, and bears numerous analogies with Bakhtin's description of the grotesque, Rabelaisian body. This is a body that is constantly in the process of becoming
and therefore remains open to the outside world through orifices functioning as
channels of "interchange and interorientation . . . . Eating, drinking, defecation,
and other elimination" (Bakhtin, *Rabelais and His World*, 317).

   34. The novel also textualizes love between women. In the episode of Sophie, for
example, Ferdinand comments that this woman understood the necessity of change
in sexual habits and, for this reason, navigated between hetero- and homosexuality
(*Voyage*, 600 ff.).

   35. Blondiaux, *Louis-Ferdinand Céline: Une écriture psychotique*, 19.

   36. On the issue of unstable time and space, see Schoolcraft, "'Honi soit qui mal
y danse,'" 833–56; Krance, *The I of the Storm*; Ifri, "Temps et chronologie dans Voyage au bout de la nuit*," 27–37; Carson, *Céline's Imaginary Space*; and Cresciucci,
Les Territoires Céliniens.

   37. Compare also the following pages from *Voyage*, 17, 28, 80, 135, 147, 230–1, 631–
2. In Céline's later works, madness will overshadow conscious narration, as in *Féerie
pour une autre fois*. For additional discussion on the madness theme, a constant in
Céline's production from his 1924 doctoral dissertation onward, see the already cited
volume by Thiher, *The Novel as Delirium*, Blondiaux's *Louis-Ferdinand Céline: Une
écriture psychotique*, as well as Verdaguer's "Tendances fantastiques et merveilleux

raciste chez Louis-Ferdinand Céline," 284–300, and Dunwoodie's "Merveilleux, étrange et fantastique dans les romans de Louis-Ferdinand Céline," 82–111.

38. Céline, 1932 "Lettre à Léon Daudet," in Céline, *Romans I*, 1108 ("Appendices").

39. ". . . type d'expression propre à celui qui ne se sent pas tout à fait sûr de son énonciation" (Leo Spitzer, "Une habitude de style, le rappel chez Céline," 443 [my translation]). The essay was originally published in 1935.

40. For a good study of archaisms, see de Boissieu, "Quelques effets 'littéraires' ou archaïsants dans *Voyage au bout de la nuit*," 33–51. The critic addresses archaic lexical and morphosyntactic constructions such as "*ne . . . mie*," substantivated infinitives as in "*le manger peu*" (sixteenth century), decimal numbers with "*et*," as in "*vingt-et-quatre*," use of "*en*" with determined nouns, as in "*en la paix*," and much more.

41. For additional discussion on the spoken aspect of Céline's style, see Holtus "Code parlé et code écrit," 36–46. For *Voyage* only, see de la Quérière, *Etude stylistique*. The issue of a stylized version of spoken French is also treated by Godard in *Poétique de Céline*, and by Latin-Racelle in "*Voyage au bout de la nuit* ou l'inauguration d'une poétique argotique," 53–77, and "Fonction de l'argot dans la narration," 151–63.

42. Rouayrenc Vigneau, "Parlé et narration dans *Voyage au bout de la nuit*," 148. On this point, see also Spear: "Le développement des voix narratives multiples," 258–68.

43. For a discussion focused on emotion, of interest are Blank, "Discours émotif et discours contrastif," 33–45, and Hokenson, "Céline's Impressionist in Language," 329–39.

44. On deformation, see the fascinating study by Juilland, *Les Verbes de Céline*.

45. For further discussion of the musicality of the Célinian sentence, I recommend Mambrino, "Céline and His Touch of Music," 163–85; Nettelbeck, "Coordonnées musicales de l'esthétique romanesque de Céline," 80–87; Bonnefis, "'Gone are the days . . . :' L'invention de la musique dans l'oeuvre de Céline," 800–23; Mur Lorda, "Oralité et littéralité dans les romans de Céline," 123–32.

46. Barthes, in "L'effet de réel," 84–9, explains how the effect of reality is achieved when the passage from text to referent effaces the presence of the linguistic sign. This is precisely what Céline intends to undo by forcing the reader to focus on the items of the code as opposed to what they may represent.

47. Chesneau, in *La Langue sauvage de Louis-Ferdinand Céline*, 88 ff., also notices the following in relation to other proper names from *Voyage*: Ganate suggests "*ganache*," [lower jaw], Entrayes "*des entrailles*," [guts] Bestombes "*des tombes*," [graves] Protiste "*proteste*," [protest], Baryton "*baryton*," [baritone]. In *Céline*, Muray also notices *Mort*'s consistent play on "*or*," ["gold"] in the proper names of Gwend*or*, N*or*a, G*or*loge, Kr*o*g*old*.

48. Louis-Ferdinand Céline, *Lettres à la N.R.F. 1931–1961*, 14.

49. " . . . faire jouer le paradigme dans et contre le syntagme," in Montaut, "Poésie de la grammaire chez Céline," 228. On the same topic, compare also

Spitzer, "La enumeracíon caótica en la poesía moderna," 247–300, where an example of enumeration from Céline's *Bagatelles* is connected to the taste for baroque fragmentation.

50. Aposiopesis also plays an important role in impeding the movement of a proposition toward closure. Sentences such as "Ils posaient leurs loupes pour mieux voir . . . Si on n'était pas des bandits . . . " (*Mort*, 162) [They'd put down their lenses . . . to take a better look at us], or "Au bout de tous les efforts, la dernière voilure lui est retombée de la misaine . . . étalée comme un goéland" (*Mort*, 125), [At the end of all these efforts, the last sail fluttered down . . . sinking to the deck like a sea-gull], would be cognitively adequate if the "three dots" were omitted.

51. Céline also refers in passing to Joyce and notes that, like Proust, Joyce is a "Puissant écrivain" [powerful writer] and has a "style lourd. Architecture lourde" [a heavy style. Heavy architecture] (*Le style contre les idées*, 85). In an essay on Rabelais, again Céline will mention Joyce, only to dismiss all Joycean influence: "Moi, y a des gens qui sont venus me demander si je n'avais pas pris tel ou tel passage de mes livres dans Joyce. Oui, on me l'a demandé! . . . Aller prendre quelque chose dans Joyce! Non. " (*Le style contre les idées*, 121) [Some people have asked me if I hadn't taken this or that passage of my books in Joyce. Yes, they did ask me that! . . . Taking something from Joyce! No].

52. On the Proustian sentence compare also Céline's 1943 "Lettre à Lucien Combelle," 106.

53. I owe this observation to Noble, *Language and Narration in Céline's Writings*, 192–93.

54. A section from *Le style contre les idées* 61–73, titled "Ma grande attaque contre le Verbe," provides further insights into Céline's conflation of Judaism as it relates to the inauthenticity of language. At a precise historical moment, comments Céline, the authors of the Book of Genesis willed the exclusion of life's contradiction and open-ended temporality by positing a language of self-identical and stable images: the Word, or "le Verbe." In open polemic against such a reappropriative move, Céline unveils the secondariness and historicity of Genesis' Word: "Vous savez, dans les Ecritures il est écrit: 'Au commencement était le Verbe.' Non! Au commencement était l'émotion. Le Verbe est venu ensuite. . . . On a sorti l'homme de la poésie émotive pour le faire entrer dans la dialectique, c'est-à-dire le bafouillage, n'est-ce pas? Ou les idées. Les idées, rien n'est plus vulgaire (*Le style contre les idées*, 67) [As you know, in the Scriptures it is written: "In the beginning was the Word." This is false. In the beginning there was emotion. The Word came afterwards. . . . Man has been taken out of the emotive poetry and has been made to enter into the dialectics, that is to say the babble, isn't it? Oh, the ideas. The ideas, nothing is more vulgar]. And yet, since the Word is a model of symbolization legitimized by the Torah and the vulgate Bible, it becomes increasingly implicated in the establishment and reproduction of an existential and social rationality. Finally, from the seventeenth century onward, it is institutionalized in the modist grammar of classical French—

in a language, that is, which conflates the order of thought, symbols, and world (*Le style contre les idées*, 119–25). For additional discussion on this topic, see Chesneau, "Céline et l'ordre des mots," 34–47.

55. Additional discussions on the paranoid aspects of the pamphlet are provided by Solomon, "The Plot as Conspiracy," 47–63; Spear, "Virility and the Jewish 'Invasion' in Céline's Pamphlets," 98–119; and Kaplan, *Reproductions of Banality*.

56. Gide's "Les Juifs, Céline et Maritain" (originally published in *La Nouvelle Revue Française*), 468–70.

57. Sartre, "Portrait de l'anti-sémite" (1945), cited in Noble, *Language and Narration in Céline's Writings*, 167.

58. Godard, *Céline Scandale*, 18, notes that in France Céline's reputation remains tainted by his anti-Semitic writings, as witnessed by two 1994 articles in *Le Figaro Magazine* and *La Quinzaine Littéraire*. As for what concerns the American reception, Kaplan recently has extended an invitation not to reprint Céline's pamphlets: "Any future republication of this text, which seeks to draw its readers into the most demented racist furor, carries, even for scholars, some degree of risk" ("Sources and quotations in Céline's *Bagatelles pour un massacre*," 30).

59. O'Neill, *The Poverty of Postmodernism*, 191. Compare also Callinicos, *Against Postmodernism*; John McGowan, *Postmodernism and Its Critics*; and Krysinski, "Rethinking Postmodernism." Krysinski writes that postmodernism lacks "socio-political finality above and beyond the legitimation of either ethical arguments, such as the emancipation of humanity, or philosophical arguments, such as the dialectics of reason.... Postmodernism can be seen as an autotelic discourse that is conscious of its non-finality, and does not adhere to what Lyotard calls the 'hermeneutics of meaning'" (12).

60. Compare Lyotard, "Rewriting Modernity," 24–35.

3. Meandering with Gadda's "Heuristic" Words

1. Gadda, "Meditazione breve circa il dire e il fare," *I viaggi la morte, Saggi giornali favole e altri scritti I*, 454; my translation.

2. This metaphysical interpretation of Gadda's writings was initiated by Giancarlo Roscioni, the administrator of the Gaddian archive and obviously the only critic to have access to the author's unpublished material. In *La disarmonia prestabilita*, Roscioni formulated Gadda's project as the Cartesian "*Singula enumerare*" in order to "*Omnia circumspicere*." Because Gadda, argued Roscioni, sought to establish the identity of the single by taking into account encyclopedic frames of knowledge, the project was doomed, as Leibnitz's history of the house of Braunschwig in *Annales Brunsvicienses* had been. Following Roscioni, a number of critics have made analogous arguments. For an excellent sampling of this reception, see Ceccaroni, *Leggere Gadda*. Other works from the 1980s and the 1990s continue this interpretative tradition. Benedetti, for example, in *Una trappola di parole*, reads Gadda's narratives as the unsuccessful attempt to turn chaos into cosmos. Sbragia,

"From the Novel of Self-Ridicule to the Modern Macaronic," 169–70, sees Gadda as a mythopoetic modernist, questing for wholeness and transcendence; so do Stragà, "La scrittura del disordine," 85–101; Stellardi, "'La luce che recede,'" 123–36; and Gabetta, "Gadda e il caledoscopio dell'euresi," 15–43. The few studies to have resisted Roscioni's school of interpretation, and to which I am much indebted, are Contini, *Quarant'anni d'amicizia*; Guglielmi, "Gadda e la tradizione del romanzo," 17–37, *La prosa italiana del novecento*, 211–43; and Fratnik, *L'écriture détournée*.

3. On this point, see Dombroski, *Introduzione allo studio di Carlo E. Gadda*; Bertone, "I diari 'del tempo perduto,'" in *Il romanzo come sistema*, 35–54; Guglielminetti, "Gadda/Gaddus: diari, giornali e note autobiografiche di guerra," 127–39, and Sbragia, *C. E. Gadda and the Modern Macaronic*, 43ff.

4. Gadda, "Giornale di guerra e di prigionia 1915–1919," in *Saggi giornali favole II*, 441; all citations will be from this collective edition and will be given parenthetically in text.

5. This is true if one excludes the short tale "La passeggiata autunnale" written during his imprisonment, and a handful of poems that Gadda wrote between 1919 and 1921, while working as an engineer for various companies.

6. Gadda, *Racconto italiano di ignoto del novecento*, *Scritti vari e postumi*, 393.

7. In a later note, Gadda even goes as far as to suggest that he may have more than five voices, and if he were to describe them, he would need a very large painter's paillette: "non basterebbe nemmeno la mia propria tavolozza; ho il violetto e l'indaco, il bleu e il verde, ma mi mancano il cioccolato e l'arancione" (*Racconto*, 602) [not even my pallette would suffice; I have the purple and the indigo, the blue and the green, but I am missing the chocolate and the orange].

8. ". . . l'impossibilità del romanzo novecentesco di proporre ancora una volta . . . una rappresentazione globale, omnicomprensiva, della vita," (Isella, "Prefazione," xviii; my translation).

9. Galdenzi Capobianco, in "Cronache da un labirinto," 173–207, points out that the composition of *Racconto* corresponds to the appearance of several new theoretical approaches to the novel. These include Ortega y Gasset's *Ideas sobra la novela* (1925), Thibaudet's *Le liseur de roman* (1925), Muir's *The Structure of the Novel* (1928), and Sklovskji's *Theory of Prose* (1929).

10. In addition to a chronological concomitance with Mikhail Bakhtin's work (*Freudianism* dates from 1927, *The Formal Method in Literary Scholarship* 1928, *Problems of Dostoevsky's Art* and *Marxism and the Philosophy of Language* 1929, "Discourse in the Novel" 1934–35) Gadda's conceptualization of the novel's form bears striking resemblance to Bakhtin's. On this point, see Raimondi, *Barocco moderno*, and particularly Segre, "Novità su Gadda," 3–4, and *Intrecci di voci*.

11. On the notion of a baroque reality, compare also Gadda's 1952 piece "L'Editore chiede venia del recupero chiamando in causa l'Autore," now printed as appendix to Gadda, *La cognizione del dolore*, 480: "grottesco e barocco . . . legati alla natura e alla storia" [grotesque and baroque . . . . tied to nature and history]. Gadda's interest

in French and Spanish baroque literature is also well documented. He often alludes to Rabelais and Cervantes and translated Quevedo's *El mundo por de dentro,* Barbadillo's *La peregrinacíon sabia* for the volume *Narratori Spagnoli.* In 1945, he wrote "Rappresentare la 'Celestina,'" *I viaggi la morte, Saggi giornali favole e altri scritti I,* 534–38. For additional discussion on Gadda and the baroque, see Stellardi, "Il barocco nella scrittura di Gadda," Raimondi, *Barocco moderno,* Manganaro, *Le Baroque et l'ingénieur,* and Dombroski, *Creative Entanglements.*

12. The work of Saussure was recommended to Gadda by Contini. See Contini, *Lettere a Gianfranco Contini,* 108.

13. Gadda, *Meditazione milanese, Scritti vari e postumi,* 621.

14. As does Deleuze in his *The Fold: Leibnitz and the Baroque.* See, in particular, the chapter "What Is Baroque?," 27–38.

15. ". . . elle ne peut jamais se refermer en système, puisque ce qu'elle travaille, c'est précisément 'l'impossibilité'—du système—," (Risset, "Carlo Emilio Gadda," 950).

16. Compare also the following statement in Gadda's "Tecnica e poesia," *Gli Anni, Saggi giornali favole e altri scritti I,* 246: "Esistono limiti. La cognizione e la confessione dei propri limiti è un dovere; ed è un motivo essenziale della verità" [Limits exist. The knowledge and the confession of one's limits is a duty; and it is an essential motive for truth].

17. I owe this observation to Guglielmi's "Gadda e la tradizione del romanzo," 30. In *La prosa italiana del novecento,* 213, Guglielmi had also noticed how Gadda "interrogandosi sulle *res* è ricondotto al problema dei *nomina.*"

18. A similarity not surprising considering Gadda's exposure to German culture. He had been a pupil of the German physicist Max Abrahams, a reader of Wittgenstein and von Hofmannsthal, and a student of German philosophy. Between 1925 and 1931, his work as an engineer also took him on numerous trips to the Ruhr. For additional discussion on Gadda and Musil via Mach's conception of the "real," see Roscioni, "Introduzione," Gadda, *Meditazione milanese,* xvi, n. 3, and De Benedictis, *La piega nera,* 203 ff. However, the most interesting comparison between the two writers remains the one provided by Calvino, *Lezioni Americane,* 101–20.

19. There are references to Schopenhauer both in *Racconto,* 450, and *Meditazione,* 834. Lucchini, in "Gli studi filosofici di Gadda," 230, n. 23, notices that Gadda's copy of Kant's *Critique of Judgment* is unmarked except for the section "analitica del bello, analitica del sublime" [analytic of the beautiful, analytic of the sublime].

20. Roscioni, in "Introduzione" to Gadda, *Meditazione milanese,* xviii, n. 1, acknowledges the similarities between this text and the 1915 *Course in General Linguistics* and imputes them to Gadda's and Saussure's reading of Vilfredo Pareto's theories of interactive economies. The similarities include Gadda's use of the comparison with the chess game and the relational and differential value of the pieces on the board. However, mirroring the outcome of his earlier *La disarmonia prestabilita,* Roscioni ends by neutralizing Gadda's project and suggests that it tends to a hyper-

model of structuralism. Elio Gioanola has made analogous observations and has described Gadda's project as a type of ur-structuralism: "Struttura delle strutture" [structure of structures] (*L'uomo dei topazi*, 173). An analogy between Gadda and Saussure has also been noticed in Cannon, "Notes on Gadda's Critical Essays," 67–71, and Manganaro, *Le Baroque et l'ingénieur*, 92.

21. It is well known that the composition of *Meditazione* coincides with Gadda's reading of "La Scienza Nuova" for a contribution to "Fiera Letteraria" of 1929. The piece is reprinted as "La 'Scienza Nuova,'" *Scritti dispersi, Saggi giornali favole e altri scritti I*, 691–97. On the issue, see also Battistini, "Gadda, Vico e un'edizione della 'Scienza nuova,'" 381–86.

22. Both essays are reprinted in *I viaggi la morte, Saggi giornali favole e altri scritti I*, 561–86 and 444–54 respectively.

23. Compare also the 1936 essay "Meditazione breve circa il dire e il fare," *I viaggi la morte, Saggi giornali favole e altri scritti I*, 444–54. Here Gadda declares that his endeavor is so stripped of aura that it might not even reach the most immediate audience of family members: "non perverrò nemmanco ai figlioli, non che ai nepoti" ("Meditazione breve," 444), [I will neither reach the children nor the nephews].

24. On the issue of parody, compare again "Meditazione breve circa il dire e il fare" 452–53, where Gadda promises to shake "le terminologie e i sistemi fraseologici inadeguati" [inadequate terminologies and phrases], and the following preface from the prose collection *Il castello di Udine*, "Tendo al mio fine" (1934): "Tendo a una brutale deformazione dei temi che il destino s'è creduto di proponermi come formate cose ed obbietti: come paragrafi immoti della sapiente sua legge" (*Romanzi e racconti I*, 119) [I tend towards a brutal deformation of the themes that fate has attempted to present to me as final things and absolute objects: as immutable paragraphs of its wise law].

25. Gadda, "La scapigliatura milanese," *Scritti dispersi, Saggi giornali favole e altri scritti I*, 970.

26. For additional discussion on the relation between Gadda and the *scapigliati*, see Contini's *Quarant'anni d'amicizia*, particularly the sections "Introduzione alla 'Cognizione del dolore'" and "C. E. Gadda traduttore espressionista," 15–35; 55–60. Of interest is also Bettini, "La rivolta di Gadda," 11–34.

27. I am referring to such recent publications as Sbragia, C. E. *Gadda and the Modern Macaronic*, Dombroski and Bertone, eds. *Carlo Emilio Gadda*, and Dombroski, *Creative Entanglements*.

28. The first reference to futurism occurs in *Diario di guerra e di prigionia 1915–1919, Saggi giornali favole II*, 801. Gadda uses the epithet of "*futurista*" to describe the toilets of the camp of Celle Lager and the mediocre poetry of Captain Casello. In the 1928 *Meditazione, Scritti vari e postumi*, 659, there is a reference to the theatrical synthesis of the minor futurist Ruggero Vasari as soporific, while in the story "L'incendio di Via Keplero," *Accoppiamenti Giudiziosi, Romanzi e racconti II*, 701, an anonymous narrator opens the diegesis by commenting that fire is capable of

better synthesis than "Sua Eccellenza Filippo Tommaso Marinetti." Finally, in the
1943 article "L'uomo e la macchina," *Gli Anni, Saggi giornali favole e altri scritti I*,
255–61, Gadda accuses the futurists of lacking technical knowledge. It comes as no
surprise, then, that Sbragia denies any connection between Gadda and futurism.
Summarizing the view held by other North American critics, Sbragia decidedly
comments that Gadda was "Outwardly adverse to avant-gardist movements in general, with never a kind word for Futurist experimentation" (*C. E. Gadda and the
Modern Macaronic*, 40).

29. Contini *Quarant'anni d'amicizia*, 57, 7.

30. Turolo, *Teoria e prassi linguistica nel primo Gadda*, 108 ff.

31. Lipparini, *Le metafore del vero*, 61 ff.

32. As Eco recalls in his recent *La ricerca di una lingua*, the "*questione*" began as
early as the fourteenth century, when Dante saw the medieval fragmentation of
tongues in "*sì*" as a curse to be transcended at the theoretical and artistic level of *De
Vulgari Eloquentia* (1303–5) and *La Commedia*, respectively. In *Inferno* XXXI the
speech of the devil Nimrod is a pastiche of "Raphèl maí amèche zabì almi," while
La Commedia as a whole is a practical attempt to create a language predicative
enough to foster the illusion of unambiguously wording the material and intellectual world. Dante's project was continued by Petrarch and extended by Bembo,
Castiglione, and Machiavelli, ultimately to become institutionalized in the "Voca-
bolario" of Accademia della Crusca in 1612. Linguistic fragmentation, however, was
by no means so easily totalized. As in the case of François Rabelais, the Renaissance
writings of Teofilo Folengo (particularly his *Baldus*) foregrounded the artificiality of
symbolic stability by way of extensive linguistic hybridizations, as did the theater of
Goldoni in the eighteenth century. In the nineteenth century, Manzoni's effort to
achieve an ever-receding linguistic unity was illustrated by the purging of Lombard
in the final version of his *Promessi Sposi* (1827–40). Nonetheless, the babelic "*koiné*"
still dwelt within and outside the text. *Promessi Sposi* are certainly not immune from
plurilinguism and traffic with Latin, "*latinorum*," Spanish and parodic versions of
seventeenth-century style. The novel itself emerged in a context of social and literary
heteroglossia. In fact, despite the official decree of 1869 for a national language, Italy
remained a country of deep-seated plurilinguism. In literature, Giovanni Verga's *I
Malavoglia* (1881) experimented with a free-indirect discourse modeled on the syntax and metaphors of Sicilian speakers. Carlo Porta and Gioachino Belli wrote dialect literature, while the *scapigliati* practiced a radical linguistic expressionism.

33. I owe this definition to Gianni Scalia, quoted in Luciano De Maria, "Introduzione," xlix.

34. The texts that comprise the theory of *paroliberismo* are the following: "Manifesto tecnico della letteratura futurista," (May 11, 1912), "Distruzione della sintassi—
Immaginazione senza fili—Parole in libertà" (May 11, 1913), and "Lo splendore
geometrico e meccanico e la sensibilità numerica," (March 18, 1914). These works
are reprinted in Marinetti, *Teoria e invenzione*, 40–48; 57–84; 84–92.

35. Marinetti, *Teoria e invenzione*, 48.

36. For further discussion of the unfinished, compare Marinetti, "Guerra sola igiene del mondo" (1915) and "Il teatro futurista sintetico" (1915) in *Teoria e invenzione,* 269–73, 97–109.

37. Concerning Dante, see the essay "Un fatto personale . . . o quasi," *I viaggi la morte, Saggi giornali favole e altri scritti I,* 495–501, where Gadda reminds the reader that canto XXI of the *Inferno* presents linguistic pluralization as a curse. As regards Manzoni, in "Lingua letteraria e lingua dell'uso," *I viaggi la morte,* 489–94, Gadda will voice a clearly negative opinion on what he considers to be Manzoni's philological teleology. The relation between Gadda and Manzoni has been much studied and is rapidly reaching exhaustion. Representative pieces are Nava, "C. E. Gadda lettore di Manzoni," 339–52, Contini's "Premessa su Gadda manzonista" and "Gadda Milanese," in *Quarant'anni d'amicizia,* 69–72; 73–79. Good discussions are also provided by: Pecoraro, *Gadda e Manzoni;* Flores, *Accessioni Gaddiane,* 46 ff.; and Cavallini, *Lingua e dialetto in Gadda,* 61 ff.

38. Gadda, "L'arte del Belli," in *I viaggi la morte, Saggi giornali favole e altri scritti I,* 548–560.

39. Gadda, "Una mostra di Ensor," in *I viaggi la morte, Saggi giornali favole e altri scritti I,* 590.

40. See the 1938 "Autografo per Giorgio de Chirico," *Scritti dispersi, Saggi giornali favole e altri scritti I,* 824–25.

41. Gadda, *Lettere a Solaria,* 16.

42. Marinetti, "La cinematografia futurista," in *Teoria e invenzione futurista,* 118–23. The piece argues that film fulfills the need for a symphony of expressions.

43. Fragments are "Teatro" (1927) and "Cinema" (1928), now in *La madonna dei filosofi, Romanzi e racconti I,* 9–20; 49–68. For a brief, yet insightful discussion on the relationship between Gadda's prose and the cinematic medium, see also Micaela Lipparini, *Le metafore del vero,* 67 ff.

44. Cook, *A History of Narrative Film,* 179. Compare also Eisenstein's 1929 "The Cinematographic Principle," 28–44.

45. Vertov, *Kino-Eye,* 14.

46. Quoted in Perloff, *The Futurist Moment,* 90.

47. On this point, compare Dombroski, "Gadda and Fascism," in *Creative Entanglements,* 117–34, and Hainsworth, "Fascism and Anti-Fascism in Gadda," 221–41. Like the futurists, Gadda had been an active interventionist also. Sbragia, *C. E. Gadda and the Modern Macaronic,* reminds the reader that on May 22, 1915 (and therefore just two days before Italy's entrance into World War I), Gadda had written a letter with his classmates Emilio Fornasini and Luigi Semenza asking the Ministry of Education to allow early examinations so that students could participate in the war. It should be pointed out, however, that Gadda's interventionism never shared Marinetti's penchant for heroic violence. As my previous discussion of *Diario* suggests, Gadda hoped that the conflict might restore Italy's sociopolitical and moral values. To tell it with Sbragia, "Gadda justified the war "as a trial of discipline, order, and abnegation of the self for the nation," while Marinetti's vision was "a disinhibiting liberation of instinctual drives" (*C.E. Gadda and the Modern Macaronic,* 45).

48. Gadda, "La casa," *Novella seconda, Romanzi e racconti II*, 1107–32 and "San Giorgio in casa Brocchi," *Accoppiamenti Giudiziosi, Romanzi e racconti II*, 643–97.

49. Cases was among the first to establish the ideological approach to Gadda's novels in "Un ingegnere di letteratura," 7–17. Cases' approach has had an illustrious progeny and includes Pasolini's *Passione e Ideologia*, Seroni, *Gadda*, Ferrero, *Invito alla lettura di C. E. Gadda*, and Baldi, *Carlo Emilio Gadda*.

50. Gadda, *La meccanica, Romanzi e racconti II*, 461–89.

51. All quotations from this novel are drawn from Manzotti's annotated edition of Gadda, *La cognizione del dolore*. For the translation, I have drawn freely from William Weaver, *Acquainted with Grief*.

52. Gadda, *"Per favore mi lasci nell'ombra" Interviste 1950–1972*, 141.

53. Gadda, "Giuseppe Berto, 'Il male oscuro,'" in *Scritti dispersi, Saggi giornali favole e altri scritti I*, 1200–1208.

54. Gonzalo's paternal lineage includes a governor, Gonzalo Pirobutirro d'Eltino, known for his ideals of morality and justice and, of course, "Signor Francisco," Gonzalo's father. On his maternal side flows the Germanic rage for order and "certo rovello interno a voler risalire il deflusso delle significazioni e delle cause" (*La cognizione*, 107), [a certain inner torment in wanting to ascend the flow of meanings and causes].

55. "Gonzalo è al centro di una tensione esistenziale e narrativa particolare, fra la fenomenicità del mondo e l'astrazione dell'idea, fra il corpo e lo spirito, fra il rumore e il silenzio" (Gian Paolo Biasin, "La cornucopia del mondo," 33).

56. The dream is represented as the disclosure of a "truth" that remains veiled by consciousness: "Ma sognare è fiume profondo, che precipita a una lontana sorgiva, ripúllula nel mattino di verità" (*La cognizione*, 168) [But to dream is a deep river, which rushes to a distant spring, bubbling up in the morning of truth]. Further, the dream connects the absence of coordination with a *"vis omicida,"* which, born from Gonzalo, has fallen on the mother: "E questa forza nera, ineluttabile . . . . più greve di coperchio di tomba . . . . cadeva su di lei! come cade l'oltraggio . . . . Ed era sorta in me, da me! . . . . E io rimanevo solo" (*La cognizione*, 171) [And this black, ineluctable force . . . heavier than a tombstone . . . was falling upon her! As the outrage falls . . . And it had risen in me, from me! . . . . And I remained alone]. For additional discussion on this aspect of the dream, see also Dombroski, "Overcoming Oedipus," 125–43.

57. For additional discussion on Gadda's practice on *non finito*, see Oddenino, "Gadda o la creatività del non finito," 367–90; Bertone, "'L'incompiutezza necessaria,'" 182–88; Borelli, "A proposito degli incompiuti di Gadda," 493–98.

58. This phenomenon is pervasive and extends well beyond these texts. In the 1944 *L'Adalgisa*, for example, *Romanzi e racconti I*, 283–564, Gadda will include two sections from *La cognizione*: "Strane dicerie contristano i Bertoloni" and "Navi approdano al Parapagal."

59. ". . . un complesso sistema a vasi comunicanti," Isella, "Presentazione," xx.

60. As early as 1906, Marinetti had promoted Romains in his literary magazine *Poesia*, and specifically in issues 6, 7, 9 of the journal. By 1913, Gian Pietro Lucini's

Filosofi ultimi, 48, had connected the two. For additional discussion on the relationship between Romains and Marinetti, see Nicholls, *Modernisms: A Literary Guide*, 84, and Pinottini, "L'Unanimismo e l'estetica del futurismo," 95–112.

61. An excellent discussion of what has been defined as Gadda's "*sternismo*," is Roscioni, "Gadda umorista," in *Strumenti Critici*, 147–62.

62. In 1972, a year before his death, Gadda located his own work on the revisionary and transitional path of Louis-Ferdinand Céline. In reply to a question from an interviewer from *L'approdo letterario* on the possibility of a filiation with the French author, Gadda comments: "Credo che il rapporto sia giusto, esatto insomma, perché veramente Céline mi ha preceduto nell'impostazione narrativa e stilistica" (*Per favore mi lasci nell'ombra" Interviste 1950–1972*, 213) [I believe that the relationship is correct, in a word, exact, because truly Céline has preceded me in narrative and stylistic organization]. Quite possibly the interviewer's question had been suggested by some observations made by Contini and Barilli. In the 1963 preface to the Einaudi edition of *L'Adalgisa*, Contini mentioned the name of Céline in connection with Gadda. The introduction, now reprinted in *Quarant'anni d'amicizia*, 11–13, suggests that Gadda might bear some resemblance to some fellow countrymen of Rabelais, from Céline to Audiberti. In the following year, Barilli, in *La barriera del naturalismo*, built upon Contini's intuition but argued that Gadda, like Céline, was a reactionary nineteenth-century naturalist in a twentieth-century panorama traversed by the experimentation of modernist writers. Despite its weaknesses, Barilli's argument foregrounded the possibility of a filiation between the two writers and fostered a long essay by Francesco Muzzioli: "Il 'Voyage' di Céline e il 'Pasticciaccio di Gadda,'" 101–42. This essay is in general brilliantly intuitive in arguing that the novels shared thematic and formal concerns. However, because it disregards *Meditazione milanese* (1928), available in print as early as 1974, and cannot draw on *Racconto italiano di ignoto del novecento* (1924), which was not published until 1983, it ends by flattening Gadda's historical specificity in the late twenties and throughout the thirties. In short, what Muzzioli locates in Gadda's 1957 novel are issues common by then to a host of other writers. Borges had been very active since *Ficciones* (1945) and *El Aleph* (1949); Raymond Queneau had published *Exercices de style* in 1947 and *Zazie dans le métro* in 1959. The period, also witnessed the publication of major works by the "*nouveaux romanciers*," such as Michel Butor's *Passage de Milan* (1954), *L'emploi du temps* (1956), *La modification* (1957), Robbe-Grillet's *Les Gommes* (1953), *Le voyeur* (1955), and *La jalousie* (1957). One should also recall Italo Calvino's *Il visconte dimezzato*, published in 1951, as was Samuel Beckett's *Molloy*. Beckett's *Malone meurt* dates from 1952, *Watt* and *L'innomable* 1953. Two very recent works—Amigoni, *La più semplice macchina*, and Krysinski, "Carlo Emilio Gadda and Louis-Ferdinand Céline," 195–220—address the possibility of a connection between Gadda and Céline in terms of style and themes but do not see any historical specificity in these artists' endeavors. Moreover, Amigoni connects Céline only to Gadda's work of the 1950s.

63. De Benedictis, *La Piega nera*, 205. For additional discussion on the availabil-

ity of Céline's novels to the Italian public, see Carile, "Editeurs, critiques," 150–61, and "La critique italienne," 101–85.

64. Pasolini, *Passione e ideologia*, 313–24. The classic study of Gadda's style is Devoto, *Itinerario Stilistico*. Good analyses are also Barbolini "Gadda: Anatomia della visione," 114–27, Lucchini, "Strategia retorica," 57–94. On Gadda's use of dialect, see Cavallini, *Lingua e dialetto in Gadda*, and Grassi, "L'aspetto figurale-simbolico," 245–64.

65. Ungaretti writes that Gadda uses language to "décharger sa rage . . . pétrir les mots, les dilater, les massacrer . . . selon l'urgence de sa critique" (Ungaretti, *Correspondance*, 611) [to vent his rage . . . to knead words, to dilate or massacre them . . . according to the urgency of his critique]. For additional analogies between the emotional language of Gadda and of Céline, compare also Manganaro, *Le Baroque et l'ingenieur*, 153 and Krysinski, "Carlo Emilio Gadda and Louis-Ferdinand Céline" 207.

66. ". . . qualche gioco di parole (c'est mon alcool à moi)" (Gadda, *"Per favore mi lasci nell'ombra" Interviste 1950–1972*, 53) ["a few word-plays (c'est mon alcool à moi)"]. See also passages such as the following: "a bilicar billi biffi," "i moccoli gocciolavano goccioloni," and "ecco un cocco, ecco un cocco, — ecco un cocco che è" (*La cognizione*, 316, 226, 465). For additional discussion on Gadda's poetic logic, see also Terzoli, "Emilio o della rima," 85–94, where she connects the author's lyrical experimentation to poems by Giovanni Pascoli and Ugo Betti.

67. Manzotti, "Introduzione"; Gadda, *La cognizione*, IX.

68. For additional discussion on this point, see Dombroski, "Overcoming Oedipus" and "Carlo Emilio Gadda: Travesties," 107–36; Pucci, "The Obscure Sickness," 43–62.

69. Derrida, *Dissemination*, 1–59, and "Living On: Border Lines," 75–176.

70. "Ogni sostantivo deve avere il suo doppio . . . Esempio: uomo-torpediniera, donna-golfo, folla-risacca, piazza-imbuto," (Marinetti, "Manifesto tecnico della letteratura futurista, in *Teoria e invenzione futurista*, 41).

71. Eco, *Semiotics and the Philosophy of Language*, 46–86. Eco distinguishes between dictionary- and encyclopedia-like models of representations. Whereas the former circumscribes definitions, the latter opens them to a process of "unilimited semiosis"—that is to say, to the expenditure and regress allowed by the archive of culture.

72. ". . . the loophole left open, accompanies the word like a shadow. Judged by its meaning alone, the word with a loophole should be an ultimate word . . . but in fact it is only the penultimate word and places after itself only a conditional, not a final period" (Bakhtin, *Problems of Dostoevsky's Poetics*, 233).

73. The problematization of the detective convention merits further reflection. A constant aspect of Gadda's narratives, it is present as late as *Quer pasticciaccio di Via Merulana* and as early as "Novella seconda" where, in a compositional note, Gadda confesses his desire to be "Conandoyliano" (*Romanzi e racconti II*, 1317). Interestingly, the note also suggests a thematic complication to put to test the conventions of the detective novel.

74. The bibliography on the reversal of convention is so extensive that only few representative titles can be cited here. See Spanos, "The Detective and the Boundary," 17–39; Hutcheon, *Narcissistic Narratives*; and Mc Hale, *Postmodernist Fiction*. In the panorama of Italian literature, see Cannon, *Post-modern Italian Fiction*, and Tani, *The Doomed Detective*.

75. Girard, *Mensonge romantique et verité romanesque*.

4. Rite of Passage: The Early Beckett between "Unwording" and "Linkwriting"

1. Beckett, "La peinture des van Velde ou le Monde et le Pantalon," in *Disjecta*, 128.

2. Because the young Beckett was a scholar of Proust and had many contacts with Joyce (as documented in Bair's monumental but unauthorized biography, *Samuel Beckett: A Biography*), his "English period" generally has been interpreted as derivative. See, for example, Kenner, *Samuel Beckett: A Critical Study*; Federman, *Journey to Chaos*; Harvey, *Samuel Beckett: Poet and Critic*; Hesla, *The Shape of Chaos*; Kenner, *A Reader's Guide to Samuel Beckett*; Gluck, *Beckett and Joyce*; Dearlove, *Accomodating the Chaos*; and Lawrence Miller, *Samuel Beckett: The Expressive Dilemma*. Among those who have escaped this tendency, and in whose frame of enquiry my discussion is located, are Melvin Friedman, "The Novels of Samuel Beckett"; Fletcher, *Samuel Beckett's Art*; Abbott, *The Fiction of Samuel Beckett*; Rabinovitz, *The Development of Samuel Beckett's Fiction*; Zurbrugg, *Beckett and Proust*; Hill, *Beckett's Fiction in Different Words*; and Begam, *Samuel Beckett and the End of Modernity*.

3. I have found no direct connection between Beckett and Gadda, with the sole exception of a common acquaintance, Nino Frank. According to Bair's *Samuel Beckett: A Biography*, like Beckett, Frank was part of Joyce's circle in 1928–29. Frank's name also appears frequently next to Gadda's as one of the steady correspondents of the journal *Solaria*, in Manacorda, *Lettere a Solaria*. Later on, Frank wrote an essay on Gadda, "Le cas Gadda," where he compared Gadda's work to *Ulysses* and the *Wake*. From a number of other sources, however, it is possible to point out Beckett's and Gadda's common interests in literature, philosophy, and linguistics. These are interests that explain their many similarities. Besides being fluent in French and German, the young Beckett was, of course, well trained in Gadda's national literature. While at Trinity College, between 1923 and 1928, he took Rudmose Brown's course on Dante's *Commedia*, was introduced to Pirandello's work by Walter Starkie, and traveled to Florence in 1927. Between 1929 and 1930, he translated Comisso, Montale, and Franchi for the fourth issue of *This Quarter* of 1930. The work of his "English decade," also abounds in allusions to Ariosto, Vico, Leopardi, Manzoni, and D'Annunzio. In addition, Beckett's interest in those same philosophers who inhabit many of Gadda's pages is well documented. At Trinity, he was tutored on Bergson by Aston Luce, who was also an authority on Descartes and Berkeley. In the same period, he was reading the pre-Socratics, possibly by way of Jean Beaufret. According to Knowlson, *Damned to Fame*, Beaufret was a specialist of

Greek thought and Heidegger. Moreover, Beckett was well acquainted with the same anti-idealistic philosophic tradition represented by Bruno, Leibnitz, Spinoza, and Kant, which had played a great role in Gadda's education. For additional discussion, see, besides Bair's biography, also Murphy, "Beckett and the Philosophers," and Pilling, "From a (W)horoscope to *Murphy*." Pilling's piece contains a detailed description of Beckett's notebook to *Murphy*. The notebook includes Beckett's references to Kant's *Critique of Pure Reason*, and his refutation of Descartes' idealism, allusions to Lucretius, Quixote, annotations in different languages, words from the fourteenth to the nineteenth centuries, and citations from *Inferno* XXXI on Nimbrot's babelization of the Word.

4. According to Bair, Beckett mentions Céline as early as 1933 in a letter to McGreevy, where he comments that he has not been able to get a copy of *Voyage* (*Samuel Beckett: A Biography*, 165). In 1935, in the essay "Censorship in the Saorstat" (*Disjecta*, 84–8), Beckett does includes Céline among the practitioners of "unwholesome literature" and seems to be, to some extent, familiar with the novelist. Knowlson observes that Beckett read *Mort à crédit* in his journey between Le Havre and Cuxhaven in 1936, and even cites Beckett's comments on the novel, from a diary entry of October 1, from the same year (*Damned to Fame*, 217). Yet, Ruby Cohn claims that Beckett wrote a letter to her on February 16, 1952, stating that he read the French author just before the war (*The Comic Gamut*, 319). Simon confirms Cohn and comments that Beckett read *Voyage* in 1937 and found it to be "le plus grand roman des littératures anglaise et française au risque de déplaire à James Joyce" (*Beckett*, 177) [the best novel of English and French literature, at the risk of displeasing James Joyce]. On the basis of Beckett's comments, several critics have suggested thematic comparisons, particularly as they relate to the issue of madness, the dehumanization of characters by nosology, and the journey motif of Beckett's later novels. See, for example Hoffman, *Samuel Beckett: The Language of Self*; Robinson, *The Long Sonata of the Dead*; Melvin Friedman, *Samuel Beckett Now*; and Rosen, *Samuel Beckett and the Pessimistic Tradition*. Cohn (*The Comic Gamut*, 100 ff.) has also suggested stylistic similarities between the two writers but, again, has done so in relation to Beckett's post-1945 French fiction. Most recently, Amiran, (*Wandering and Home*) has suggested that the relation between Beckett and Céline might not be simply one of influence but, rather, of a shared concern with language.

5. Samuel Beckett, *Proust*.

6. For the complete text, see Leopardi, *Canti*, 251–52. As Italy's most famous poet of negation, Leopardi not only departed from romantic aesthetics by rooting his poetry in the pessimism of classical thought, but his most theoretical work, *Zibaldone* (1817–32), endorses that same Vichian theory of poetry as the antithesis of abstract, philosophical language that Beckett explores in the essay on *Finnegan's Wake* (*Disjecta*, 19–33). For additional discussion on Beckett's interest in Leopardi—an area that certainly would need additional investigation—see Oliva, *Samuel Beckett. Prima del silenzio*; Brun, "Sur le Proust de Beckett"; and Caselli, "Beckett's Intertextual Modalities of Appropriation."

7. "The Proustian equation is never simple. . . . And the quality of its action falls under two signatures. In Proust each spear may be a spear of Telephus" (*Proust*, 1).

8. Drawing upon the earlier insights of Rosen, *Samuel Beckett and the Pessimistic Tradition*, and Pilling, "Beckett's Proust," Zurbrugg, *Beckett and Proust*, makes very convincing arguments concerning Beckett's consistently idiosyncratic reading of the Proustian novel.

9. Lyotard, *The Postmodern Condition*, 81. Another document from 1934 further suggests Beckett's interest in the postmodern side of Proust. The piece criticizes Albert Feuillerat's approach to *A la recherche* on the grounds that it interprets the whole of the novel in light of the retotalization of life—"the resolution . . . consummated in the Hôtel de Guermantes"—whereas in effect, continues Beckett, the text also documents a lack of uniformity and cohesion, a "material" often communicated "in dribs and drabs" ("Proust in Pieces," *Disjecta*, 65).

10. Beckett, "Casket of Pralinen for a Daughter of a Dissipated Mandarin," reprinted in Harvey, *Samuel Beckett, Poet and Critic*, 278–83.

11. *Disjecta*, 136. A point worth noting is the unsettling force that these writers of the thirties have on the legislative primacy of postmodern theory over the fictional text. A line of enquiry certainly worth exploring, would be Beckett's shaping influence on the work of Deleuze, whose last work and epitaph is a long essay on the languages of Beckett, "L'Epuisé."

12. I owe this observation on the Corneillean ascendance of Beckett's concept of a "visible darkness" to Knowlson and Pilling, *Frescoes of the Skull*, 18. These critics observe that this concept derives from *Le Cid*, known to Beckett as an undergraduate. The equation of a type of visibility that depends on darkness is often made in Beckett's work. See, for example, "Intercessions by Devis Devlin" and "McGreevy on Yeats," (*Disjecta*, 91–97).

13. Going against reductive metafictional approaches to Beckett, Gontarski reminds us that "Beckett's is an aesthetics of compromise . . . repelled by mimesis . . . yet unwilling to abandon representation wholly," ("The Intent of Undoing," 5). Of late, Gontarski's view has been gaining currency. See, for example, Ricks, *Beckett's Dying Words*; Farrow, *Early Beckett*, where it is argued that Beckett's art represents a move to a different realism. For a good introduction to metafictional approaches to Beckett's prose—all regrettably founded on the notion that where metaphysical representation fails only self-referential and ludic writing opens—see Bernal, *Langage et fiction dans le roman de Beckett*, Moorjani, *Abysmal Games*, and Brienza, *Samuel Beckett New Worlds*.

14. See also "Words about Painters" (*Disjecta*, 115–52). For additional discussion on the relation between Beckett's prose and painting, compare O'Brien, *Beckett Country*, which describes Beckett's love for Caravaggio and the two Brueghels. On painting as it relates to the issue of "dark visibility," see McMillan, "Samuel Beckett and the Visual Arts." The author discusses how as early as "Casket of Pralinen," Beckett was already connecting his work to painters: Velasquez, Epstein, Botticelli,

Bellini, Mantegna, Chinnery, and others. An excellent piece is also Read's "Beckett's Search for Unseeable and Unmakeable," which describes Beckett's long relationship with and writings on the Israeli artist Avigdor Arikha.

15. Wood, "An Endgame of Aesthetics: Beckett as Essayist," 14.

16. I am well aware of the tradition of scholars for whom Beckett would be a writer of nihilism and despair. This is a tradition that certainly owes much to Martin Esslin's "Introduction" to his edited volume *Samuel Beckett: A Collection of Critical Essays*; Rosen, *Samuel Beckett and the Pessimistic Tradition*; and Robinson, *The Long Sonata of the Dead*. However, as Henning has most recently argued in *Beckett's Critical Complicity*, these approaches function only within a metaphysical horizon of totality and closure, one certainly alien to Beckett's work.

17. Knowlson and Pilling, *Frescoes of the Skull*, 249.

18. In the "The Shenker Interview" of May 5, 1956 (Federman and Graver, *Samuel Beckett: The Critical Heritage*, 146–49), Beckett admits to having read *The Castle* in the original. Hence, numerous critics have suggested analogies with Kafka and other writers of the *Sprachkrise*, such as Rilke and Hofmannsthal. Linda Ben-Zvi, "Samuel Beckett, Fritz Mauthner, and the Limits of Language," has associated his prose to Mauthner's *Beiträge zu einer Kritik der Sprache* (1901–2), read by Beckett in 1932, and therefore at the time of his first fictional and theoretical works.

19. "To be an artist is to fail, as no other dare fail . . . all that is required now . . . is to make of this submission, this admission, this fidelity to failure, a new occasion, a new term of relation, and of the act which, unable to act, obliged to act, he makes, an expressive act" (Beckett, *Disjecta*, 145). Compare also the 1961 interview with Tom Driver: "To find a form that accommodates the mess, that is the task of the artist now" (Federman and Graver, *Samuel Beckett: The Critical Heritage*, 219).

20. Barker, "Paysage to Passage." On this issue, compare also Read, "Artistic Theory in the Work of Samuel Beckett," Amiran, *Wandering and Home*, which develops the concept of a positive logic to describe Beckett's depiction of the unending process of life. An older but still valid work is Abbott, *The Fiction of Samuel Beckett*.

21. Trezise, *Into the Breach*. It should be noted, however, that Trezise locates the break in Beckett's *Trilogy*, and therefore ends by effacing the author's specificity in the thirties' decade.

22. Current scholarship is giving much attention to the issue of mortality in Beckett's work. See for example, Ricks, *Beckett's Dying Words*, ties Beckett to a tradition of writers fascinated by death, and then discusses the theme of death as metaphor for language's contingency. A good discussion is also Locatelli, *Unwording the World*, even if, as its title suggests, the focus of the study is on *Company* (1980), *Ill seen/Ill said* (1982), and *Worstward Ho* (1983). Locatelli also connects death with the philosophy of Heidegger, well known to Beckett. See on this point, the 1961 interview with Tom Driver (Federman and Graver, *Samuel Beckett: The Critical Heritage*, 219), as well as Bair's *Samuel Beckett: A Biography*, 97.

23. The piece was commissioned to Beckett by Joyce, who was trying to publicize "Work in Progress" through a collection of laudatory essays. On this point, see Bair's *Samuel Beckett: A Biography*, 71 ff.

24. Joyce, *Finnegans Wake*, 614.

25. Mitchell argues how Joyce and Beckett represent opposite tendencies: "one which stresses the creative and infinite power of the word, and another which sees language as impotent in the face of reality" ("Samuel Beckett and the Postmodernism Controversy," 117).

26. Vattimo, "Art and Oscillation," in *The Transparent Society*, 51.

27. The topic as a whole certainly merits deeper reflection that I can offer in this context, particularly since it is one of the less explored avenues in the literary formation of the early Beckett. While some critics have obscured the importance of Beckett's involvement with the avant-garde, others have dedicated to it only a very cursory treatment, generally in relation to his poetry and drama. Among those who have downplayed Beckett's involvement with the avant-garde is Bair, who discusses Beckett's deep-seated interest in unanimism as a way "to satisfy the moderatorship" (*A Biography*, 54). Among the critics more receptive to the topic, have been Kennedy, *Murphy's Bed*, who discusses *Murphy* in relation to surrealism; Zurbrugg, "Beckett, Proust, and Burroughs," 172–87 and "Beyond Beckett," 37–56; and Gontarski, "The Intent of Undoing," 5–23. This critic observes that Beckett's "struggle against representation . . . is in the critical and creative avant-garde" ("The Intent of Undoing," 20). Worthy of mention is also Lois Gordon, *The World of Samuel Beckett*. Gordon offers valuable discussion on the Parisian avant-gardist scene of the late twenties and thirties. Others have focused on the drama and the poetry only. See, for example, Taxidou, "Modernist Drama/Postmodernist Performance," 171–85; Lamont, "Yesterday's Avant-garde, Today's Great Classics," 37–56; and Fletcher, "The Private Pain and the Whey of Words," in which Fletcher points out—and often laments—the influence of Jouve, Apollinaire, and the surrealists on Beckett's verse.

28. "Assumption" and "Dante . . . Bruno . Vico . . Joyce" appeared in *Transition* 16/17; "For Future Reference" in 19/20; "Sedendo et Quiescendo" in 21; "Malacoda—Enueg II—Dortmunder" in 24; "Ooftish" and "Denis Devlin" in 27.

29. McMillan, *Transition*, 235–78.

30. Eisenstein, "The Cinematographic Principle," 30.

31. For additional discussion concerning Beckett's involvement with the verticalists, see Kennedy, *Murphy's Bed*, 274–99, and Dearlove, "'Syntax Upended,'" 122–28.

32. O'Brien, *Beckett Country*, 271.

33. Fowlie observes that Joyce ought not be connected to the surrealist avant-garde because of his verbal mastery (*Age of Surrealism*, 184). This point has also been made by Hassan in "Joyce, Beckett, and the Postmodern Imagination" (179–200). Hassan points out that the onirism of the *Wake* is quite removed from the surrealist loss of control.

34. I owe this observation to a paper titled "Behind and Beyond the Camera Eye" delivered at the Strasbourg Conference on Samuel Beckett on April 2, 1996, by Lois Overbeck, who is the coeditor of Beckett's forthcoming correspondence.

35. For some interesting observations on the influence of avant-gardist cinema on Beckett's later work, see Brater's *Beyond Minimalism*. Brater comments that in addition to Dalí's *Un chien andalou,* Beckett might have been influenced by Vertov's experimental film *Man with a Movie Camera* (1928).

36. Bair, "*Dream of Fair to Middling Women:* A Preface and a Postscript," 21–27, mentions rejections by Chatto and Windus, Hogarth Press, Jonathan Cape. Bair also cites a letter from Beckett to George Reavey describing the rejections (*Samuel Beckett: A Biography,* 154).

37. O'Brien, "Foreword" to Beckett, *Dream of Fair to Middling Women,* xi.

38. Knowlson and Pilling, *Frescoes of the Skull,* 13.

39. "The more Joyce knew the more he could. He's tending toward omniscience and omnipotency as an artist" ("The Shenker Interview," Federman and Graver, *Samuel Beckett: The Critical Heritage,* 148).

40. Gontarski, "The Intent of Undoing," 13.

41. Levinas, "Ethics as First Philosophy," in *The Levinas Reader,* 75–87.

42. For further discussion, see also the essays edited by Ben-Zvi, *Women in Beckett,* and Mary Bryden, *Women in Samuel Beckett's Prose and Drama.* These publications argue that Beckett's earlier works, at least to *Happy Days,* are informed by "phallologocentric" practices, whereby woman functions as darkness, multiplicity, and ultimate obstacle to the reconciliatory quests of the male. I would like to comment that I disagree with these writers' arguments and suggest that they fail to take into account the narrator's point of view vis-à-vis that of the male characters.

43. Kroll, "'I Create, Therefore I Am,'" 44 ff.

44. Knowlson and Pilling, *Frescoes of the Skulls,* 9.

45. The same force is at work in Beckett's first published story, "Assumption," 41–44. In a third-person narrative voice, the story begins by introducing a world of coexisting opposites. Words are incongruous; "the unread intelligentsia" (41). Images clash; a buffoon swings while an organist sits, chess players strategically move "Pawn to King's fourth" but also reply by the elementary, beginner's strategy of "Pawn to Rook's third" (41). A part of the heterogeneity of this space—"He could have shouted and could not" (41)—an artist attempts to fence and contain inner and outer confusion. However, in an ironic mode, the narrative voice observes that this is a desperate act by a "whispering prestidigitator" (42), since the "damming" (43) walls are threatened on both sides by the forces of eventuality. One day, the dam does indeed break open; the "great storm of sound" is released and joins the discordant liveliness of the cosmos: "the breadth of the forest and the throbbing cry of the sea" (44). The narrative ends with a baffling image, a scene resisting all structures of explanation: the woman is touching the dead hair of the artist.

46. Zurbrugg, "Beckett, Proust, and *Dream of Fair to Middling Women,*" 43–64, argues that the tunnel imagery functions for Marcel as relief from the flight of Albertine.

47. Bair consistently employed biographical criticism to read the text. Her approach was certainly much criticized but has had many followers. Even Knowlson's *Damned to Fame* is not immune from this temptation and seeks to locate in *Dream's*

characters a number of historical figures, perhaps forgetting Beckett's statement that "The danger is in the neatness of identifications" (*Disjecta*, 19).

48. See Iser, *The Implied Reader*, 257–73, *The Act of Reading*, 222 ff., *Prospecting*, 140–51; Keir, "Not I: Beckett's Mouth and the Ars(e) Rhetorica," 124–48, Gibson, *Reading Narrative Discourse*, 140–72. Gibson argues that texts like those of Beckett (and, I might add, of Gadda and Céline) require a dialogical model of reading, one attentive to deviations and lack of coherency.

49. ". . . se noient toutes les différences" (Pasquier, "Blanc, Gris, Noir, Gris, Blanc," 77).

50. For further discussion of these points see Arthur, "Murphy, Gerontion and Dante," 54–67, and Stevenson Gilliland, "Belacqua in the Moon," 36–46.

51. Beckett, *More Pricks than Kicks*, 9.

52. The representations that follow question one of the most enduring myths of Beckett's criticism, notably the one established by Lukács' notion of the "surface" exploration of Beckett generating a political escapism, despite Adorno's attempt to argue for the political resistance in Beckett's work, in his "Trying to Understand *Endgame*," 119–50. Recently, however, critics have began to question Lukács' premises. From a neo-Marxist perspective, Bruck, "Beckett, Benjamin, and the Modern Crisis in Communication," 159–71, notices how Beckett's narratives contemptuously reflect on bourgeois myths. Vincenzo, *La fine di un inizio*, has defended Beckett from the Lukácsian argument of sociological disengagement, as has Moriconi, *Beckett e altro assurdo*. Also worth mentioning is Harrington, *The Irish Beckett*, who places Beckett's *More Pricks than Kicks* and *Murphy* in the context of satire directed against Irish morality and cultural history.

53. See, for example, the passage where the narrator comments that although he had been a friend of Belacqua — "We were Pylades and Orestes for a period" (37) — he eventually severed all connections: "He was an impossible person in the end. I gave him up in the end because he was not serious" (38).

54. Zurbrugg, *Beckett and Proust*, 222–23.

55. The short and unpublished eleventh story of *More Pricks than Kicks*, "Echo's Bones," (1934–35 ca.) follows a similar mode of "poetic justice." The story deals with Belacqua's afterlife, where he serves as a stud for Lord Gall's barren wife. Here, however, Belacqua appears to have achieved some kind of recognition, and ponders "if on the whole he had not been a great deal deader before rather than after his formal departure, so to speak" (quoted by Zurbrugg, *Beckett and Proust*, 224). Additional discussion of the story is to be found in Rabinovitz's chapter "Learning to Live with Death: 'Echo's Bones,'" in *The Development of Samuel Beckett's Fiction*, 55–63.

56. Quoted in Harrington, *The Irish Beckett* 105.

57. Beckett, *Murphy*, 25.

58. For additional discussion on the connections to Leibnitz, see Hesla, *The Shape of Chaos*, 33 ff., and Levy, *Beckett and the Voice of the Species*, 19 ff.

59. An excellent discussion of Murphy's punning habits is to be found in Ackerley, "'In the Beginning was the Pun,'" 15–22.

60. On the issue of repetition, see also Connor, *Samuel Beckett: Repetition, Theory, and Text*; Hill, "Duality, Repetition, Aporia," in *Beckett's Fiction in Different Words*, 59–78. Also Rabinovitz, *Innovation in Samuel Beckett's Fiction*, addresses the issue but, and via Cohn, sees it as a device for unity, and therefore "bare" in Deleuze's sense.

61. For additional discussion, particularly on Beckett's parody of psychology, see Rabinovitz, "Beckett and Psychology," 65–77, and Culik, "The Place of *Watt* in Beckett's Development," 62 ff.

62. Mintz, "Beckett's *Murphy*: A 'Cartesian' Novel," 156–65.

63. It is well known that Beckett had little sympathy for Descartes, as witnessed by his poem "Whoroscope." For additional discussion on Murphy's Cartesianism, see also Morot-Sir, "Samuel Beckett and Cartesian Emblems," 25–104, and particularly Henning, "The Guffaw of the Abderite," 5–20. Henning has argued successfully that the novel satirizes the monistic heritage of Western idealism by placing it into a dialogic relation with pre-Socratic atomism and Democritus. Good discussions are provided by Henning, *Beckett's Critical Complicity*, and Acheson, "Murphy's Metaphysics."

64. On this point, see also Wood, "Murphy, Beckett; Guelincx, God," 27–51.

65. Derrida, *La vérité en peinture*, develops the concept of "parergonality" to describe the dislocation and ultimately the eclipse of frames. Quite suggestively, Derrida's argument relies on Kant's *Critique of Judgment*.

66. Loughrey and Taylor, "Murphy's Surrender to Symmetry," 79–90.

67. Compare Henning, "The Guffaw of the Abderite," 5–20. Worthy of mention in this context is also Beckett's 1936 letter to McGreevy (*Disjecta*, 102), in which Beckett comments on Murphy.

68. ". . . atomique, disjonctive, coupée, hachée, où l'énumération remplace les propositions, et les relations combinatoires, les relations syntaxiques: une langue des noms" (Deleuze, "L'Epuisé," 66). The theorist distinguishes between three models of language in Beckett; the one of words, before *The Unnamable* and up to *Watt*, and those of voices and images, both belonging to later works.

69. I owe these observations to Farrow, *Early Beckett: Art and Allusion in More Pricks than Kicks and Murphy*, 60–1, and Kennedy, *Murphy's Bed*, 61.

70. Coe, "Beckett's English," 36–57. For additional discussion on Beckett's style, see also Frederick Smith, "Beckett's Verbal Slapstick," 43–55.

71. Topia, "Murphy ou Beckett baroque," 93–119.

72. This technique clearly justifies a comment by Kenner that Beckett's syntax is perhaps only the shade of one ("Shades of Syntax," 21–31).

5. Postponing A Conclusion . . .

1. McFarlane, "The Mind of Modernism," 93.

2. "El *ethos* de la escritura vienesa . . . presupone una superación de las categorías negativas y se funda sobre un postulado creador del lenguaje artístico que sería verdadero, apofánico y dialéctico más allá de las negatividades petrificadas. La

Sprachkritik presupones entonces una *Sprackpraxis*. El metatexto . . . es una especie de semiosis terapéutica de la lengua y del lenguaje novelesco" (Krysinski, "El metatexto vienés," 131; my translation).

3. de Beauvoir, *La Force des Choses*, 29–30.

4. Eco, "Form as Social Commitment," 239.

5. See, for example, some of the essays collected in Calvino, *Una pietra sopra*.

6. Gadda, "Un'opinione sul neorealismo," in *I viaggi la morte, Saggi giornali favole e altri scritti I*, 629.

7. For further discussion see Baranski and Pertile, *The New Italian Novel*, and Stefano Tani, "La giovane narrativa," 161–192. I would like to add that Gadda's work has even inspired an Argentinian writer Enrique M. Butti, who in 1993 published a Borgesian rewriting of *Quer Pasticciaccio*, titled *Indí* and translated into Italian as *Pasticciaccio Argentino* (1994).

8. Tani, "La giovane narrativa," 177.

9. Barthes, *Writing Degree Zero*, 77.

10. Kristeva, *Desire in Language*.

11. Kristeva, *Powers of Horror*, 133–206.

12. Jean-Bloch, *Le présent de l'indicatif*.

13. See, in particular, the statements made by Kerouac, "Jack Kerouac," and Miller, "Henry Miller," *Cahier de l'Herne*, 423, 426.

14. Kaplan, "The Céline Effect," 117–36.

15. Ibid., 120.

16. Friedman, *Black Humor*.

17. In "Cry Havoc," 35–47, Steiner observes how the possibility of creating fine art does not imply a heteronomous relation with high moral standards. Challenging Ruskin's statement, voiced in 1870 during a lecture in Oxford, that "you must be good men before you can either paint or sing" (35), Steiner writes that the endeavors of novelists such as Rebatet and Céline illustrate how "the ability to play and love Bach can be conjoined in the same human spirit with the will to exterminate a ghetto or napalm a village" (46).

18. See the conclusion of chapter two in this volume.

19. Mauriac, *The New Literature*.

20. Breon Mitchell, "Samuel Beckett and the Postmodernism Controversy," 114.

BIBLIOGRAPHY

Abbott, Porter H. *The Fiction of Samuel Beckett: Form and Effect*. Berkeley: University of California Press, 1973.

Acheson, James. "Murphy's Metaphysics." In *The Beckett Studies Reader*. Ed. Stanley Gontarski. Gainesville: University Presses of Florida, 1993. 78–93.

Ackerley, C. J. "'In the Beginning Was the Pun': Samuel Beckett's *Murphy*." *AUMLA* 55 (May 1981): 15–22.

Adams, Hazard, and Leroy Searle, eds. *Critical Theory since 1965*. Tallahassee: Florida State University Press, 1986.

Adorno, Theodore, and Max Horkheimer. *Dialectics of Enlightenment*. New York: Herder and Herder, 1972.

———. "Trying to Understand *Endgame*." *New German Critique* 26 (1982): 119–50.

Althusser, Louis. *Lenin and Philosophy*. London: Monthly Review Press, 1971.

Amigoni, Ferdinando. *La più semplice macchina*. Bologna: Il Mulino, 1995.

Amiran, Eyal. *Wandering and Home: Beckett's Metaphysical Narrative*. University Park: Pennsylvania State University Press, 1993.

Andreini, Alba, and Marziano Guglielminetti, eds. *C. E Gadda: La coscienza infelice*. Milan: Guerini Studio, 1996.

Apollinaire, Guillaume. *L'Esprit Nouveau et les poètes*. Paris: Haumont, 1946.

Artaud, Antonin. *Selected Writings*. Ed. Susan Sontag. New York: Farrar, Straus and Giroux, 1976.

Arthur, Kateryna. "Murphy, Gerontion and Dante." *AUMLA* 55 (May 1981): 54–67.

Astier, Pierre, Morris Beja, and Stanley Gontarski, eds. *Samuel Beckett: Humanistic Perspectives*. Columbus: Ohio State University Press, 1983.

Attridge, Derek, and Daniel Ferrer. *Post-structuralist Joyce: Essays from the French.* Cambridge: Cambridge University Press, 1984.

Auerbach, Eric. *Mimesis.* Princeton, N.J.: Princeton University Press, 1953.

Bair, Deirdre. *Samuel Beckett: A Biography.* New York and London: Jonathan Cape, 1978.

———. "*Dream of Fair to Middling Women*: A Preface and a Postscript." *The Review of Contemporary Fiction* 7 (1987): 21–27.

Bakhtin, Mikhail. *The Dialogic Imagination.* Ed. Michael Holquist. Austin: University of Texas Press, 1981.

———. *Problems of Dostoevsky's Poetics.* Minneapolis: University of Minnesota Press, 1984.

———. *Rabelais and His World.* Bloomington: Indiana University Press, 1984.

———. *Speech Genres and Other Late Essays.* Ed. Caryl Emerson and Michael Holquist. Austin: University of Texas Press, 1986.

Baldi, Guido. *Carlo Emilio Gadda.* Milan: Mursia, 1972.

Baranski, Zygmunt, and Lino Pertile, eds. *The New Italian Novel.* Edinburgh: University of Edinburgh Press, 1993.

Barbolini, Roberto. "Gadda: Anatomia della visione." *Il Verri* 20 (1980–81): 114–27.

Barilli, Renato. *La barriera del naturalismo.* Milan: Mursia, 1964.

Barker, Stephen. "Paysage to Passage: Beckett's Poiesis of the World." *Journal of Beckett Studies* 1 (1992): 15–38.

Barthes, Roland. "L'Effet de réel." *Communications* 11 (1968): 84–89.

———. *Writing Degree Zero.* New York: Farrar, Straus and Giroux, 1968.

Bataille, Georges. "Louis-Ferdinand Céline: *Voyage au bout de la nuit.*" *La critique sociale* 7 (January 1933): 47.

———. *Visions of Excess: Selected Writings 1927–1939.* Ed. Allan Stoekl. Minneapolis: University of Minnesota Press, 1985.

Battistini, Andrea. "Gadda, Vico e un'edizione della 'Scienza nuova'." *Bollettino del Centro di Studi Vichiani* 12–13 (1982–83): 381–86.

Baudelaire, Charles. In *My Heart Laid Bare and Other Prose Writings.* London: Soho Books, 1906. 37–41.

Beaujour, Michel. "Céline: Artist of the Repulsive." In *Céline and His Critics: Scandal and Paradox.* Ed. Luce Stanford. Saratoga, Calif.: ANMA Libri, 1986. 52–63.

Beaujour, Michel, Dominique Le Roux, and Michel Thélia, eds. *Cahier de l'Herne* 3–5 (1972).

Beckett, Samuel. "Assumption." *Transition* 16–17 (June 1929): 41–44.

———. *Proust.* New York: Grove Press, 1931.

———. *Murphy.* New York: Grove Press, 1957.

———. *Three Novels by Samuel Beckett.* New York: Grove Press, 1965.

———. *More Pricks than Kicks.* New York: Grove Press, 1972.

———. *Disjecta.* Ed. Ruby Cohn. New York: Grove Press, 1984.

———. *Dream of Fair to Middling Women.* New York: Arcade Publishing, 1992.

Begam, Richard. *Samuel Beckett and the End of Modernity.* Stanford: Stanford University Press, 1996.

Bellosta, Marie-Christine. "Le capharnaüm Célinien ou la place des objets dans *Mort à crédit.*" *Archives des lettres modernes* 164 (1976): 3–126.

———. *Céline ou l'art de la contradiction.* Paris: Presses Universitaires de France, 1990.

Ben-Zvi, Linda. "Samuel Beckett, Fritz Mauthner, and the Limits of Language." *PMLA* 95 (1980): 183–200.

———, ed. *Women in Beckett.* Urbana and Chicago: University of Illinois Press, 1990.

Benedetti, Carla. *Una trappola di parole.* Pisa: ETS Editrice, 1980.

Benjamin, Walter. *Illuminations.* New York: Schoken Books, 1968.

———. *The Origin of German Tragic Drama.* London: Lowe and Brydone, 1977.

———. *Reflections.* New York: Schocken Books, 1978.

Benveniste, Emile. *Problems in General Linguistics.* Coral Gables, Fla.: Miami University Press, 1971.

Bernal, Olga. *Langage et fiction dans le roman de Beckett.* Paris: Gallimard, 1969.

Bernardini, Napoletano Francesca. "Il modello Manzoniano nella scrittura gaddiana, tra apologia e parodizzazione." In *Gadda: Progettualità e scrittura.* Ed. Carlino Fabrizio, Aldo Mastropasqua, and Francesco Muzzioli. Rome: Editori Riuniti, 1987. 203–29.

Bertone, Manuela. *Il romanzo come sistema.* Rome: Editori Riuniti, 1993.

———. "'L'incompiutezza necessaria': Carlo Emilio Gadda tra finitezza e non finito." *RLA* 2 (1990): 182–88.

Bertone, Manuela, and Robert Dombroski, eds. *Carlo Emilio Gadda: Contemporary Perpsectives.* Toronto: University of Toronto Press, 1997.

Bettini, Filippo. "La rivolta di Gadda e i rapporti con l'avanguardia scapigliata." In *L'alternativa letteraria del '900: Gadda.* Ed. Filippo Bettini, Mirko Bevilacqua, and Fabrizio Carlino. Rome: Savelli, 1975. 11–34.

Bettini, Filippo, Mirko Bevilacqua, and Fabrizio Carlino, eds. *L'alternativa letteraria del '900: Gadda.* Rome: Savelli, 1975.

Biasin, Gian-Paolo. *Literary Diseases: Theme and Metaphor in the Italian Novel.* Austin and London: University of Texas Press, 1975.

———. "La cornucopia del mondo." *Forum Italicum* 23 (1989): 30–50.

Blank, Andréas. "Discours émotif et discours contrastif." *Actes du colloque international de Toulouse 5–7 juillet 1990.* 33–45.

Blondiaux, Isabelle. *Louis-Ferdinand Céline: Une écriture psychotique.* Paris: Nizet, 1985.

Bo, Carlo, ed. *Narratori Spagnoli.* Milan: Bompiani, 1941.

Bonnefis, Philippe. "'Gone are the days . . .' L'invention de la musique dans l'oeuvre de Céline." *Modern Language Notes* 4 (1988): 800–823.

Borelli, Francesca. "A proposito degli incompiuti di Gadda." *Rassegna della Letteratura Italiana* 89 (1985): 493–98.

Bové, Paul, ed. *Early Postmodernism.* Durham, N.C.: Duke University Press, 1995.

Brater, Enoch, ed. *Beckett at 80/Beckett in Context.* Oxford and New York: Oxford University Press, 1986.

————. *Beyond Minimalism*. Oxford: Oxford University Press, 1987.

Breton, André. *Manifeste du surréalisme*. Paris: Sagittaire, 1924.

————. *Manifestes du surréalisme*. Montreuil: Pauvert, 1962.

————. *Nadja*. Paris: Gallimard, 1964.

Brienza, Susan. *Samuel Beckett's New Worlds: Style in Metafiction*. Norman and London: University of Oklahoma Press, 1987.

Bruck, Jan. "Beckett, Benjamin, and the Modern Crisis in Communication." *New German Critique* 26 (1982): 159–71.

Brun, Bernard. "Sur le Proust de Beckett." In *Beckett avant Beckett—Essais sur le jeune Beckett (1930–1945)*. Ed. Jean-Michel Rabaté. Paris: Presses de l'Ecole Normale Superieure. 79–91.

Bryden, Mary. *Women in Samuel Beckett's Prose and Drama*. N.Y.: Barnes and Noble Books, 1993.

Bryden, Mary, and John Pilling, eds. *The Ideal Core of the Onion: Reading Beckett Archives*. Bristol: Longdunn Press, 1992.

Buccheri, Mauro, and Elio Costa, eds. *Italo Svevo: Tra moderno e postmoderno*. Ravenna: Longo, 1995.

Buck-Morss, Susan. *The Origin of Negative Dialectics*. New York and London: Free Press, 1977.

Buckley, William, ed. *Critical Essays on Louis-Ferdinand Céline*. Boston: G. K. Hall, 1989.

Budgen, Frank. *James Joyce and the Making of Ulysses*. London: Grayson, 1934.

Burch, Noël. *Life to Those Shadows*. London: British Film Institute, 1990.

Bürger, Peter. *Theory of the Avant-garde*. Minneapolis: University of Minnesota Press, 1984.

————. *The Decline of Modernism*. University Park: Pennsylvania State University Press, 1992).

Burns, Wayne. *A Contextualized Reading of Journey at the End of Night and Death on the Installment Plan*. New York: Lang, 1988.

Calinescu, Matei. *Five Faces of Modernity*. Durham, N.C.: Duke University Press, 1987.

Calinescu, Matei, and Douwe Fokkema, eds. *Exploring Postmodernism*. Amsterdam and Philadelphia: John Benjamins, 1986.

Callinicos, Alex. *Against Postmodernism*. New York: St. Martin's Press, 1990.

Calvino, Italo. *Lezioni Americane*. Milan: Garzanti, 1988.

————. *Una pietra sopra*. Torino: Einaudi, 1980.

Cannon, Jo-Ann. "Notes on Gadda's Critical Essays." *Canadian Journal of Italian Studies* 5 (1981–82): 67–71.

————. *Post-modern Italian Fiction*. Cranbury: Associated University Press, 1989.

Carey, Phyllis, and Ed Jewinski, eds. *Re: Joyce 'n Beckett*. New York: Fordham University Press, 1992.

Carile, Paolo. "Editeurs, critiques, et public italiens face à Céline." *Australian Journal of French Studies* 13 (1976): 150–61.

————. "La critique italienne." *La Revue des lettres modernes: Louis-Ferdinand Céline* 5 (1988): 101–85.

Carson, Jane. *Céline's Imaginary Space*. New York: Peter Lang, 1987.

Caselli, Daniela. "Beckett's Intertextual Modalities of Appropriation." *Journal of Beckett Studies* 1 (Autumn 1996): 1–24.

Cases, Cesare. "Un ingegnere di letteratura." *Mondo operaio* 5 (1958): 7–17.

Cavallini, Giorgio. *Lingua e dialetto in Gadda*. Messina and Firenze: D'Anna, 1977.

Ceccaroni, Arnaldo, ed. *Leggere Gadda: Antologia della critica gaddiana*. Bologna: Zanichelli, 1977.

Céline, Louis-Ferdinand. *Bagatelles pour un massacre*. Paris: Denoël, 1937.

————. *La Vie et l'oeuvre de Philippe-Ignace Semmelweis*. Paris: Denoël and Steele, 1937.

————. *L'Ecole des cadavres*. Paris: Denoël, 1938.

————. *Les Beaux Draps*. Paris: Denoël, 1941.

————. *Féerie pour une autre fois*. Paris: Gallimard, 1952.

————. *Mort à crédit*. Paris: Gallimard, 1952.

————. *Voyage au bout de la nuit*. Paris: Gallimard, 1952.

————. *Casse-pipe*. Paris: Gallimard, 1970.

————. "Lettre à Lucien Combelle." Ed. Michel Beaujour, Dominique Le Roux, and Michel Thélia. *Cahier de l'Herne* 3–5 (1972):106.

————. *Mea Culpa*. Ed. Club de l'Honnête Homme. Paris: Gallimard, 1981.

————. *Romans I*, Collection "La Pléiade." Paris: Gallimard, 1981.

————. *Entretiens avec le Professeur Y*. Hanover, N.H., and London: Brandeis University Press, 1986.

————. *Le style contre les idées*. Ed. Lucien Combelle. Paris: Editions Complexe, 1987.

————. *Lettres à la N.R.F 1931–1961*. Ed. Pascal Fouché. Paris, Gallimard, 1991.

Chesneau, Albert. *La Langue sauvage de Louis-Ferdinand Céline*. Lille: Service de reproduction de thèse, 1974.

————. "Céline et l'ordre des mots." *Actes du Colloque International de Paris, 20–21 juin 1986*. 34–47.

Coe, Richard. "Beckett's English." In *Samuel Beckett: Humanistic Perspectives*. Ed. Pierre Astier, Morris Beja, and Stanley Gontarski. Columbus: Ohio State University Press, 1983. 36–57.

Cohn, Ruby. *The Comic Gamut*. New Brunswick, N.J.: Rutgers University Press, 1962.

————, ed. *Samuel Beckett: A Collection of Criticism*. New York: McGraw-Hill, 1975.

Colum, Mary, and Padraic Colum. *Our Friend James Joyce*. Garden City, N.Y.: Doubleday, 1958.

Connor, Steven. *Samuel Beckett: Repetition, Theory, and Text*. Oxford: Basil Blackwell, 1988.

Contini, Gianfranco. *Lettere a Gianfranco Contini, a cura del destinatario 1934–1966*. Milan: Garzanti, 1988.

————. *Quarant'anni d'amicizia*. Torino: Einaudi, 1989.

Cook, David. *A History of Narrative Film*. New York: W. W. Norton, 1990.

Coward, Rosalind, and John Ellis. *Language and Materialism*. London and New York: Routledge and Kegan Paul, 1977.

Cresciucci, Alain. *Les Territoires Céliniens*. Paris: Klincksieck, 1990.

————, ed. *Céline: Voyage au bout de la nuit*. Paris: Klincksieck, 1993.

Culik, Hugh. "The Place of *Watt* in Beckett's Development." *Modern Fiction Studies* 29 (1983).

Culler, Jonathan. "Phenomenology and Structuralism." *The Human Context* 5 (1973): 35–42.

————. *The Pursuit of Signs: Semiotics, Literature, Deconstruction*. Ithaca, N.Y.: Cornell University Press, 1981.

————. *On Deconstruction*. Ithaca, N.Y.: Cornell University Press, 1982.

Cunningham, Valentine. *British Writers of the Thirties*. Oxford and New York: Oxford University Press, 1988.

Dearlove, J. E. *Accommodating the Chaos*. Durham, N.C.: Duke University Press, 1982.

————. "Syntax Upended in Opposite Corners: Alterations in Beckett's Linguistic Theories." In *Samuel Beckett: Humanistic Perspectives*. Ed. Pierre Astier, Morris Beja, and Stanley Gontarski. Columbus: Ohio State University Press, 1983. 122–28.

de Beauvoir Simone, *La Force des Choses*. Paris: Gallimard, 1963.

DeBenedetti, Giacomo. *Il romanzo italiano del 900*. Milan: Garzanti, 1971.

De Benedictis, Maurizio. *La piega nera*. Anzio: De Rubeis, 1991.

de Boissieu, Jean-Louis. "Quelques effets 'littéraires' ou archaïsants dans *Voyage au bout de la nuit*." *La Revue des lettres modernes* 462–467 (1976): 33–51.

de la Quérière, Yves. *Etude stylistique des effets de mots dans Voyage au bout de la nuit*. Lexington: University Press of Kentucky, 1973.

————. "'Sacer Esto:' Reading Céline through Georges Bataille." In *Critical Essays on Louis-Ferdinand Céline*. Ed. William Buckley. Boston: G. K. Hall, 1989. 278–300.

Deleuze, Gilles. *Kafka: Toward a Minor Literature*. Minneapolis: University of Minnesota Press, 1986.

————. "L'Epuisé." Appendix to *Quad et autres pièces pour la télévision*. Paris: Minuit, 1992.

————. *The Deleuze Reader*. Ed. Constantin Boundas. New York: Columbia University Press, 1993.

————. *The Fold: Leibnitz and the Baroque*. Minneapolis: University of Minnesota Press, 1993.

————. *Difference and Repetition*. N.Y.: Columbia University Press, 1994.

de Man, Paul. *Blindness and Insight: Rhetoric of Contemporary Criticism*. New York: Oxford University Press, 1971.

————. *Allegories of Reading: Figural Language in Rousseau, Nietzsche, Rilke, and Proust*. New Haven: Yale University Press, 1979.

————. *The Resistance to Theory.* Minneapolis: University of Minnesota Press, 1986.

De Maria. "Introduzione." Marinetti. *Teoria e invenzione futurista.* Milan: Mondadori, 1968. xix–lxxi.

Derrida, Jacques. *Speech and Phenomena, and Other Essays on Husserl's Theory of Signs.* Evanston, Ill.: Northwestern University Press, 1973.

————. *Of Grammatology.* Baltimore and London: Johns Hopkins University Press, 1974.

————. *La Vérité en peinture.* Paris: Flammarion, 1978.

————. *Writing and Difference.* Chicago: University of Chicago Press, 1978.

————. *Dissemination.* Chicago: University of Chicago Press, 1981.

————. *Positions.* Chicago: University of Chicago Press, 1981.

————. "Two Words for Joyce." In *Post-structuralist Joyce.* Ed. Derek Attridge and Daniel Ferrer. Cambridge: Cambridge University Press, 1984.

————. "Living On: Border Lines." *Deconstruction and Criticism.* New York: Continuum, 1987. 75–176.

————. *Between the Blinds: A Derrida Reader.* New York: Columbia University Press, 1991.

De Saussure, Ferdinand. *Course in General Linguistics.* New York and Toronto: McGraw Hill, 1966.

Devoto, Giacomo. *Itinerario Stilistico.* Firenze: Le Monnier, 1975.

Dherbey, Gilbert Romeyer. "L'Esthétique de Louis-Ferdinand Céline." *Nouvelle Revue Française* 400 (1986): 53–67.

Dombroski, Robert. *Introduzione allo studio di C. E. Gadda.* Firenze: Nuove Edizioni Vallecchi, 1974.

————. *La totalità dell'artificio: Ideologia e forma nel romanzo di Pirandello.* Padova: Liviana Editrice, 1978.

————. "Overcoming Oedipus: Self and Society in *La cognizione del dolore.*" *Modern Language Notes* 99 (1984): 125–43.

————. *Properties of Writing: Ideological Discourse in Modern Italian Fiction.* Baltimore, Md.: Johns Hopkins University Press, 1994.

————. and Manuela Bertone, eds. *Contemporary Perspectives on Carlo Emilio Gadda.* Toronto: University of Toronto Press, 1997.

————. *Creative Entanglements: Gadda and the Baroque.* Toronto: University of Toronto Press, 1999.

Doubrovsky, Serge. *Autobiographies: De Corneille à Sartre.* Paris: Presses Universitaires de France, 1988.

Dunwoodie, Peter. "Merveilleux, étrange et fantastique dans les romans de Louis-Ferdinand Céline." *Les Lettres Romanes* 37 (1983): 82–111.

Eagleton, Terry. *Literary Theory.* Minneapolis: University of Minnesota Press, 1983.

Eco, Umberto. *The Name of the Rose.* New York: Harcourt Brace Jovanovich, 1983.

————. *Semiotics and the Philosophy of Language.* Bloomington: Indiana University Press, 1984.

―――. *The Aesthetics of Chaosmos*. Hutchinson and Cambridge, Mass.: Harvard University Press, 1989.

―――. "Form as Social Commitment." *The Open Work*. Cambridge, Mass.: Harvard University Press, 1989. 123–57.

―――. *Foucault's Pendulum*. New York: Harcourt Brace Jovanovich, 1989.

―――. *La ricerca della lingua perfetta nella cultura europea*. Bari: Laterza, 1993.

Eisenstein Sergei. "The Cinematographic Principle and the Ideogram." *Film Form: Essays in Form*. New York: Harcourt, Brace and World, 1949.

Eliot, T. S. "Ulysses, Order and Myth." In *James Joyce: Two Decades of Criticism*. Ed. Seon Givens. New York: Vangard Press, 1948.

Esslin, Martin, ed. *Samuel Beckett: A Collection of Critical Essays*. Englewood Cliffs, N.J.: Prentice-Hall, 1965.

Farrow, Anthony. *Early Beckett: Art and Allusion in More Pricks than Kicks and Murphy*. Troy, N.Y.: Whitston, 1991.

Federman, Raymond. *Journey to Chaos*. Berkeley and Los Angeles: University of California Press, 1965.

Federman, Raymond, and Lawrence Graver, eds. *Samuel Beckett: The Critical Heritage*. London: Routledge and Kegan Paul, 1979.

Ferrero, Ernesto. *Invito alla lettura di C. E. Gadda*. Milan: Mursia, 1972.

Figueras, André, ed. *Poètes d'Aujourd'hui: Jules Romains*. Paris: Seghers, 1952.

Flaubert, Gustave. *Letters*. Ed. Francis Steegmuller. Cambridge, Mass: Belknap Press, 1980.

Fletcher, John. "The Private Pain and the Whey of Words: A Survey of Beckett's Verse. In *Samuel Beckett: A Collection of Critical Essays*. Ed. Martin Esslin. Englewood Cliffs, N.J.: Prentice Hall, 1965. 23–32.

―――. *Samuel Beckett's Art*. London: Chatto and Windus, 1971.

Flores, Enrico. *Accessioni Gaddiane*. Napoli: Loffredo, 1973.

Foucault, Michel. *The Archeology of Knowledge and the Discourse on Language*. New York: Pantheon Books, 1972.

―――. *The Order of Things*. New York: Random House, 1973.

Fowlie, Wallace. *Age of Surrealism*. New York: Swallow Press, 1950.

Frank, Nino. "Le cas Gadda." *Le Mercure de France* 1133 (1958): 131–34.

Fratnik, Marina. *L'écriture détournée: Essai sur le texte narratif de C.E. Gadda*. Torino: Albert Meynier, 1990.

Friedman, Bruce Jay, ed. *Black Humor*. New York: Bantam, 1965.

Friedman, Melvin. *Samuel Beckett Now*. Chicago: University of Chicago Press, 1970.

―――. "The Novels of Samuel Beckett: An Amalgam of Joyce and Proust." In *Critical Essays on Samuel Beckett*. Ed. Patrick McCarthy. Boston: G. K. Hall, 1986. 11–21.

Gabetta, Gianfranco. "Gadda e il caledoscopio dell'euresi." *Aut Aut* 256 (1993): 15–43.

Gadda, Carlo Emilio. *Meditazione milanese*, a cura di Gian Carlo Roscioni. Torino: Einaudi, 1974.

————. *Lettere a Solaria*, a cura di Giuliano Manacorda. Rome: Editori Riuniti, 1979.

————. *Racconto italiano di ignoto del novecento, Scritti vari e postumi*. Torino: Einaudi, 1983.

————. *La cognizione del dolore*, a cura di Emilio Manzotti. Torino: Einaudi, 1987.

————. *Lettere a Gianfranco Contini*, a cura del destinatario 1934–1966. Milan: Garzanti, 1988.

————. *Romanzi e racconti I*, a cura di Raffaella Rotondi, Guido Lucchini, Emilio Manzotti. Milan: Garzanti, 1988.

————. *Romanzi e racconti II*, a cura di Giorgio Pinotti, Dante Isella, Raffaella Rotondi. Milan: Garzanti, 1989.

————. *Saggi giornali favole e altri scritti I*, a cura di Liliana Orlando, Clelia Martignoni, Dante Isella. Milan: Garzanti, 1991.

————. *Saggi giornali favole II*, a cura di Claudio Vela, Gianmarco Gaspari, Giorgio Pinotti, Franco Gavazzeni, Dante Isella, Maria Antonietta Terzoli. Milan: Garzanti, 1992.

————. *"Per favore mi lasci nell'ombra" Interviste 1950–1972*, a cura di Claudio Vela. Milan: Adelphi, 1993.

————. *Scritti vari e postumi*, a cura di Andrea Silvestri, Claudio Vela, Dante Isella, Paola Italia, Giorgio Pinotti. Milan: Garzanti, 1993.

Galdenzi Capobianco, Mirella. "Cronache da un labirinto: appunti per la poetica di Gadda." *Annali dell'Istituto Orientale di Napoli, Sezione Romanza* 26 (1984): 173–207.

Gasché, Rodolphe. *The Tain of the Mirror: Derrida and the Philosophy of Reflection*. Cambridge, Mass.: Harvard University Press, 1986.

Ghidetti Enrico. *Italo Svevo: La coscienza di un borghese triestino*. Rome: Editori Riuniti, 1992.

Gibson, Andrew. *Reading Narrative Discourse: Studies in the Novel from Cervantes to Beckett*. New York: St. Martin's Press, 1990.

Gide, André. "Les Juifs, Céline et Maritain." Ed. Michel Beaujour, Dominique Le Roux, Michel Thélia. *Cahier de l'Herne* 3–5 (1972): 468–70.

Gilbert, Stuart. *James Joyce's Ulysses*. New York: Vintage Books, 1930.

Gioanola, Elio. *L'uomo dei topazi: Saggio psicoanalitico su C.E. Gadda*. Genoa: Il melangolo, 1977.

Giordano, Paolo, Albert Mancini, and Anthony Tamburri, eds. *Italiana 1988*. River Forest, Ill.: Rosary College, 1990.

Gindin, James. *British Fiction in the Thirties*. New York: St. Martin's Press, 1992.

Girard, René. *Mensonge romantique et verité romanesque*. Paris: Grasset, 1961.

Gluck, Barbara. *Beckett and Joyce: Friendship and Fiction*. Lewisburg, Pa.: Bucknell University Press, 1979.

Godard, Henri. "Un art poétique." *La Revue des lettres modernes* 398–402 (1974): 7–40.

————. "Préface." Louis-Ferdinand Céline, *Romans I*. Collection "La Pléiade." Paris: Gallimard, 1981. ix–liii.

————. *Poétique de Céline*. Paris: Gallimard, 1985.

————. *Céline Scandale*. Paris: Gallimard. 1994.

Gontarski, Stanley, ed. "The Intent of Undoing in Samuel Beckett's Art." *Modern Fiction Studies* 29 (1983): 5–23.

————. *The Beckett Studies Reader*. Gainesville: University Presses of Florida, 1993.

Gordon, Lois. *The World of Samuel Beckett 1906–1946*. New Haven: Yale University Press, 1996.

Grassi, Letizia. "L'aspetto figurale-simbolico e la polifonia dei linguaggi nella *Cognizione del dolore* di C. E. Gadda." *Lingua e stile* 2 (1989): 245–64.

Gray, Margaret. *Postmodern Proust*. Philadelphia: University of Pennsylvania Press, 1992.

Green, Matthews Mary Jean. *Fiction in the Historical Present: French Writers and the Thirties*. Hanover, N.H.: University Press of New England, 1986.

Guénot, Jean. *Louis-Ferdinand Céline damné par l'écriture* (1973).

Guglielmi, Guido. *La prosa italiana del novecento*. Torino: Einaudi, 1986.

————. "Gadda e la tradizione del romanzo." *Carlo Emilio Gadda: La coscienza infelice*, ed. Andreini Alba and Marziano Guglieminetti. Milan: Guerini Studio, 1996. 17–37.

Guglielminetti, Marziano. "Gadda/Gaddus: diari, giornali e note autobiografiche di geurra." In *C.E. Gadda: La coscienza infelice*. Ed. Andreini Alba and Marziano Guglielminetti. Milan: Guerini Studio, 1996. 17–37.

Hainsworth, Peter. "Fascism and Anti-Fascism in Gadda." In *Carlo Emilio Gadda: Contemporary Perspectives*. Ed. Manuela Bertone and Robert Dombroski. Toronto: University of Toronto Press, 1997. 221–41.

Harrington, John. *The Irish Beckett*. Syracuse, N.Y.: Syracuse University Press, 1991.

Harvey, Lawrence. *Samuel Beckett: Poet and Critic*. Princeton, N.J.: Princeton University Press, 1970.

Hassan, Ihab. "Joyce, Beckett, and the Postmodern Imagination." *Triquarterly* 34 (1975): 179–200.

Hayman, David. *The "Wake" in Transit*. Ithaca, N.Y.: Cornell University Press, 1990.

Heidegger, Martin. "The Origin of the Work of Art." *Poetry, Language, Thought*. New York: Harper and Row, 1971. 17–87.

Henning Debevec, Sylvie. "The Guffaw of the Abderite: Murphy and the Democritean Universe." *Journal of Beckett Studies* 10 (1985): 5–20.

————. *Beckett's Critical Complicity: Carnival, Contestation, and Tradition*. Lexington: University Press of Kentucky, 1991.

Hertz, Neil. "The Notion of Blockage in the Literature of the Sublime." In *Psychoanalysis and the Question of the Text*. Ed. Geoffrey Hartman. Baltimore and London: Johns Hopkins University Press, 1978. 62–85.

Hesla, David. *The Shape of Chaos: An Interpretation of the Art of Samuel Beckett*. Minneapolis: University of Minnesota Press, 1971.

Hewitt, Nicholas. "*Mort à crédit* et la crise de la petite bourgeoisie." *Australian Journal of French Studies* 13, no. 1–2 (1976): 110–18.

———. *The Golden Age of Louis-Ferdinand Céline*. Hamburg and New York: Berg Publishers, 1987.

Hill, Leslie. *Beckett's Fiction in Different Words*. Cambridge: Cambridge University Press, 1990.

Hjelmslev, Louis. *Prolegomena to a Theory of Language*. Madison: University of Wisconsin Press, 1973.

Hoffman, Frederick. *Samuel Beckett: The Language of Self*. Carbondale: Southern Illinois University Press, 1962.

Hokenson, Ian. "Céline's Impressionist in Language," *Esprit Créateur* 13 (1973): 329–39.

Holtus, Günther. "Code parlé et code écrit." *Australian Journal of French Studies* 1–2 (1976): 36–46.

Hutcheon, Linda. *Narcissistic Narratives: The Metafictional Paradox*. Waterloo, Ont.: Wilfrid Laurier Press, 1980.

Huyssen, Andreas. *After the Great Divide: Modernism, Mass Culture, Postmodernism*. Bloomington: Indiana University Press, 1986.

Ifri, Pascal. "Temps et chronologie dans *Voyage au bout de la nuit*." *Romance Quarterly* 36 (1989): 27–37.

Isella, Dante. "Prefazione." Gadda, Carlo Emilio. *Racconto italiano di ignoto del novecento*. Torino: Einaudi, 1983. v–xxvii.

———. "Presentazione." Gadda. *Romanzi e racconti I*, a cura di Raffaella Rotondi, Guido Lucchini, Emilio Manzotti. Milan: Garzanti, 1988. xvii–xxiii.

Iser, Wolfgang. *The Implied Reader: Patterns of Communication in Prose from Bunyan to Beckett*. Baltimore and London: Johns Hopkins University Press, 1974.

———. *The Act of Reading: A Theory of Aesthetic Response*. Baltimore and London: Johns Hopkins University Press, 1978.

———. *Prospecting: From Reader Response to Literary Anthropology*. Baltimore and London: Johns Hopkins University Press, 1989.

Jakobson, Roman. "Linguistics and Poetics." In *Language and Literature*. Ed. Krystyna Pomorska and Stephen Rudy. Cambridge, Mass.: Harvard University Press, 1987. 62–94

———. "Two Aspects of Language and Two Types of Aphasic Disturbances." In *Language and Literature*. Ed. Krystyna Pomorska and Stephen Rudy. Cambridge, Mass.: Harvard University Press, 1987. 94–114.

James, Henry. *The Portrait of a Lady*. Boston: Houghton Mifflin, 1963.

Jameson, Fredric. *The Political Unconscious*. Ithaca, N.Y.: Cornell University Press, 1981.

———. *Postmodernism, or the Cultural Logic of Late Capitalism*. Durham, N.C.: Duke University Press, 1991.

Jannini P. A., and Sergio Zoppi, eds. *Quaderni del Novecento Francese 4*. Rome: Bulzoni, 1978.

Jean-Bloch, Michel. *Le présent de l'indicatif: Essai sur le nouveau roman*. Paris: Gallimard, 1973.

Joyce, James. *Ulysses*. New York: Random House, 1966.

———. *A Portrait of the Artist as a Young Man*. New York: The Viking Press, 1968.

———. *Finnegans Wake*. New York: Penguin, 1976.

Juilland, Alphonse. *Les Verbes de Céline*. Saratoga, Calif.: ANMA Libri, 1985.

Kaplan, Alice Y. *Reproductions of Banality*. Minneapolis: University of Minnesota Press, 1986.

———. "Sources and Quotations in Céline's *Bagatelles pour un massacre*." In *Céline and the Politics of Difference*. Ed. Rosemarie Scullion, Philip Solomon, and Thomas Spear. Hanover, N.H., and London: University of New England Press, 1995.

———. "The Céline Effect: A 1992 Survey of Contemporary American Writers." *Modernism/Modernity* 3, no. 1 (1996): 117–36.

Kearney, Richard. *Dialogues with Contemporary Continental Thinkers*. Manchester: Manchester University Press, 1984.

Keir, Elam. "Not I: Beckett's Mouth and the Ars(e) Rhetorica." In *Beckett at 80/ Beckett in Context*. Ed. Enoch Brater. Oxford and New York: Oxford University Press, 1986. 124–48.

Kennedy, Sighle. *Murphy's Bed*. Lewisburg: Bucknell University Press, 1971.

Kenner, Hugh. *Samuel Beckett: A Critical Study*. New York: Grove Press, 1961.

———. *A Reader's Guide to Samuel Beckett*. New York: Farrar, Straus and Giroux, 1973.

———. "Shades of Syntax." In *Samuel Beckett: A Collection of Criticism*. Ed. Ruby Cohn. New York: McGraw-Hill, 1975. 21–31.

Kerouac, Jack. "Jack Kerouac." Ed. Michel Beaujour, Dominique Le Roux, Michel Thélia. *Cahier de l'Herne* 3–5 (1972): 423.

Knapp, Bettina. *Céline: Man of Hate*. Alabama: University of Alabama Press, 1974.

Knowlson, James and John Pilling. *Frescoes of the Skull*. London: John Calder, 1979.

———. *Damned to Fame: The Life of Samuel Beckett*. London: Bloomsbury Publishing, 1996.

Krance, Charles. *The I of the Storm*. Lexington: University Press of Kentucky, 1992.

Kristeva, Julia. *Desire in Language*. New York: Columbia University Press, 1980.

———. *Powers of Horror: An Essay on Abjection*. New York: Columbia University Press, 1982.

Kroll, Jeri. "'I Create, Therefore I Am': The Artist's Mind in Samuel Beckett's Fiction." *AUMLA* 55 (1981).

Krysinski, Wladimir. *La novela en sus modernidades*. Madrid and Frankfurt: Vervuert Verlag and Iberoamericana, 1988. 119–31.

———. "Carlo Emilio Gadda and Louis-Ferdinand Céline: Some Considerations on the Novel in Progress." In *Contemporary Perspectives on Carlo Emilio Gadda*. Ed. Manuela Bertone and Robert Dombroski. Toronto: University of Toronto Press, 1996. 195–220.

———. "Rethinking Postmodernism (with some Latin American Excurses). In *Latin American Postmodernisms*. Ed. Richard Young. Amsterdam: Rodopi, 1997. 9–27.

Lacan, Jacques. *Ecrits: A Selection.* London: Tavistock, 1977.

———. "The Mirror Stage as Formative of the Function of the I as Revealed in Psychoanalytical Experience." In *Critical Theory since 1965.* Ed. Hazard Adams and Leroy Searle. Tallahassee: Florida State University Press, 1986. 734–38.

Lamont, Rosette. "Yesterday's Avant-garde, Today's Great Classics: Beckett, Ionesco, Tardieu." *Laurels* (Spring 1985): 37–56.

Latin Racelle, Danièle. "*Voyage au bout de la nuit* ou l'inauguration d'une poétique argotique." *La Revue des lettres modernes* 462–67 (1976). 53–77.

———. "*Voyage au bout de la nuit:* de la phrase segmentée à la 'petite musique" de Céline." *Au bonheur des mots: Mélanges en l'honneur de Gerald Antoine.* Nancy: Presses Universitaires de Nancy, 1984. 301–7.

———. "Fonction de l'argot dans la narration." *Le Voyage au bout de la nuit: Roman de la subversion et subversion du roman.* Bruxelles: Palais des Academies, 1988. 151–63.

LeBlanc, James. "On Excrement, Time and Style in Céline's *Mort à crédit.*" *Degree Second* 12 (1989): 77–86.

Leopardi, Giacomo. *Canti.* Milan: Mursia, 1977.

Levinas, Emmanuel. *The Levinas Reader.* Ed. Sean Hand. Cambridge, Mass.: Blackwell, 1986.

Levy, Press. Eric. *Beckett and the Voice of the Species: A Study of the Prose Fiction.* Totowa, N.J.: Gill and Macmillan, 1980.

Lipparini, Micaela. *Le metafore del vero.* Pisa: Pacini, 1994.

Locatelli, Carla. *Unwording the World: Samuel Beckett's Prose Works after the Nobel Prize.* Philadelphia: Pennsylvania University Press, 1990.

Loselle, Andrea. "Bardamu's American Dream: Censorship and Prostitution." *South Atlantic Quarterly* 93, no. 2 (1994): 225–42.

Loughrey, Bryan, and Neil Taylor. "Murphy's Surrender to Symmetry." *Journal of Beckett Studies* 11 (1989): 79–90.

Lucchini, Guido. "Strategia retorica nelle scelte lessicali del primo Gadda." *Studi Novecenteschi* 10 (1983): 57–94.

———. "Gli studi filosofici di Gadda." *Strumenti Critici* 75 (1994): 223–45.

Lucente, Gregory. "'Non conclude': Self-Consciousness and the Boundaries of Modernism in Pirandello's Narrative." *Criticism* 1 (1984): 21–47.

Lucini, Gian Pietro. *Filosofi ultimi.* Rome: Libreria Moderna, 1913.

Lukács, Georg. *Realism in Our Time.* New York: Harper and Row, 1964.

Luperini, Romano. *L'allegoria del moderno.* Rome: Editori Riuniti, 1990. 203–19.

Lyotard, Jean-François. *Discours, figure.* Paris: Klincksieck, 1971.

———. *The Postmodern Condition: A Report on Knowledge.* Minneapolis: University of Minnesota Press, 1984.

———. *Phenomenology.* Albany: State University of New York Press, 1991.

———. *The Inhuman: Reflections on Time.* Stanford, Calif.: Stanford University Press, 1991. 24–35.

———. *The Postmodern Explained.* Minneapolis: University of Minnesota Press, 1992.

————. "The Sublime and the Avant-Garde." In *Postmodernism: A Reader*. Ed. Thomas Docherty. New York: Columbia University Press, 1993. 244–56.

————. *Lessons on the Analytic of the Sublime*. Stanford, Calif: Stanford University Press, 1994.

Mambrino, Jean. "Céline and His Touch of Music." In *Céline and His Critics: Scandals and Paradox*. Ed. Luce Stanford. Saratoga, Calif.: ANMA Libri, 1986. 163–85.

Manacorda, Giuliano, ed. *Lettere a Solaria*. Rome: Editori Riuniti, 1979.

Mancini, Albert, Paolo Giordano, and Anthony Tamburry, eds. *Italiana 1988*. River Forest, Ill: Rosary College, 1990.

Manganaro, Jean-Paul. *Le Baroque et l'ingénieur*. Paris: Seuil, 1994.

Manzotti, Emilio. "Introduzione." Gadda. *La cognizione del dolore*. Torino: Einaudi, 1987. vii–li.

Marcuse, Herbert. *Negations: Essays in Critical Theory*. London: Penguin Books, 1986. 88–133.

Marinetti, Filippo Tommaso. *Teoria e invenzione futurista*, a cura di Luciano de Maria. Milan: Mondadori, 1968.

Marx, Karl. *The Communist Manifesto*. Ed. David McLellan. Oxford: Oxford University Press, 1988. 20–47.

Mauriac, Claude. *The New Literature*. New York: Braziller, 1959.

Mauthner, Fritz. *Beiträge zu einer Kritick der Sprache*. Leipzig: Felix Meiner, 1923.

————. *Wörterbuch der Philosophie*. Vienna: Böhlau, 1923.

Mazzacurati, Giancarlo. *Pirandello nel romanzo europeo*. Bologna: Il Mulino, 1987.

McCarthy, Patrick, ed. *Critical Essays on Samuel Beckett*. Boston: G. K. Hall, 1986.

McFarlane, James. "The Mind of Modernism." In *Modernism: A Guide to European Literature 1890–1930*. Ed. Malcom Bradbury and James McFarlane. New York: Penguin, 1976. 71–93.

————. "The Name and Nature of Modernism." In *Modernism: A Guide to European Literature 1890–1930*. Ed. Malcom Bradbury and James McFarlane. New York: Penguin, 1976. 19–55.

McGowan, John. *Postmodernism and Its Critics*. Ithaca, N.Y.: Cornell University Press, 1991.

McHale, Brian. *Postmodernist Fiction*. London: Methuen, 1987.

McMillan, Dougald, ed. "Samuel Beckett and the Visual Arts." In *Samuel Beckett: A Collection of Criticism*. Ed. Ruby Cohn. New York: McGraw-Hill, 1975. 121–35.

————. *Transition: The History of a Literary Era 1927–1938*. New York: George Braziller, 1976.

Miller, Henry. "Henry Miller." Ed. Michel Beaujour, Dominique Le Roux, Michel Thélia. *Cahier de l'Herne* 3–5 (1972): 426.

Miller, Lawrence. *Samuel Beckett: The Expressive Dilemma*. New York: St. Martin's Press, 1992.

Mintz, Samuel. "Beckett's *Murphy*: A 'Cartesian' Novel." *Perspectives* 11 (1959): 156–65.

Mitchell, Breon. "Samuel Beckett and the Postmodernism Controversy." In *Exploring Postmodernism*. Ed. Matei Calinescu and Douwe Fokkema. Amsterdam and Philadelphia: John Benjamins, 1986. 109–21.

Montaut, Annie. "Poésie de la grammaire chez Céline." *Poétique* 50 (1982): 226–35.

Moorjani, Angela. *Abysmal Games in the Novels of Samuel Beckett*. Chapel Hill: University of North Carolina Press, 1982.

Moretti, Franco. *Opera Mondo*. Torino: Einaudi, 1994.

Moriconi, Bernardina. *Beckett e altro assurdo*. Naples: Guida, 1990.

Morot-Sir, Edouard, ed. *Samuel Beckett: The Art of Rhetoric*. Chapel Hill, University of North Carolina Press, 1976.

———. "Samuel Beckett and Cartesian Emblems." In *Samuel Beckett: The Art of Rhetoric*. Ed. Edouard Morot-Sir. Chapel Hill: University of North Carolina Press, 1976. 25–104.

Mur Lorda, Clara. "Oralité et littéralité dans les romans de Céline. Quelques aspects du rhythme dans la prose Célinienne." *Colloque International de Toulouse 5–7 juillet 1990*. 123–32.

Muray, Philippe. *Céline*. Paris: Seuil, 1981.

Murphy, P. J. "Beckett and the Philosophers." In *The Cambridge Companion to Beckett*. Ed. John Pilling. Cambridge: Cambridge University Press, 1994. 222–40.

Muzzioli, Francesco. "Il 'Voyage' di Céline e il 'Pasticciaccio' di Gadda: due percorsi dall'allegoria alla tautegoria." *L'alternativa letteraria del '900*, a cura di Filippo Bettini, Mirko Bevilacqua, Fabrizio Carlino. Rome: Savelli, 1975. 101–42.

Nava, Giuseppe. "C. E. Gadda lettore di Manzoni." *Belfagor* 3 (1965): 339–52.

Nettelbeck, Colin. "Coordonnées musicales de l'esthétique romanesque de Céline." *Australian Journal of French Studies* 1–2 (1976): 80–87.

———. "Notion and Function of Transposition." In *Céline and His Critics: Scandals and Paradox*. Ed. Luce Stanford. Saratoga, Calif.: ANMA Libri, 1986. 186–95.

Nicholls, Peter. *Modernisms: A Literary Guide*. Berkeley and Los Angeles: University of California Press, 1995.

Nietzsche, Friedrich. *The Birth of Tragedy and The Genealogy of Morals*. New York: Doubleday, 1956.

———. *Human, All Too Human*. New York: Routledge, 1996.

Noble, Ian. *Language and Narration in Céline's Writings: The Challenge of Disorder*. Atlantic Highlands, N.J.: Humanities Press International, 1987.

Norman, Page. *The Thirties*. Basingstoke: McMillan Education, 1990.

O'Brien, Eoin. *The Beckett Country*. London: Faber and Faber and Black Cat Press, 1986.

———. "Foreword." Samuel Beckett. *Dream of Fair to Middling Women*. New York: Arcade Publishing, 1992. xi–xx.

Oddenino, Giuseppina. "Gadda o la creatività del non finito," *Metamorfosi della novella*, a cura di Giorgio Barberi Squarotti. Foggia: Bastogi, 1985. 367–90.

Oliva, Renato. *Samuel Beckett. Prima del silenzio*. Milan: Mursia, 1967.

O'Neill. John. *The Poverty of Postmodernism*. London: Routledge, 1995.

Overbeck, Lois. "Behind and beyond the Camera Eye." Unpublished paper. *The Strasbourg Conference on Samuel Beckett*. April 2, 1996.

Panofsky, Erwin. "Style and Medium in the Motion Pictures." In *Three Essays on Style*. Ed. Irving Lavin. Cambridge, Mass.: MIT Press, 1995. 91–125.

Pasolini, Pier Paolo. *Passione e Ideologia*. Milan: Garzanti, 1960.

Pasquier, Marie-Claire. "Blanc, Gris, Noir, Gris, Blanc." *Cahiers Renaud-Barrault* 106 (1983): 61–79.

Patrizi, Giorgio, ed. *La critica e Gadda*. Bologna: Cappelli, 1975.

Pecoraro, Aldo. *Gadda e Manzoni. Il giallo della Cognizione del dolore*. Pisa: ETS, 1996.

Pefanis, Julian. *Heterology and the Postmodern*. Durham, N.C.: Duke University Press, 1991.

Perloff, Marjorie. *The Futurist Moment*. Chicago: University of Chicago Press, 1986.

Pilling, John. "Beckett's Proust." *Journal of Beckett Studies* 1 (Winter 1976): 8–29.

———. "From a (W)horoscope to *Murphy*." In *The Ideal Core of the Onion: Reading Beckett Archives*. Ed. Mary Bryden and John Pilling. Bristol: Longdunn Press, 1992. 1–20.

———, ed. *The Cambridge Companion to Beckett*. Cambridge: Cambridge University Press, 1994.

Pinottini, Marzio. "L'Unanimismo e l'estetica del futurismo." *Quaderni del novecento francese* 4, a cura di P. A. Jannini e Sergio Zoppi. Rome: Bulzoni, 1978. 95–112.

Pirandello, Luigi. *Saggi, poesie, scritti varii*, a cura di Manlio Lo Vecchio Musti. Milan: Mondadori, 1960.

———. *Il fu Mattia Pascal*. Milan: Mondadori, 1988.

———. *Uno, nessuno e centomila*. Milan: Mondadori, 1991.

———. *Novelle per un anno*. Firenze: Giunti, 1994.

Poulet, Robert. *Entretiens familiers avec Louis-Ferdinand Céline*. Paris: Plon, 1958.

Proust, Marcel. *Du côté de chez Swann*. Paris: Gallimard, 1954.

———. *Le Temps retrouvé*. Paris: Gallimard, 1989.

Pucci, Pietro. "The Obscure Sickness." *Italian Quarterly* 42 (1967): 43–62.

Queneau, Raymond. "Préface" to Gustave Flaubert, *Bouvard et Pécuchet*. Paris: Brodard et Taupin, 1959. 7–11.

Rabaté, Jean, ed. *Beckett avant Beckett—Essais sur le jeune Beckett*. Paris: Presses de l'Ecole Normale Supérieure, 1984.

Rabinovitz, Rubin. *The Development of Samuel Beckett's Fiction*. Urbana: University of Illinois Press, 1984.

———. "Beckett and Psychology." *Journal of Beckett Studies* 11, 1989: 65–77.

———. *Innovation in Samuel Beckett's Fiction*. Urbana: University of Illinois Press, 1992.

Raimondi, Ezio. *Barocco moderno: C.E. Gadda e Roberto Longhi*. Bologna: CUSL, 1990.

Ray, Robert. *A Certain Tendency of Hollywood Cinema: 1930–1980*. Princeton, N.J.: Princeton University Press, 1985.

Read, David. "Artistic Theory in the Work of Samuel Beckett." *Journal of Beckett Studies* 8 (1982): 7–22.

———. "Beckett's Search for Unseeable and Unmakeable: *Company* and *Ill Seen Ill Said*." *Modern Fiction Studies* 29 (1983): 111–25.

Richard, Jean-Pierre. *Microlectures*. Paris: Éditions du Seuil, 1979.

Ricks, Christopher. *Beckett's Dying Words—The Clarendon Lectures 1990*. Oxford: Clarendon Press, 1993.

Rilke, Rainer Maria. *Die Aufzeichnungen des Maltes Laurids Brigge*. In Rilke, *Gesammelte werke*. Leipzig: Insel-Verlag, 1951.

———. *Duisener Elegien*. Zurich: Manesse Verlag, 1951.

Risset, Jacqueline. "Carlo Emilio Gadda ou la philosophie à l'envers." *Critique* 282 (1970): 944–51.

Robbe-Grillet, Alain. *For a New Novel*. Evanston, Ill.: Northwestern University Press, 1989.

Robinson, Michael. *The Long Sonata of the Dead: A Study of Samuel Beckett*. New York: Grove Press, 1969.

Roscioni, Giancarlo. "La conclusione alla 'Cognizione del dolore'." *Paragone* 238 (1969): 86–99.

———. *La disarmonia prestabilita*. Torino: Einaudi, 1969.

———. "Introduzione." Gadda. *Meditazione milanese*. Torino: Einaudi, 1974. v–xl.

———. "Gadda umorista." *Strumenti Critici* 75 (1994): 147–62.

Rosen, Steven. *Samuel Beckett and the Pessimistic Tradition*. New Brunswick, N.J.: Rutgers University Press, 1976.

Rouayrenc Vigneau, Catherine. "Parlé et narration dans *Voyage au bout de la nuit*." In *Céline: Voyage au bout de la nuit*. Ed. Alain Cresciucci. Paris: Klincksieck, 1993. 141–49.

Sarraute, Nathalie. *L'Ere du soupçon*. Paris: Gallimard, 1956.

———. *The Age of Suspicion*. New York: George Braziller, 1963.

Sartre, Jean-Paul. *What Is Literature?* New York: Washington Square Press, 1966.

Sbragia, Albert. "From the Novel of Self-Ridicule to the Modern Macaronic." In *Italiana 1988*. Ed. Paolo Giordano, Albert Mancini, and Anthony Tamburri. River Forest, Ill.: Rosary College, 1990. 169–70.

———. *C. E. Gadda and the Modern Macaronic*. Gainesville and Tallahassee: University Presses of Florida, 1996.

Schatz, Thomas. *Old Hollywood/New Hollywood: Ritual, Art, and Industry*. Ann Harbor: UMI Research Press, 1983.

Schoolcraft, Ralph. "'Honi soit qui mal y danse:' Circulation and Transport in Céline's Early Novels." *Modern Language Notes* 105 (1990): 833–56.

Scullion, Rosemary, Philip Solomon, and Thomas Spear, eds. *Céline and the Politics of Difference*. Hanover, N.H., and London: University of New England Press, 1995.

Segre, Cesare. "Novità su Gadda," *Alfabeta* 55 (1983): 3–4.

———. *Intrecci di voci: La polifonia nella letteratura del novecento*. Torino: Einaudi, 1991.

Seroni, Adriano. *Gadda*. Firenze: La Nuova Italia, 1969.

Shaw Sailer, Susan. *On the Void To Be*. Ann Arbor: University of Michigan Press, 1993.

Silverman, Kaja. *The Subject of Semiotics*. New York: Oxford University Press, 1983.

Simon, Alfred. *Beckett*. Paris: Belfond, 1981.

Smith, André. *La Nuit de Louis-Ferdinand Céline*. Paris: Grasset, 1973.

Smith, Frederick N. "Beckett's Verbal Slapstick." *Modern Fiction Studies* 29 (1983): 43–55.

Solomon, Philippe. "The Plot as Conspiracy: Céline's Review of Renoir's *La Grande Illusion* in *Bagatelles pour un massacre*." In *Céline and the Politics of Difference*. Ed. Rosemarie Scullion, Philip Solomon, and Thomas Spear. Hanover, N.H., and London: University of New England Press, 1995. 47–63.

Spanos, William. "The Detective and the Boundary." In *Early Postmodernism*. Ed. Paul Bové. Durham, N.C.: Duke University Press, 1995. 17–39.

Spear, Thomas. "Le dévelopment des vois narratives multiples: L'émergence du narrataire Célinien." *Actes du Colloque International de Paris 20–21 juin 1986*. 258–68.

———. "Céline and 'Autofictional' First-person Narration." *Studies in the Novel* 23 (1991): 357–70.

———. "Virility and the Jewish 'Invasion' in Céline's Pamphlets." In *Céline and the Politics of Difference*. Ed. Rosemarie Scullion, Philip Solomon, and Thomas Spear. Hanover, N.H., and London: University of New England Press, 1995. 98–119.

Spengler, Oswald. *The Decline of the West*. New York: Alfred Knopf, 1962.

Spitzer, Leo. *Marcel Proust e altri saggi di letteratura francese moderna*. Torino: Einaudi, 1959.

———. "La enuméracion caótica en la poesía moderna," *Linguística e Historia Literaria*. Madrid: Gredos, 1968. 247–300.

———. "Une habitude de style, le rappel chez Céline." Ed. Michel Beaujour, Dominique Le Roux, Michel Thélia. *Cahier de l' Herne* 3–5 (1972): 443–51.

Stanford, Luce, ed. *Céline and His Critics: Scandals and Paradox*. Saratoga, Calif.: ANMA Libri, 1986.

———. "Céline's Sources: A Contradiction in Terms?." In *Alphonse Juilland: D'une passion l'autre*. Ed. Brigitte Cazelles and René Girard. Saratoga, Calif.: ANMA Libri, 1987. 141–53.

Steiner, George. "Cry Havoc." In *Extra-Territorial*. New York: Atheneum, 1971. 35–47.

Stellardi, Giuseppe. "Il barocco nella scrittura di Gadda." *Studi d'Italianistica nell'Africa Australe* 1 (1984): 53–64.

―――. "'La luce che recede . . . ": Il miraggio del Libro nella scrittura di Gadda." *Studi e problemi di critica testuale* 45 (1992): 123–36.

Stevenson Gilliland, Kay. "Belacqua in the Moon: Beckett's Revision of Dante and the Lobster." In *Critical Essays on Samuel Beckett.* Ed. Patrick McCarthy. Boston: G. K. Hall, 1986.

Stevenson, Randall. *The British Novel since the Thirties.* London: Batsford, 1986.

Stragà, Antonio. "La scrittura del disordine." *Lingua e stile* 25 (1990): 85–101.

Svevo, Italo. *Il vecchione, Racconti, saggi, pagine sparse,* a cura di Bruno Maier. Milan: Dall'Oglio, 1968.

―――. *La coscienza di Zeno.* Milan: Dall'Oglio, 1976.

Swingle, L. J. "Virginia Woolf and Romantic Prometheanism." In *Bucknell Review: Romanticism, Modernism, Postmodernism.* Cranbury, N.J.: Associated University Press, 1980. 88–106.

Tani, Stefano. *The Doomed Detective.* Carbondale: Southern Illinois University Press, 1984.

―――. "La giovane narrativa." In *Postmodern Fiction in Europe and Americas.* Ed. Theo D'haen and Hans Berthens. Amsterdam: Rodopi, 1988. 161–92.

Taxidou, Olga. "Modernist Drama/Postmodernist Performance: The Case of Samuel Beckett." *Gramma* 2 (1994): 171–85.

Terracini, Benvenuto. *Analisi stilistica.* Milan: Feltrinelli, 1966.

Terzoli, Maria Antonietta. "Emilio o della rima. Appunti sulla metrica di Gadda." *Il Cenobio* 1 (1993): 85–94.

Thiher, Alan. *The Novel as Delirium.* New Brunswick, N.J.: Rutgers University Press, 1972.

―――. "Le 'Je' Célinien: ouverture, extase, clôture." *Australian Journal of French Studies* 13, no. 1–2 (1976): 47–54.

Thomas, Merlin. *Louis-Ferdinand Céline.* New York: New Directions, 1979.

Todorov, Tzvetan. *The Fantastic: A Structural Approach to a Literary Genre.* Ithaca, N.Y.: Cornell University Press, 1975.

―――. *Théories du symbole.* Paris: Seuil, 1977.

Topia, André. "Murphy ou Beckett baroque." In *Beckett avant Beckett—Essais sur le jeune Beckett (1930–1945).* Ed. Jean-Michel Rabaté. Paris: Presses de l'Ecole Normale Superieure. 93–119.

Trezise, Thomas. *Into the Breach: Samuel Beckett and the Ends of Literature.* Princeton, N.J.: Princeton University Press, 1990.

Turolo, Antonio. *Teoria e prassi linguistica nel primo Gadda.* Pisa: Giardini, 1995.

Ungaretti, Giuseppe. *Correspondance Jean Paulhan-Giuseppe Ungaretti 1921–1968.* Paris: Gallimard, 1989.

Vattimo, Gianni. "The End of (Hi)story." In *Zeitgeist in Babel.* Ed. Ingeborg Hoesterey. Bloomington: University of Indiana Press, 1991. 132–41.

―――. *The End of Modernity.* Baltimore: Johns Hopkins University Press, 1991.

―――. *The Transparent Society.* Baltimore: Johns Hopkins University Press, 1992.

Verdaguer, Pierre. "Tendances fantastiques et merveilleux raciste chez Louis-Ferdinand Céline." *Symposium* 39 (1985–86): 284–300.

Vertov, Dziga. *Kino-Eye*. Ed. Annette Michelson. Berkeley and Los Angeles: University of California Press, 1984.

Vincenzo, Romano. *La fine di un inizio*. Bari: Grandolfo Editore, 1975.

Vitoux, Frédéric. *Louis-Ferdinand Céline: Misère et parole*. Paris: Gallimard, 1973.

———. *Céline*. Paris: Belfond, 1978.

———. *A Biography*. New York: Paragon House, 1992.

Von Hofmannsthal, Hugo. "The Letter of Lord Chandos." In *Selected Prose*. London: Routledge and Kegan Paul, n.d. 134–35.

Weaver, William. *Acquainted with Grief*. New York: George Braziller, 1969.

Wilde, Alan. *Horizons of Assents: Modernism, Postmodernism, and the Ironic Imagination*. Baltimore and London: Johns Hopkins University Press, 1981.

Wolf, Nelly. "Un mauvais français." In *Céline: Voyage au bout de la nuit*. Ed. Alain Cresciucci. Paris: Klincksieck, 1993. 123–40.

Wood, Rupert. "Murphy, Beckett; Guelincx, God." *Journal of Beckett Studies* 2 (1993): 27–51.

———. "An Endgame of Aesthetics: Beckett as Essayist." In *The Cambridge Companion to Beckett*. Ed. John Pilling. Cambridge: Cambridge University Press, 1994.

Woolf, Virginia. *Mrs. Dalloway*. New York: Harcourt, Brace and World, 1953.

———. *To the Lighthouse*. New York: Harcourt Brace Jovanovich, 1955.

Zurbrugg, Nicholas. "Beyond Beckett: Reckless Writing and the Concept of the Avant-Garde within Postmodern Literature." *Yearbook of General and Comparative Literature* 30 (1981): 37–56.

———. "Beckett, Proust, and Burroughs and the Perils of 'Image Warfare'." In *Samuel Beckett: Humanistic Perspectives*. Ed. Pierre Astier, Morris Beja, and Stanley Gontarski. Columbus: Ohio State University Press, 1983. 172–87.

———. "Beckett, Proust, and *Dream of Fair to Middling Women*." *Journal of Beckett Studies* 9 (1984): 43–64.

———. *Beckett and Proust*. Gerrards Cross, Bucks: Colin Smythe, 1988.

Index

Norma Bouchard is an assistant professor of Italian and comparative literature at the University of Connecticut, Storrs. She is the editor of *Umberto Eco's Alternative: The Politics of Culture and the Ambiguities of Interpretation* (1998). She specializes in nineteenth- and twentieth-century literature and cultural theory.